Becoming a Social Worker

WITHDRAWN

This is a book about social workers and social work. It tells the story of the journey into and through social work of people from around the world living and working in social work today. We hear what has brought them into social work and what has kept them in it since. Their lively accounts demonstrate that commitment and passion remain at the heart of social work today.

This new edition of *Becoming a Social Worker* is made up of entirely new stories. It describes what it is like to be a social worker in a range of different practice settings in different countries. While many of the narratives are from practitioners and educators who either grew up in, or came as adults to, the UK, half of the narratives explore the experiences of social workers and educators working in different parts of the world, in countries as diverse as Australia and New Zealand, India and Bangladesh, Ireland, Sweden and Eastern Europe, Nigeria, the USA and Canada. The book ends with a commentary, which argues that social work is truly a global profession.

Some of the contributors will be recognised as those who have played a key part in shaping social work over the years and they provide valuable insights into how the profession has developed over time. Other contributors, less well known but no less interesting, give a vivid account of the challenges that social work education and practice face, and the shared values that underpin social work wherever it is located. Social work is a demanding and difficult job that goes largely unseen within society. We only ever hear about social work and social workers when something goes wrong and a vulnerable adult or child is hurt. *Becoming a Social Worker* sets out to change that – to make social work visible, so that those considering a career in the caring professions across the world can make an informed choice about whether social work is the career for them.

Viviene E. Cree is Professor of Social Work Studies in the School of Social and Political Science at the University of Edinburgh, UK. She previously worked as a social worker and practice teacher in statutory and voluntary agencies for sixteen years. She has researched and written extensively on social work and social work education, including publishing numerous journal articles and chapters in edited collections and nine books. She is co-editor of the book series, 'Social Work in Practice', BASW/Policy Press.

 7/3/2013

Student Social Work

This exciting new textbook series is ideal for all students studying to be qualified social workers, whether at undergraduate or masters level. Covering key elements of the social work curriculum, the books are accessible, interactive and thought-provoking.

New titles

Human Growth and Development
John Sudbery

Mental Health Social Work in Context
Nick Gould

Social Work and Social Policy
An introduction
Jonathan Dickens

Social Work Placements
Mark Doel

Social Work
A reader
Viviene E. Cree

Sociology for Social Workers and Probation Officers
Viviene E. Cree

Integrating Social Work Theory and Practice
A practical skills guide
Pam Green Lister

Social Work, Law and Ethics
Jonathan Dickens

Becoming a Social Worker, 2nd edn
Global narratives
Viviene E. Cree

Forthcoming titles

Social Work with Children and Young People, their Families and Carers
Janet Warren

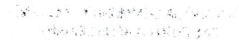

Becoming a Social Worker

Global narratives

Second edition

Edited by Viviene E. Cree

Routledge
Taylor & Francis Group

LONDON AND NEW YORK

First published 2013
by Routledge
2 Park Square, Milton Park, Abingdon, Oxon, OX14 4RN

Simultaneously published in the USA and Canada
by Routledge
711 Third Avenue, New York, NY 10017

Routledge is an imprint of the Taylor & Francis Group, an informa business

British Library Cataloguing in Publication Data
A catalogue record for this book is available from the British Library

Library of Congress Cataloging-in-Publication Data
Becoming a social worker : global narratives / edited by Viviene E. Cree. — 2nd ed.
        p. cm. — (Student social work)
    1. Social workers—Great Britain—Case studies. 2. Social service—Great Britain.
    I. Cree, Viviene E., 1954–
    HV247.B395 2013
    361.3023'41—dc23   2012032223

ISBN: 978–0–415–66595–7 (hbk)
ISBN: 978–0–415–66694–7 (pbk)
ISBN: 978–0–203–06687–4 (ebk)

Typeset in Rotis
by Keystroke, Station Road, Codsall, Wolverhampton

MIX
Paper from
responsible sources
FSC® C004839
www.fsc.org

Printed and bound in Great Britain by
TJ International Ltd, Padstow, Cornwall

Contents

Contents

Contributors

Gary Bailey is Professor of Practice at the Simmons College School of Social Work, Boston, Massachusetts, USA, and President of the International Federation of Social Workers (IFSW).

Kenneth Bolger is Manager of a community mental health team in the Highlands of Scotland.

Jim Campbell is Professor of Social Work at Goldsmith's, University of London, England, and co-editor of the *British Journal of Social Work*.

Marie Connolly is Professor of Social Work at the University of Melbourne, Australia.

Viviene E. Cree is Professor of Social Work Studies at the University of Edinburgh, Scotland.

Hilton Dawson was Chief Executive of the British Association of Social Workers (BASW) at the time of writing.

Lena Dominelli is Professor of Applied Social Sciences and Academician in the Academy of the Learned Societies for Social Sciences.

Merlyn D'Souza is Director of Justice and Care, an NGO based in India.

Gudrun Elvhage and Pernilla Liedgren Dobronravoff are Lecturers in Social Work at Ersta Sköndal University College in Sweden.

Moana Eruera is a Māori social work consultant and trainer based in the North Island, Aotearoa New Zealand.

Bill Foley is a social worker within the infectious diseases team of an acute Dublin teaching hospital in Ireland.

Jan Fook is Director of the School of Social Work at Dalhousie University, Nova Scotia, Canada.

Mekada J. Graham is Director/Chair of the Department of Social Work at California State University, Los Angeles, CA, USA.

Contributors

Md. Tuhinul Islam is Assistant Director, leading the Education and Child Development Programme, of an NGO based in Bangladesh.

Robyn Kemp is a social care and social pedagogy consultant and trainer working across the UK.

Petra Matuvi was studying for her Master of Social Work degree in Wales at the time of writing her chapter.

Carla Nzombe is a criminal justice social worker in Scotland.

Uzoma Odera Okoye is a Lecturer in Social Work in Nigeria.

Sally Paul is a social worker at Strathcarron Hospice in Scotland.

Richard Pearl works in Wales as a social worker in a community team for adults over the age of 65.

June Sadd is a survivor consultant, practice educator and trainer based in England.

Gaylene Stevens is a trainer for the Anglican Māori Diocese of Te Waipounamu based in Christchurch, Aotearoa New Zealand.

Pauline Sung-Chan is Associate Professor at the Hong Kong Polytechnic University, Hung Hom, Kowloon, Hong Kong.

Neil Whettam is Regional Child Protection Adviser for the children's charity, Terre des Hommes (TDH) in the Balkans.

Acknowledgements

With thanks to the following people for their help in sourcing potential authors: Dina Sidhva and George Palattiyil, Maeve Foreman, Mark Smith, Rosemary Okoli, Ruth Stark, Sally Holland.

Introduction

Viviene E. Cree

This is a book about social workers and social work. It tells the story of the journey into and through social work of twenty-three social workers living and working in different parts of the world today. It demonstrates that although social work is a very diverse activity across the world, with different legal, policy and institutional contexts, the commitment and the passion that social workers demonstrate remain the same; social workers, wherever they are located, are people who fundamentally want to help others and to make society a better place. The book also provides evidence that social work is now a truly globalised profession. The social workers who have shared their narratives are a mix of people on the move and people who have chosen to stay, or to return, to their place of origin. For some, this has meant reclaiming indigenous practices and valuing traditional belief systems as viable alternatives to the 'Western' (or 'Northern') orthodoxy in social work. For others, becoming a social worker has been about leaving behind communities and countries, for all the familiar 'push-and-pull' factors that accompany migration stories. Whichever is the case, what we see is that we are in the midst of creating a new, global, 'glocal'[1] social work, one that is unique to specific settings, yet shares a value-base and commitment to social justice wherever it is located.

In the book, we hear about the driving forces that have brought people into social work – that most 'unloved profession'[2] – and we learn what has kept them in social work through the ups and downs over the years. For some, this has been about the influence of key people in their lives: parents and children, teachers and mentors, friends and colleagues, and, significantly, service users (clients) whose lives have affected them deeply and given them the strength to go on. Many of the social workers who

1

have written chapters for the book are critical of the never-ending administrative machine that gets in the way of their relationship with service users. But most have found their own creative solutions and have been able to continue to value their work in spite of what is often experienced as the constraining context within which they practise. (A similar message is to be found in Cree and Davis (2007), in which social workers often describe 'going the extra mile' and stepping outside procedures in order to give the support that they felt was needed.)

Some of the narrators in the book will be recognised as famous names in social work; they are some of the 'movers and shakers' who have played a key part in shaping social work over the course of their careers. Most, however, are not. Although they may be less well known, they are no less interesting, as we learn first hand about social work practice and social work education from those 'on the ground'.

Context of the book

This is the second edition of *Becoming a Social Worker*, which was first published in 2000. The first book set out to describe social work in the UK to a lay audience, recognising that social work was an activity that was largely hidden from public view. I argued that while school and university students are likely to have a good idea about the role and tasks of other professionals (such as teachers, doctors, priests or lawyers), they are much less likely to have come across social workers, or to have a clear understanding of what social workers do. I suggested that there were a number of obvious reasons for this:

- Social work services have never been institutionalised as a 'service for all' within the welfare state, in the way that education and health services have been. Instead, social work remains a service focused on disadvantaged and marginalised individuals and groups. It is a 'last resort service', rationed by tests of income and need (Hill 2000). Arguably, the impact of this is felt even more keenly today, as global economic pressures bite and services are cut back across statutory and voluntary sectors alike.

- Social work practice often takes place in service users' homes and in offices where it is not usually observed by anyone else; it is largely an unseen and unfamiliar activity. In the words of Pithouse (1987), it is an 'invisible trade'.

- The code of confidentiality which is fundamental to social work values makes it difficult for social workers to promote or defend their practice. Confidentiality is crucial 'as a basis for social work interventions based on trust and honesty' (Thompson 2000: 112). But confidentiality can lead to secrecy, and secrecy may create mistrust and suspicion. Social workers need to be able to tell others about their achievements without feeling that they are breaking rules of confidentiality.

But social work, I argue, is more than an invisible occupation: it is also, at times, a detested one, or so we might believe if we were to take at face value the popular presentation of social workers in the media and in the tabloid press. Over the past thirty years or so, social work has been subjected to a fairly consistent hammering in the popular press. A series of child abuse scandals and subsequent public inquiries have left social workers feeling 'damned if they do' and 'damned if they don't'; either blamed for taking too heavy measures to protect children and vulnerable adults or condemned for not doing enough (Ayre 2001). Social workers have also been lambasted for being sandal-wearing, 'wet' liberals, criticised for over-identifying with their clients, particularly young offenders and some families (Jones 1998). At the same time, they have been portrayed as 'politically correct' zealots who are out to privilege the experiences of some members of society (often presented as black and gay people), to the detriment of other, 'more deserving' members of society (Dominelli 1997). Things reached an all-time low for social workers in the UK in 2007 when 'Baby P' (Peter Connelly) died in London, and 1.6 million *Sun* readers signed a petition for the social workers involved to be fired.

Various commentators have tried to explain why social work has had such a bad press to date. It is clear that the very nature of social work with those who are stigmatised as deviant or disadvantaged in society leads social workers, in turn, to be stigmatised and discriminated against. Social work, writes Jones, is 'immersed in poverty and social exclusion' (2002: 7). The majority of those who use social work services are poor and drawn from the most disadvantaged sectors of the population. The job of social work is to mediate on behalf of those who are oppressed and disadvantaged, and at the same time to ration and gatekeep resources to some of the most needy in society (Jones 2002: 17). Social work is thus situated in the middle, pulled between the individual and society, the powerful and the excluded, negotiating and at times in conflict with both (Cree 2012). Beyond this, however, it is known that there is widespread ignorance about what it is that social workers actually do, as identified in two Scottish studies (Davidson and King 2005; Gallilee 2005).

Social work is not, however, only criticised by those outside the profession. Social workers have themselves been quite critical of social work and social workers. During the 1970s and 1980s, radical social workers drew attention to the 'social control' aspects of social work practice, and argued instead for a social work practice that aligned itself more fully with service users and with the trade union movement (see Langan 1993). There was a feeling that the only legitimate social work was community social work or community development; all other kinds of social work were about maintaining the status quo and keeping poor people down. Feminist social workers similarly pointed out that state services, while claiming to support women, reinforced gender stereotypes and confirmed women's oppression (Langan and Day 1992); meanwhile disabled people campaigned against the paternalism of state provision, and fought for a measure of control over how services should be delivered (Campbell and Oliver 1996).

More recently, social workers have been vociferous in their complaints about the impact of managerialism and cutbacks in services on social work. There is a sense in which social workers on the ground are concerned that they can no longer 'do social work'. They are so busy managing and delivering packages of care that they are no longer able to perform the support functions which give them job satisfaction in social work. Jones' (2001) research into state social workers in Northern

England found deep unhappiness among those who felt that they had inadequate resources to be able to help their clients. A study of social work in the UK and Sweden by Harlow *et al.* (2012) mirrors this finding. The researchers argue that neoliberalism, through the processes of managerialism, has impacted negatively on social work in the UK and Sweden, through the managerial drive for increased performance in economy, efficiency and effectiveness, and also in the development of evidence-based practice. More optimistically, the researchers detect resistance among social workers themselves, as has also been recognised in the accounts in Cree and Davis (2007), as well as in the narratives in this book. This issue is also explored in Munro's (2012) review of child protection services in England. Here she argues that professionals have been 'too focused on complying with rules and regulations and so spending less time assessing children's needs', and she is critical of 'a target-driven culture meaning social workers are unable to exercise their professional judgement'. The Munro Review findings have been widely welcomed by social workers who see this as giving them an opportunity to 'do social work' again in the future.

Reviewing the picture overall, we can see that social work is a demanding and difficult job, for which social workers can expect little thanks from the general public. It is also, however, a vitally important job, which is carried out with and on behalf of some of the most vulnerable people in society. But what is social work?

What is social work?

As I pointed out in the 2000 edition of this book, it is almost impossible to find a simple definition of social work with which everyone is likely to agree. 'Social work is', Thompson suggests, 'what social workers do' (2000: 13). From this perspective, social work is what the contributors to this volume depict. But is this enough? Even with the accounts of twenty-three social workers, there are a great many gaps in coverage; social work is always greater than the sum of its individual parts. In the 'real world' of social work, there can be no single answer to the question, 'What is social work?', because there is always a gap between what people think it ought to be and what it really is. This means that the definition of social work agreed in 2001 by the International Association of Schools of Social Work and the International Federation of Social Workers may demonstrate more about the aspirations of its authors than about social work practice in the member countries which were signatories to the definition:

> The social work profession promotes social change, problem-solving in human relationships, and the empowerment and liberation of people to enhance well-being. Utilising theories of human behaviour and social systems, social work intervenes at points where people interact with their environments. Principles of human rights and social justice are fundamental to social work.
>
> (http://www.ifsw.org)

My own view is that there is no essential social work task. Rather, social work is best understood as a collection of competing and contradictory discourses that come together at a particular moment in time to frame the task of social work, defining not just its capabilities but also its potential (Cree 1995). This means that we should not expect to find unanimity in books about social work or even in accounts of social workers. Social work is always subject to competing claims of definition and practice, and cannot be separated from the society in which it is located. What we will see in this book are some of the many facets and contexts of social work practice across the world today. We will also gain access to some of the changes (and some of the controversies) that have rocked social work over the past thirty years or so. This may, in turn, give us some clues about the future of social work.

Focus of the book

It is easiest to start with what this book is not, before outlining what it is. It is not a 'how to do' manual for social workers: a book that describes social work across its many settings, introducing 'good practice' examples along the way. There are many useful books of this nature already, and this book does not try to compete with them. It is, moreover, not a book whose primary function is to deconstruct the meaning of social work; again, readers can find many such books on the market. Finally, this is not a book that aims to present a definitive account of social work in all countries of the world, if that were ever possible. Again, other books offer alternatives here, including Cox and Pawar (2012), Gray and Webb (2010), Hall (2012) and Lyons *et al.* (2012).

What this book does instead is to look at social work from the inside: from the highly individualised and unique experiences of social work practitioners, educators and students located in different parts of the world. It is therefore primarily a piece of autobiography, in which social workers set out to explore what social work means to them, by telling the story of why they became social workers and how their careers in social work have progressed until the present day. Autobiographical and biographical accounts have become increasingly popular within social sciences and within sociological research in particular. Auto/biographical research is best explained as 'part of a movement to reveal and understand the "personal" and its interlinking with the immediate and wider social context and political practices' (Roberts 2002: 31). In other words, it allows us to see at first hand the connections between the individual and society, and between 'public issues' and 'private troubles' (Mills 1959). This does not, of course, imply that the accounts given in this book are 'true' for all social workers and for all time. It is inevitable that in asking people to look back over their lives and careers, the narratives will be partial and subjective; they will tell us as much about the author as they do about social work. But this is always the case, whatever the subject of writing. These stories give us access not only to the autobiography of the person who is writing, but to a large degree they also open a window on the biographies of all the other actors who have played a part in the authors' lives: the parents, the teachers, the colleagues, the clients and service users with whom they have worked over the years. Consequently, they present a rich and multi-layered testimony of social work and social workers over the past thirty years or so.

Vivienne E. Cree

My own story

I will retell my own story now for those who are new to this book. I have puzzled about social work and my place in it for the whole of my professional career, lasting over thirty years in social work practice and social work education. The questions 'What is social work? and 'Why am I a social worker?' have remained key questions for me, first pursued in my Ph.D. study (Cree 1992, 1995) and later through research into career motivations of beginning social work students (Cree 1996a). Throughout this time, I now realise that I have been trying to resolve central contradictions in my own background and upbringing, as I will now discuss.

I was brought up in a strongly Christian family, with a firm set of injunctions towards 'putting the needs of others first' and 'looking after the less fortunate in society'. The idea of 'service' was fundamental to this, and my childhood was an active and social one, busy with visits to grandparents, church choir, uniformed organisations, voluntary work and playing with my sisters and friends (Cree 1996b). This might suggest that a career in social work was an obvious step for me, but nothing could be further from the truth. Social workers were viewed by my parents as 'busybodies' who meddled in the lives of others, and more than this, they were social misfits who interfered in others' lives to make up for shortcomings in their own. Those who received social work help were little better. They were either calculating scroungers or poor souls who were better off without social work interference.

Of course, real life is never so starkly contrasted; there is always much that is less certain and may even be contradictory. One of my mother's best friends was a social worker. She keenly felt my mum's disapproval at times, and yet was able to regularly share some of her work frustrations with her. My father – who had what I always thought was a hilarious notion that everyone who lived in the council-owned houses at the back of our town had colour TVs (then a real sign of wealth!) and played golf – was a wholly generous man who had little concern for his own self-interest. Once retired, my mother became District Organiser for the Women's Royal Voluntary Society (WRVS), and my father delivered meals-on-wheels and ran (with my mother and her friends) tea-bars at local hospitals and a Young Offenders' Institution. So it was no surprise to either of my parents that I ended up in social work, and they were delighted when I got my first job lecturing at the University of Edinburgh, although even then, I heard my mum tell someone that I was 'teaching sociology' (which was, of course, partly true, because this is one of my teaching areas).

My own story, like all the stories in this collection, is a unique and particular story, reflecting as it does my own white, aspiring middle-class, small-town-Scotland upbringing in the 1950s and 1960s. But it is important to recognise how many of the stories in this book have echoes of similar conflicts and contradictions. Choosing to become a social worker is a difficult decision to make. It begs a deeper and far more intractable question: 'What do you have to offer others?' Or even more challenging, '*Why* do you think that you have something to offer others?' It is the familiar 'Who do you think you are?' question which plagued me in adolescence, and remains with me today. Social work is, first and last, about *you*; about walking alongside someone and using yourself, as well as your professional knowledge and values. This was understood by the early social work pioneers, including Octavia Hill, who saw the relationship between social worker and service user as ultimately one of friendship: 'Do not trust any plan of relief, however methodical which leaves intimate personal action out of account.'[3] So becoming a social worker is inevitably complicated, just as social work practice is hugely diverse and complex.

Organisation of the book

The chapters in this book are ordered alphabetically by author, not country by country, because it is the individuals and their stories that are the focus of attention, first and foremost. The contributors are people of different ages who work in different settings in social work across the world. They are women and men, students and social workers, practitioners, educators and managers, from a range of ethnic, religious and cultural backgrounds. Two identify themselves as gay; two discuss serious mental health difficulties at times in their lives. They all have different stories to tell, but there are also some shared themes which emerge across the chapters, and these will be discussed in the final chapter where I review the book as a whole, identifying areas of common interest and setting the individual accounts in the wider context of social work practice.

Each contributor was invited to address three topics:

1   Career choice: why they chose a career in social work; any defining moments or people who have had special significance to them; their experience of social work education and training.

2   Current job: what they are doing now – tasks and responsibilities (including how social work operates in their country and an account of 'My typical week'); any specific challenges or successes; what keeps them going in their work.

3   Looking ahead: their thoughts for the future; hopes and fears for social work in their country and more globally.

I have been an involved, though (I hope) not dictatorial editor. While I have sought to maintain clarity and readability throughout the book, I have not tried to impose too strict a 'house style' on the contributors. As a result, some chapters read a little differently to others. I hope that the end result is a book that has something for everyone; that readers will find something in the accounts that speaks to them and to their ideas and experience, and that this, in turn, informs their own 'becoming a social worker' journey.

Notes

1 The sociologist Roland Robertson argues that rather than living in a global age in which everything has homogenised and become the same across the world, we live in a 'glocal' one. He writes: 'an age in which the quotidian, reflexive synthesis of the local and the global is an ever-present feature and, also, a dilemma of most of human life. It constitutes the most significant phenomenological dimension of the ambivalence and ambiguity of the contemporary human condition. . . . While the world-as-a-whole is characterized by much sameness and homogeneity, there are equally significant respects in which it is marked by difference and heterogeneity.' He compares this with the idea of 'indigenization', in which goods or services are produced and distributed according to particularistic, local criteria. See Robertson (1992) and http://artefact.mi2.hr/_a04/lang_en/theory_robertson_en.htm.

2 This is the title of a book published as far back as 1973, suggesting that social work's problems with self-presentation are anything but new. See Richan and Mendelsohn (1973).

3 From a printed pamphlet of a speech given by Octavia Hill in Bristol, 'The Importance of Aiding the Poor without Almsgiving', quoted in Darley (1990: 117).

References

Ayre, P. (2001) 'Child protection and the media: Lessons from the last three decades', *British Journal of Social Work* 31: 887–901.

Campbell, J. and Oliver, M. (1996) *Disability Politics: Understanding our Past, Changing our Future*, London: Routledge.

Cox, D. and Pawar, M. (2012) *International Social Work: Issues, Strategies, and Programs*, 2nd edn, London: Sage.

Cree, V.E. (1992) 'Social Work's Changing Task', Unpublished Ph.D. thesis, Edinburgh: University of Edinburgh.

—— (1995) *From Public Streets to Private Lives. The Changing Task of Social Work*, Aldershot: Avebury.

—— (1996a) 'Why do men care?' In K. Cavanagh and V.E. Cree (eds) *Working with Men. Feminism and Social Work*, London: Routledge.

—— (1996b) *Social Work: A Christian or Secular Discourse?*, Waverley Paper, Edinburgh: University of Edinburgh.

—— (2012) 'Social work and society'. In M. Davies (ed.) *Blackwell Companion to Social Work*, 4th edn, Oxford: Blackwell.

Cree, V.E. and Davis, A. (2007) *Social Work: Voices from the Inside*, London: Routledge.

Darley, G. (1990) *Octavia Hill*, London: Constable.

Davidson, S. and King, S. (2005) *Public Knowledge of and Attitudes to Social Work in Scotland*, Edinburgh: Scottish Executive.

Dominelli, L. (1997) *Sociology for Social Work*, Basingstoke: Macmillan.

Galilee, J. (2005) *Literature Review on Media Representations of Social Work and Social Workers*, Edinburgh: Scottish Executive.

Gray, M. and Webb, S. (2010) *International Social Work, Volumes I–IV*, London: Sage.

Hall, N. (2012) *Social Work Around the World V: Building the Global Agenda for Social Work and Social Development*, Geneva: IFSW.

Harlow, E., Berg, E., Barry, J. and Chandler, J. (2012) 'Neoliberalism, managerialism and the reconfiguring of social work in Sweden and the United Kingdom', *Organization*, 25, doi: 10.1177/1350508412448222 (accessed 19 July 2012).

Hill, M. (ed.) (2000) *Local Authority Social Services. An Introduction*, Oxford: Blackwell.

Jones, C. (1998) 'Social work and society'. In R. Adams, M. Payne and L. Dominelli (eds) *Social Work. Themes, Issues and Critical Debates*, Basingstoke: Macmillan.

—— (2001) 'Voices from the front line: state social workers and New Labour', *British Journal of Social Work*, 31: 547–62.

—— (2002) 'Poverty and social exclusion'. In M. Davies (ed.) *Blackwell Companion to Social Work*, 2nd edn, Oxford: Blackwell.

Langan, M. (1993) 'The rise and fall of social work'. In J. Clarke (ed.) *A Crisis in Care?*, London: Sage.

Langan, M. and Day, E. (1992) *Women, Oppression and Social Work*, London: Routledge.

Lyons, K., Hokenstad, T., Pawar, M., Huegler, N. and Hall, N. (eds) (2012) *The Sage Handbook of International Social Work*, London: Sage.

Mills, C.W. (1959) *The Sociological Imagination,* Oxford: Oxford University Press.

Munro, E. (2012) *Munro Review of Child Protection: Final Report – A Child-centred System*, London: DoE.

Pithouse, A. (1987) *Social Work: The Social Organisation of an Invisible Trade*, Aldershot: Avebury.

Richan, W.C. and Mendelsohn, A.R. (1973) *Social Work. The Unloved Profession*, New York: Franklin Watts.

Roberts, B. (2002) *Biographical Research*, Buckingham: Open University Press.

Robertson, R. (1992) *Globalization: Social Theory and Global Culture*, London: Sage.

Thompson, N. (2000) *Understanding Social Work. Preparing for Practice*, Basingstoke: Macmillan.

1 'If you ask me what I came into this life to do, I will tell you: I came to live out loud'[1]

Gary Bailey

I was born and raised in Cleveland, Ohio, an African American child and young person, and it was here that I learned about, and was first affected by, the US Civil Rights, Gay Rights and Women's movements. The 1970s was the period during which I came to terms with my sexual orientation and began to develop into the person I am today. I have lived my life as an openly gay African American male since 'coming out' (though that was not a term we used then) while in my senior year at high school. I was 17 years old. My parents had always told my brother and me that there was nothing they could not deal with, as long as we told them the truth. If we were 'rough housing', as kids will do, and despite being told not to, and we (let's say) broke a window or one of my mother's favourite ornaments, as long as we were honest about what we had done, then we were not punished. So when I realised that I was gay, all I could think back in 1973 was that I had to let my parents know; to tell them the truth as I now knew it.

In my mind, it was really more of a test for them than it was for me; would they be the people whom I had known them to be when I had told them truths in the past? If not, better that I learned it now rather than later, because I knew well enough that my independent streak, my tendency towards being mischievous (nothing serious, but I was always one to push the rules and boundaries) meant that this would not be the greatest challenge I would present to my parents and my family during my lifetime. Remember: this was the 1970s and my parents were in their early fifties, having had me and my brother later in life than was traditional at the time. My parents, understandably, were not happy with the news, but continued to stay focused on the fact that I was their child and that our home was always my home, and that I should never turn away from them or my family. So, over time, we worked through whatever discomfort they had and moved on to have an even more wonderful relationship, one in which I could be open, honest and present with them, or as much as any young person really is with their parents. I was able to involve them with the people whom I loved and whom they came to love too, and not to exclude my family from areas of my life for fear that they would 'discover' and disapprove, as I have known others who remained closeted or distant from their families, fearful of their families' rejection or abandonment.

I realise now that I learned early on what it meant to live 'doubly' within the margins of society, to be a living example of what the great educator, sociologist and civil rights leader W.E.B. DuBois referred to in his historic book (1903) as 'double consciousness'. I experienced first hand both the opportunities and oppressions in America. When I attended Cleveland's University School, one of the leading private schools in the northeast, the American Psychiatric Association was still debating whether or not to remove 'homosexuality' from the ranks of pathology in the definitive *Diagnostic and Statistical Manual*.

I am proud to say that I grew up in Cleveland, Ohio, and am proud to identify myself as a 'Buckeye', an affectionate nickname for residents of Ohio, the 'buckeye state'. Cleveland is located on the shores of Lake Erie, and when I was a child it had a strong and vibrant African American community; it also had a vibrant arts' community, including a world-class symphony orchestra, the legendary Karamu Theatre and a phenomenal museum of art, built in a Palladian style and surrounded by a lagoon with swans; a veritable oasis in the middle of the city. In 1970, a statue at the front of the museum (a bronze copy of Rodin's *The Thinker*) was irreparably damaged by a pipe bomb. No one was injured in the blast, but the statue was destroyed. This reminds us that this was a time of political activism, with campaigns against the continuing military action in Vietnam and against the American government in general. The 1960s was also still a time of racial segregation across the USA. Cleveland was the first city to elect an African American as its mayor, the late Carl Stokes, in 1967, and the following year, his brother, Louis Stokes, was elected as Ohio's first African American US Congressman.

My family, like our neighbours, owned their own home. We lived in what I remember as being a very diverse community. Our next-door neighbours included a Japanese family who had been interned in a detention camp in California during World War Two and had moved to Cleveland; on the other side, an older Polish couple who had left Poland to escape the war; and across the street, a German family, which included an elderly mother and her single adult son. We were one of three African American families on our block. I was too young to remember moving to Decker Avenue but I do recall that we had what at the time seemed like an enormous backyard full of flowers and fruit trees, as well as a grape arbour. My brother and I had lots of places to play, catching bugs and digging worms and playing with our first dog Skippy, a collie mix, as well as a rabbit named Peter and chickens, given to us at Easter time as gifts in our Easter baskets. There were county fairs and amusement parks to be enjoyed, and cherry cokes when we went bowling and foot-long hot dogs at the circus when it came to town! There was an active downtown with three major department stores, and people during that period used to get dressed up to 'go into town' to shop at the department store Higbee's, with its amazing art deco interior with beautiful chandeliers going down the length of the entire first floor. It was a wonderful place to grow up and my brother and I had a great childhood, with 'cook-outs' in the backyard and birthday parties, trips to the lake front in the summer on hot evenings, and ice-cream and walking along the breakwater with our parents. I miss my parents each day, and am grateful for the memories and the time we had together as a family, and the story of my family is one I hope to share some day in more detail.

Much of that halcyon period ended in 1968 when I was 13. The Civil Rights movement had become the Black Liberation movement, and was capturing students' imaginations, and so-called 'soul music' became the music of protest. The assassination of Dr Martin Luther King, Jr, in April 1968, resulted in our inner-city neighbourhood, like so many other major US cities, erupting in flames and riots. In the flash of an eye, our idyllic community disappeared: shops were burned and looted and most were not rebuilt; our neighbours moved away to what they considered to be 'safer' communities. My parents were committed to living in the central city so, as others left, we remained, but it was a very different experience. I don't recall it as being worse, just different from what it had been before.

Both of my parents had been born in the US South (my mother was from Georgia and my father from Alabama) and had experienced the height of 'Jim Crow' segregation, the yoke of US apartheid and discrimination. I have come to learn recently as I have worked on our family history that both were the grandchildren of slaves. They wanted the best for their children, and did all that they could to provide us with every opportunity possible that would help us to advance and succeed. My father worked at the Ford Motor Company on the assembly line and my mother went back to work outside the home after we grew older; she worked on the janitorial staff of the Cleveland public schools. Both parents were, in effect, 'community organisers', but without professional training. My mother was active in voter registration drives following the passage of the US Civil Rights and Voting Rights acts, and took part in local political action, especially as it related to education. She was often at community discussions about the quality of schools for children of colour, or hosting political events in our home, and both mum and dad spent a great deal of time advocating for our neighbourhood at Cleveland's City Hall. My dad was a great supporter, but worked long hours to make sure that we had what might be described as an upwardly mobile life; he took his role as the breadwinner and provider for his family very seriously. There was an expectation that we kids would also get involved in our community. I was often sent across the street to sit with an elderly neighbour so that her son could go out on a Friday night, and I have early memories of going to the polling place to volunteer, with my parents, on election day. Yet we had fun and always seemed to be on the go and doing something. The other family expectation was that my brother and I would go to college and pursue careers. We both attended college and graduate school without accumulating the debt that is so typical in the USA these days, thanks to the sacrifice, planning and hard work of our parents, who hoped that I would become a physician and my brother an attorney. My brother is now an attorney in Colorado, and I took some 'pre-med' courses at Tufts University, located in Medford, a town near Boston.

Undergrad study

The period at college was a challenging time. For the first time in my life I found myself not part of a community. Boston was experiencing a lot of racist hostility against the much smaller numbers of African Americans; I wasn't enjoying my courses; and, over and above this, it was as if I was the only openly gay person on campus! I often ate alone and spent a lot of time alone, alone but not lonely. Eventually, I found a community of friends at Tufts, both straight and gay, Black and White, and I came to love my time there. Our little group refers affectionately to each other as our 'Tufts family' and I am a proud godfather to four amazing children from this group, who themselves have grown into phenomenal young people.

One winter during intercession, I took a course that was taught by a professional social worker, whose name is Jane Greenspan. I loved her description of what she did for a living and realised I was on the wrong course; everything I had done and experienced until then now told me that I should train as a social worker. I switched my major to Child Study and graduated from the Eliot Pearson School of Child Study in 1977.

From social work training to practice

I enrolled at the Boston University School of Social Work to earn my Masters in Social Work (MSW) in 1979/80. There I made some great friends, several of whom remain great friends and have become part of my extended professional family. I was a Casework 'major' with a 'minor' in Group Work. My first field placement was at the Travelers' Aid Society,[2] which helped people who had travelled without a plan for housing or employment, etc. I dealt with all types of people and learned to think quickly on my feet as I might only have a person as a client for one interview. The lessons learned have since served me well in many areas of my career, as did my second-year field placement in a suburban school system where I worked with children and families in a Montessori-modelled[3] open classroom elementary school in a more affluent Boston suburb. Very different populations, but in my second year I developed the ability not to be tied to an office; I also learned how to develop relationships with those who did not immediately understand the role of the social worker. Both were great experiences and have served me well.

I completed graduate school and received my Master's degree by the time I was 23 years old. I was also discovering gay life as an adult and getting involved in relationships, and I spent a lot of time in the clubs and bars which were a part of the scene at the time. Imagine my surprise when, some years later in 1995, I received the award for Outstanding Contributions to the Field of Social Work from the Boston University School of Social Work Alumni Association. This goes to prove that you can sometimes surprise yourself just by doing the work you believe in and feel good about.

I began my career at the Family Service of Greater Boston (FSGB)[4] in 1980. Few American social service organisations claim as rich a history as this one, which traces its roots to 1835, only thirteen years after Boston's incorporation as a city. The agency served children, youth and families and older people through the wide sweep of the American experience, during the Civil War, two world wars, the Great Depression, civil rights and women's movements, and the technology revolution. My task was to provide 'in-home counselling' and supportive services to so-called 'at-risk' elders and their families. This was the best professional accident that ever occurred for me, and I remained at the agency for fourteen years. I held a range of positions, including supervising graduate students. Eventually, I was asked to teach a course on community organising as an adjunct faculty member at Boston College (BCGSW) School of Social Work and I went on to teach a course on the Dynamics of Racism and Oppression at my alma mater Boston University (BUSSW) and to head their gerontology section, which meant that I organised speakers and mini-seminars for students and community members, again while still working full time at the FSGB.

I left the FSGB after being recruited to the position of Executive Director of Parents' and Children's Services (PCS) which was founded in 1849 and is one of Boston's oldest child welfare and child protection agencies. Originally called the Children's Mission to the Children of the Destitute of the City of Boston, PCS provided needy children with shelter, education and employment. Its mission went on to become one of promoting the well-being of children and the preservation of families through culturally competent direct service, education and advocacy. I remained at PCS until 1999, when I became a Visiting Professor at Simmons School of Social Work, Simmons College, the oldest degree-granting social work programme in the USA. I have been a permanent member of the faculty at the Simmons now for over fifteen years.

Balancing academic life and community action

I am currently a Professor of Practice at the Simmons School of Social Work, Simmons College and have another appointment at the School of Nursing and Health Studies. I also hold an appointment as an adjunct Assistant Professor at the Boston University School of Public Health. I teach required introductory-level graduate courses in Social Policy, Dynamics of Racism and Oppression, and an elective in Social Action which focuses on gerontology. I am involved in a variety of college-wide activities, including the Faculty Senate, and I am a member of the Simmons President's Diversity and Inclusion Advisory Council (PDIAC) which focuses on how to recruit and retain diverse students, faculty and staff at the college in all areas. In addition, I chair the Simmons College Black Administrators, Faculty and Staff Council (BAFAS) and chair the School of Social Work (SSW) Awards Committee.

I am not particularly interested in conventional research and see myself more as a practitioner. My writing has tended to focus on areas connected to my volunteer and practice areas of interest: HIV/AIDS, diversity and inclusion, social disparities and, most recently, human rights and international social work practice. I am also called upon by the media (press, radio and television) to respond to topical issues that are related to the areas mentioned. I have testified before US Congressional committees on issues impacting upon the social work profession and frequently do the same in my state. In 2009, I was delighted to be appointed by the Governor of Massachusetts to the Board of Directors of the Massachusetts Educational Financing Authority (MEFA), which helps develop and provide financing for families so that students can attend college.

I was elected president of the National Association of Social Work (NASW)[5] in 2003. I found it interesting that while I was at my office at national headquarters in Washington, DC, near Capitol Hill, NASW staff members and others treated me with a certain degree of deference; yet when I left the confines of the building, I had difficulty catching a cab on the streets of the nation's capital. I was just another Black man, confronted by the same social disparities that exist in so many parts of the world for so many other people of colour. When my term as president ended, I chose to focus on improving the image of social workers and the profession in the United States by becoming Chairperson of the National Social Work Public Education Campaign, giving me the opportunity to travel extensively across the United States, Canada and parts of Europe promoting the profession of social work.

Currently, I am a member of the Governing Board of the Boston Teachers' Union School in Jamaica Plain, Massachusetts, and a member of the Board of the Fenway High School in Boston. I have also been involved for many years with the AIDS Action Committee (AAC) of Massachusetts,[6] one of the nation's foremost AIDS service organisations. When I was just starting my career in social work, the gay community had no idea that the AIDS crisis was around the corner, and when the AIDS epidemic struck, social workers were at the forefront of providing compassionate care, dealing with family crises and fighting hard for fair policies and equal treatment of people with AIDS. I have lost countless friends and loved ones during the course of the past thirty years of the epidemic; I was much honoured to receive the Bayard Rustin Award for Courage from the AAC in 2010.[7]

In 2010, I was elected President of the International Federation of Social Workers (IFSW),[8] the first person of colour to do so, and only the third North American. My objective in becoming President was to take the message forward about what our profession is, and what the world could be like, if we put more of our energy and intent into creating genuine opportunities for self-realisation and social justice.

MY TYPICAL WEEK

Really – is there any such thing as a typical week? My parents had great sayings about the use of time: my father would always say, 'Why touch something twice?' My mother, for her part, often said, 'When you want to get something done, always ask a busy person!' A typical day for me now usually begins at around 4.30 or 5 a.m. lying in bed with both the local morning news and the BBC on the television, so that I have a sense of what is happening locally, nationally and internationally. I get up at around 6 a.m. and before I make coffee for my partner and myself, I throw in a load of washing or fold a load that I had put in the drier the night before. Our cat insists on his morning cuddles and then I check emails while the kettle is on, to see what has come in while I was asleep. And so another working day begins!

Monday	Simmons College by 12; Policy Class 6–8.30 p.m. Home by 9 p.m. Quick dinner; read emails and 'snail mail', respond to texts, talk with family and friends. Bed around 12.30 a.m.
Tuesday	Medical appointment at 8 a.m.; into office/work, student meetings; prepare classes for the coming week. External meeting(s): Fenway High School Board Meeting (6 p.m.). Drinks with friends, then home.
Wednesday	Faculty Senate meeting 8–10 a.m.; 10.30–noon Center for Excellence in Teaching (CET) Search Committee meeting; Policy Class and meeting with students 1–3:30 p.m.; Debrief with CET co-chair 3.30–4.30 p.m.
Thursday	Personal errands; into office by 12 noon. Massachusetts Educational Finance Authority (MEFA) meeting downtown 3–6 p.m. Meet partner at his office and dinner out.
Friday	Manicure at 8 a.m. on my way to office. Meeting with my Associate Dean; covering a colleague's class from 1–3 p.m.; meeting with director of the MSW Program; meeting Black administrators, Faculty and Staff Council vice-chair to plan African American History Month.
Saturday	UUMC Men's Group Breakfast meeting at 10 a.m. to plan for Men's Day Service and Community Health Fair. Do other work (yard work, gardening, repairs, etc. at

> the church). Either go out for dinner with partner or host dinner at home with
> friends.
>
> Sunday   Attend church in the morning, followed by brunch and possibly visit to office or
>   some shopping. Read the Sunday papers and prepare for the week – meals and
>   lunches, etc.

Reflecting on where I am now

For years, my interests have been in the areas of board development, international social work practice, elder and family housing programme development; issues pertaining to diversity; social justice and human rights; and working with lesbian, gay, bisexual and transgender (LGBT) communities, so my work with IFSW provides an interesting intersection for my current areas of practice and interest. I wish I could say that racism, anti-US sentiment or shades of heterosexism or homophobia do not appear from time to time, but that would not be true, as they indeed have and do. However, I believe strongly that if you are comfortable with who you are, even though others may not agree or even be comfortable with you, they may grow to develop a greater degree of comfort and you may gain their respect. I feel that way about being gay and African American, too. What I am saying here is that I am unwilling to own other people's 'stuff' or biases or bigotry; and woe betide the people who tell me they are uncomfortable being in a room with me as an African American, or as a gay man. I have a cardinal rule: if you can't deal with me, then get out of my way, please!

My family fully accepts and loves me. I have dear friends and colleagues who respect and love me, and I have never tried to help anyone adjust to the fact that I am who I am. I continually say this: you have to set the tone. I am not asking people to agree with me about me, but I do require, no – I demand, that they treat me with respect. I do not give people the power to disapprove of me, because I approve of myself. I honestly don't care what others think of me as a man of colour or as a gay man and usually people understand this, and if they don't they soon do. In addition, my being openly gay and of colour has given me a set of skills that have helped me to navigate the world on my own terms. I understand in double digits what it means to be an outsider. There has always been a little piece of me that loves being the 'outlaw' more than being the 'inlaw'. As we LGBT folks have become more accepted, I am oddly a little less comfortable. I liked the old renegade days. We're becoming more and more mainstream. Once I was in Copenhagen, where it seemed that gay people were more readily absorbed into mainstream culture, and it felt as if it was absolutely no big deal to be gay; I missed having a more affirming and defined gay space. Because gay people are seemingly more accepted, there's no secret language, dress code, special social cues. No sense of tribe, really.

It's a different world from when I grew up. I remember when I was a kid, when a Black person appeared on the television we would all scream, 'There are Black people on TV!' and everyone in the neighbourhood would run to see who they were, and felt a sense of pride that the person on television was where they were, and had achieved what they had. I remember when that was true about gays and lesbians on TV. Now, we have become more mainstream and have our own gay-themed TV or reality shows. But being in the mainstream doesn't necessarily raise you up. Sometimes it reduces you to the lowest common denominator, and I believe that reality television is not always the best that there is of the medium. That is not to say that there is no work for us to do – there is still rampant discrimination and there is still so much to be done to truly become an inclusive global community for all. But it does get, and has got, better. The day will come when I write more fully the story of my life and the intersection of the personal and the professional; however, this is not the time. The late Dame Elizabeth Taylor is purported to have once said, 'I am too busy living my life to write about it yet.' I, too, am still busy living my dream.

The great African American feminist poet Audre Lorde said in a speech in 1987 in Montreal:

> Each of us has some power. You can use your power in the service of what you say you believe. If you do not use your power, someone will use it for you, and do it in your name.

What I want people to know is that they too can have a dream; you have to put it out there and just go for it. They, like me, can become someone who works for increased diversity, social justice and human rights for all people including LGBT communities. It's almost like being a gay Black kid from Cleveland with a dream; they too can even become president of an international organisation someday.

Notes

1   Paraphrased from a quotation by Emile Zola, cited in Winokur, J. (1989) *Writers on Writing*, London: Headline.

2   www.travelersaid.org/.

3   www.montessori.org.uk.

4   www.fsgb.org/.

5   www.naswdc.org/.

6   http://www.aac.org/.

7   Bayard Rustin was the organiser of the 1963 March on Washington, one of the largest non-violent protests ever held in the USA. Rustin was beaten, imprisoned and fired from important leadership positions, largely because he was an openly gay man in a fiercely homophobic era. See http://rustin.org/?page_id=2/.

8   Headquartered in Berne, Switzerland, IFSW consists of ninety national organisations, is divided into five regional groups, and has over 700,000 members. Its primary goal is to promote the profession of social work

and organise professional social workers and facilitate their work through international cooperation. See www.ifsw.org/.

References

DuBois, W.E.B. (1903, 1994) *The Souls of Black Folks*, New York: Dover Publications.

Lorde, A. (1978) 'Power', in *The Black Unicorn: Poems*, New York: Norton, pp. 108–109.

2 Reflections on mental health social work

Kenneth Bolger

I was brought up in a small village in the North West Highlands of Scotland during the 1960s. The village was breathtakingly beautiful but remote, with little in the way of amenities or services. There was a one-teacher primary school for the dozen or so children who would then have to move on to board away from home to attend secondary school. There was a man living in the village at that time in a house on his own (I'll call him Calum). Calum was a gaunt, unshaven man in his thirties or forties who dressed in little more than rags. He spent all his time pacing up and down the village with a cigarette permanently clamped between his teeth. Calum would rarely talk to or even acknowledge anyone else, but he would appear to have animated conversations with himself and sometimes he could be heard shouting from within his unlit and dilapidated house. The village children were wary of Calum, although he would never acknowledge their presence, but we were also curious about him. I remember asking what was wrong with Calum and being given the explanation that 'his brother was killed by a torpedo during the war' and accepting this, as children do, as a reasonable explanation. The only time I remember Calum conversing or interacting with anyone else was when he had heated arguments in the village shop with the lady who served behind the counter when she refused to sell him any more cigarettes unless he also bought some food (presumably from his welfare benefits). I also witnessed the same lady going into Calum's house with plates of food.

I am not aware of Calum being seen by any health professional. The nearest doctor was a general practitioner (GP) in the next village down fifteen miles of single-track road and at that time there were no community mental health services and no community psychiatric nurses (CPNs). I later learned that Calum had returned home from the Second World War where he had been in the merchant navy (as were many West Highland men). His ship had been sunk and he had survived. His brother, serving on another ship, was killed as the result of a torpedo attack by a U-boat. At some time during the 1970s, Calum was taken to Craig Dunain Hospital in Inverness, a large Victorian asylum that served the Highlands and North of Scotland and where he remained for the rest of his life.

Towards a career in psychiatric social work

I have always been struck by how communities provide for people with severe mental health problems and how the level of provision available impacts upon the lives of everybody else in the community. Fast-forward a number of years and I'm in my twenties, living on the Upper East Side of New York, picking up casual work, mostly on construction sites. I lived with some friends in a small flat known as a 'walk up' (it didn't have a lift) with a buzzer entry-phone system. An elderly lady with significant mental health issues somehow managed to overcome the rudimentary security system and take up residence in the hallway for a number of weeks. Reactions from the residents of the apartment block varied from 'she must be evicted immediately, the smell is appalling' (it was) to other residents who would buy her a sandwich from the deli (delicatessen) next door. This was in the late 1970s when New York was in the process of closing large psychiatric institutions, but there appeared to be little in the way of community resources in evidence. In the relatively affluent Upper East Side, it was very common to see people with obvious mental health problems sleeping in doorways, swathed in blankets and clothing against the bitter winter nights. I clearly remember one besuited, briefcase-carrying man surveying such a sight and saying to his companion with real feeling, 'Where are our programmes? Why isn't anybody helping these people?'

I am not sure to what extent these experiences influenced my later decision to train as a psychiatric social worker but I was aware of how marginalised and vulnerable this group was and I was motivated to enrol on the Post Graduate Diploma (Psychiatric) Social Work course at Manchester University. Prior to this I had been working as a residential social worker in London, working in a hostel for people with severe and enduring mental health problems. At this time (the mid-1980s), London had embarked upon the process of closing its old psychiatric hospitals, as New York had a few years earlier, and the borough I worked for was in the process of trying to establish community-based services for this client group. It was, in many ways, a challenging task for the newly formed community mental teams to resettle clients who, in some cases, had been on the psychiatric wards for most of their lives. For those who had been on what are, by today's standards, fairly unsophisticated anti-psychotic medication throughout the 1960s and 1970s, full rehabilitation back into the community was an unrealistic goal and, for these clients, the hostel and its day centre were of critical importance.

Return to New York

Prior to taking up the postgraduate training in Manchester, my partner (a social worker specialising in childcare) and I decided to take up an offer of employment in New York for eighteen months. We were employed by the Jewish Board of Family and Children's Services[1] to work with young people in residential care. My partner worked with young women in a community facility in the Bronx and I worked in a residential unit with young men aged between 14 and 19 with behavioural and mental health issues. The first thing that struck me about working in a residential social work setting in New York was the way in which race and ethnicity ran through almost every aspect of daily life. Around 95 per cent of both the clients and staff were from either African American or Hispanic communities and there was some initial wariness about the Board openly recruiting a group of mostly white British workers. As it turned out, one of the more salutary aspects of the experience was the way in which apparent racial and ethnic differences that initially seemed insurmountable all but evaporated over time as relationships were built.

This situation should be seen in the context of the often complex (and occasionally antagonistic) nature of the relationship between the Jewish and African American communities. Most of the senior professionals in the organisation were white Jewish, and the staff and clients were overwhelmingly African American with some Hispanic and other ethnic groups. To give a flavour of time and place, there was general consternation among my colleagues and the boys on the unit that Spike Lee's excellent film *Do the Right Thing*, released that year,[2] had not been nominated for an Oscar. This was seen generally as yet more evidence of how that community was marginalised and discriminated against. What struck me as a bizarre and rather sad manifestation of the way in which race permeated most aspects of life was the reaction to the growing popularity of the TV cartoon show *The Simpsons* (at that time shown as part of the Tracey Ullman Show). The boys loved the show and, in particular, the character of the wisecracking, skate-boarding son, Bart. As T-shirts and other merchandise began to appear on the streets, the boys began to acquire T-shirts and proceed to colour Bart's face and hair with black felt-tip pen. It was as though they could not, or could not be seen to, relate to an icon of the white community in that way. Enterprising T-shirt printers in Harlem soon got in on the act, and more professionally drawn 'Black Bart' shirts became commonplace.

Aside from some racial and cultural nuances, it was striking how many similarities there were in the nature of the social work tasks as compared to the UK. I was immediately struck by how hard US residential social workers worked. It was by no means unusual for people to be carrying two or even three jobs. In some cases, people were bringing up families, working full time on the unit and, at the same time, studying for a degree. Most of the boys came from Harlem or the South Bronx neigh-bourhoods and had arrived in full-time residential care for a number of reasons. A not uncommon story was that a boy had been brought up by a single mother who had succumbed to the crack cocaine scene that was then reaching epidemic proportions in certain city neighbourhoods. The boys had been assessed as having behavioural or mental health problems, but in the main appeared to be the product of poverty and dysfunctional backgrounds. They were, on the whole, remarkably resilient and, for the most part, responded well to positive reinforcement and consistent and caring boundary setting. A constant source of concern for everybody working on the unit was how the boys would fare when they left residential care and returned to their neighbourhoods. Few of the boys had any academic or vocational qualifications and in reality, for most of them, it would be likely to come down to a choice between the lucrative gang-related drug scene that was endemic in their neighbourhoods or the possibility of a minimum-wage job with few prospects.

One incident I witnessed illustrated for me the difficulties in applying social work values when they were seen to be at odds with 'neighbourhood' or 'street' culture. I came on to the unit one day and witnessed a confrontation between a 15-year-old resident and a male residential worker. Both were African American, from the same part of Harlem. The boy, frustrated at not being allowed to do something he wanted to, had grabbed a plastic knife (metal ones were not used on the unit) and brandished it towards the worker. The worker, who was about 30 years old, six feet six and built like a heavyweight boxer, walked up to the boy, pulled up his shirt exposing his stomach and said, 'Pull a knife on me? OK punk, stab me! I'll give you a free go – stick it into my stomach. After you do that, I'm going to kill you – I'll get maybe ten to fifteen [years' imprisonment] for wasting a little punk like you. I can do that standing on my head.' The worker seemed to be sincere in what he said and the boy started shaking with fear, dropped the knife and dissolved into a sobbing heap on the floor. I spoke later with the worker and told him that I did not think that threatening to murder the residents was in keeping with our role as residential social workers. He looked at me very carefully for a moment and said, 'You don't come from our neighbourhood. What you have to understand is that if that boy had done that on the street to the wrong person, he would now be dead. I know it seems tough but if we don't teach these kids how to deal with people they are going to encounter daily, then they are going to end up dead very quickly.'

I found the experience of working within the American care system a fascinating one. Although the work was often hard, as is residential social work anywhere, the experience of being able to interact and live with people from the vibrant African American community was one which undoubtedly influenced my thinking and practice. I remember taking a group of teenagers to a bowling alley in an affluent white New York suburb and watch parents call their children over to them and hold them protectively. Our boys who, five minutes earlier had been laughing and joking in the minibus, reacted to this reception by pulling down baseball caps, slouching 'Gangsta' style and generally trying to look intimidating, complying with their ascribed roles. It was possible at times like that to gain some sense of what it was like to be treated with fear and suspicion and the limited range of options which that leaves open. Labelling theory has much to offer here (Becker 1963).

Criminal justice services

In the early 1990s, I returned to the Highlands (after being away for twenty years) to take up a post as a social worker with criminal justice services (roughly equivalent to the probation service in England

and Wales). This was an interesting time as specialist criminal justice teams had just been formed and resources were being made available to develop community-based alternatives to prison sentences like probation and community service.[3] For the first two years, I worked as a main grade social worker, covering court duties, writing social enquiry reports and supervising probation orders. Because of my background in mental health, my caseload was weighted towards clients experiencing mental health problems and I also had the opportunity to train as a Mental Health Officer (the equivalent of an ASW in England).[4] I was then successful in applying for a senior social worker post in criminal justice services, with the fairly broad remit of developing services and alternatives to custody for offenders abusing drugs. People are often surprised that the Highlands have a 'drugs problem'. Although not on the same scale as the South Bronx or Manchester, the ways in which drug addiction can impact upon the lives of users and those around them are depressingly similar. At this time 'harm reduction' had clearly won out as an approach (see Newcombe 1992), and we were able to establish good working relationships with Community Psychiatric Addiction staff and the courts. The goal was that, instead of continually imprisoning offenders with addiction problems (we knew this did not impact upon re-offending), a community-based alternative such as a probation order with conditions of compliance (for example, regular attendance at a methadone clinic) could be used as a way of incentivising users to address their dependency problems.

At this time, I started running groups in the local prison for convicted prisoners thought to be at risk from drug abuse. It probably says much about the boredom of serving a prison sentence, but I have never worked with a more enthusiastic group of clients. There was real concern then, as now, about the fact that habitual heroin users' tolerance to drugs was reduced (but not always eliminated!) while they were serving a prison sentence.[5] There had been a series of deaths among young men following release from Scottish prisons because of this (see Bird and Hutchinson 2003), and the group talked candidly about ever-present thoughts of 'that first hit' following release. Harm-reduction advice of the day was subjected to rigorous assessment and analysis (and sometimes rejected as being laughably naïve). Prompted by concern about the number of young people acquiring criminal records for relatively minor drug offences (for example, the possession of small amounts of cannabis), I approached the Procurator Fiscal (similar to the Crown Prosecutor in England and Wales) who agreed to the setting up of a 'Diversion from Prosecution Scheme' whereby people charged with such an offence would be given the opportunity to participate in harm-reduction group work on the understanding that they would not be prosecuted and would not have a criminal record. This initially attracted a flurry of interest from the media which appeared to be looking for an 'Is this the first step towards legalising cannabis?' story. It became apparent fairly quickly that it was not, and was generally recognised as a proportionate and sensible response to the problem which did not involve stigmatising young people with criminal records that would follow them throughout their lives.

During the 1990s, drug use was endemic to the 'dance' scene in the Highlands, as it was in the rest of the UK. There was particular concern that young people were exposing themselves to significant risk by taking Ecstasy and other related drugs in the rapidly evolving scene, and there had, in fact, been a number of deaths (see Milroy *et al.* 1996). I was invited to be on the steering group and subsequently the board of a group set up to address this problem. Lottery funding was acquired and the organisation BLAST! was born. BLAST! worked from a base in Inverness city centre with three paid employees and a growing number of volunteers whose job was to undertake outreach work with young people who were involved with recreational drug use. From the outset, the organisation adopted a non-judgemental, harm-reduction approach and, over time, acquired the reputation for delivering credible support and advice; workers became a common sight in clubs, festivals and on the city streets. As the organisation developed, it hosted innovative workshops in most of the secondary schools in the area.

Community mental health service

For the past ten years I have been managing community mental health teams in the Highlands. This has been a momentous decade in the history of mental health provision in Scotland which has seen the drawing up, passing and implementation of the Mental Health (Care and Treatment) (Scotland) Act 2003. Prior to the Act, there was general agreement that the law in relation to mental disorder in Scotland had not kept pace with clinical practice and changing attitudes. The time was right for new legislation upon which a modern and innovative psychiatric service could be built. The new Act was implemented in 2005 and set out the circumstances in which someone suffering from a mental disorder could be subject to compulsory detention and/or treatment. The Act clearly defined responsibilities, roles, duties and safeguards, and, in a departure from the previous 1984 Act, laid down a set of guiding principles upon which the Act is based. The principles guide the interpretation of the Act and anyone using it is obliged to take them into account when making decisions. Among the ten principles (Non-discrimination, Equality, Respect for Diversity, Informal Care, Participation, Respect for Carers, Least Restrictive Alternative, Benefit, Child Welfare) is the principle of 'Reciprocity'; that is, where society imposes an obligation on an individual to comply with a programme of treatment or care, it should impose a parallel obligation on the health and social care authorities to provide safe and appropriate services, including ongoing care following discharge from compulsion. Nowhere in the country, particularly in parts of the remote and unpopulated North West Highlands, is making a reality of this principle more of a challenge.

Of course, the delivery of adequate health and social care to remote parts of the Highlands has always been challenging. The dismantling of the feudal clan system in the seventeenth century, accelerated by the defeat of the Jacobite uprising in 1745, followed by devastating rural depopulation in the nineteenth century, had left the Highland economy in a parlous state (see MacLean and Linklater 2012). The Dewar Report, published in 1912, described the desperate lack of medical provision, particularly in the more remote areas of the Highlands. The subsistence method of farming known as 'crofting' rarely produced any financial surplus to pay for doctors' visits, as was possible in the industrialised Lowlands. In the ten years prior to the Dewar Report, the national figure for uncertified deaths in Scotland was 2 per cent, in the County of Ross that figure was 47.5 per cent and in one Wester Ross Parish it was 81 per cent.

The 2003 Act has set the bar high in terms of what are acceptable standards. The challenge is, and will continue to be, that sufficient resources are made available to implement the principles of the Act.

MY TYPICAL WEEK

As with many social work jobs, it is not always possible to plan and predict work, as it often requires responding to rapidly developing situations. A typical week, however, might look something like this:

Monday	Supervision with team member. Administration and report writing – there always seem to be reports/papers required by senior management/other agencies, job descriptions to write. Coordination of work (via telephone/e-mail) with other teams and agencies.
Tuesday	Chair multi-disciplinary pre-guardianship meeting (Adults with Incapacity (Scotland) Act 2000). Coordination of work. Prepare Guardianship Application (Adults with Incapacity (Scotland) Act 2000) for Sheriff Court.
Wednesday	Visit outlying team/supervision with team member (discussing each case individually). Home visit with husband of detained patient to prepare social circumstances report.
Thursday	Chair Multi-disciplinary Pre-compulsory Treatment Order meeting (Mental Health (Care and Treatment) (Scotland) Act 2003). Team/allocation meeting.
Friday	On duty rota – attend Psychiatric Hospital and assess patient for consent to detention (Short-term Detention Certificate). Prepare social circumstances report. Mental Health Officer Service management meeting.

Towards the future

Psychiatric services in the Highlands, as throughout the UK, have seen significant changes in the past thirty years. During the 1970s, the former psychiatric hospital in Inverness housed 1,400 patients. Today, despite a significant increase in the population of the Highlands, the replacement hospital (New Craigs) has only 140 beds, representing a significant shift from hospital to the community.

If resources are made available, Scotland might have a system of treating people with mental health problems that is as good as any in the world. I often think back to Calum who lived in my village. His condition, I believe, was largely untreated and he appeared to live a lonely and tormented existence before being locked up for the remainder of his life. That would not be the case today. It is likely that Calum would have been able to stay in the village and would have been seen regularly by members of the community mental health team. CPNs would have monitored his medication, and social work and support work staff would have ensured that he would not have to live in squalor and that the quality of his life would not have deteriorated. The Dewar Report and its proposed solutions directly influenced the formation of the National Health Service which, in turn, has influenced the delivery of health and social care throughout the world. It would be nice to think that despite the current pressures on the public purse a way could be found to deliver community services that are based on the principles of the Act and would raise the standard of services for those suffering from mental ill health to a whole new level.

As I write this, we have just put in place a major restructuring of social work services in the Highlands which means that I am now managing a team of eight Mental Health Officers covering half of the Highland area. Mental Health Officers are specially trained social workers who are primarily responsible for the statutory aspects of working with mentally disordered clients (for example, making applications to the Mental Health Tribunal for compulsory treatment orders and guardianship applications to the Sheriff Court). I am responsible for the allocation of cases and supervision of team members (monthly). Although no longer part of community mental health teams, we work closely with consultant psychiatrists in particular and are at times required to work closely with other mental health professionals and other agencies including the police, with whom we may be required to closely coordinate detaining someone from the community.

The process of reflecting on my career for this chapter has enhanced the realisation that I am in the privileged position of being able to work in a job which I feel is crucially important, always interesting, if occasionally sad and frustrating, and to live in an area where the quality of life is exceptional. The deep sense of frustration, shared by many of us involved in providing services for people suffering from mental ill health, stems from the vision of a mental health service set out in the 'new' Mental Health Act, to which we all aspire, and the political and economic reality of current funding for the public sector which appears to keep the kind of service we feel people deserve, predicated on the solid principles of the Act, tantalisingly out of reach.

Notes

1   Social work agencies in the United States are often drawn up on religious/ethnic lines, reflecting the communities they were first called into being to support.

2   The film *Do the Right Thing* (1989), directed by Spike Lee, is largely concerned with racial tension in an African American community in New York which comes to a head on the hottest day in summer.

3   For more information on the operation of the criminal justice system in Scotland, see Moore and Whyte (1998).

4   For more information on MHOs in Scotland, see Scottish Government (2006).

5   This was not a Scottish-only concern. The *Guardian* newspaper reported in 2008 that heroin use in jails had overtaken cannabis use in England and Wales (Friday, 14 March 2008).

References

Becker, H. (1963) *Outsiders: Studies in the Sociology of Deviance*, New York: Free Press.

Bird, S. and Hutchinson, S. (2003) 'Male drugs-related deaths in the fortnight after release from prison: Scotland, 1996–99', *Addiction* 98: 185–190.

Dewar, Sir John (1912) *Report of Highlands and Islands Medical Services Committee*, Cmd 6559, London.

MacLean, F. and Linklater, M. (2012) *Scotland: A Concise History*, 4th edn, London: Thames & Hudson.

Milroy, C., Clark, J. and Forrest, A. (1996) 'Pathology of deaths associated with ecstasy and eve misuse', *Journal of Clinical Pathology* 49: 149–153.

Moore, G. and Whyte, B. (1998) *Social Work and Criminal Law in Scotland*, Edinburgh: Mercat Press.

Newcombe, R. (1992) 'The reduction of drug related harm: a conceptual framework for theory, practice and research', in P. O'Hare, R. Newcombe, A. Matthews, E. Buning and E. Drucker (eds) *The Reduction of Drug Related Harm*, London: Routledge.

Scottish Government (2006) *A Survey of Mental Health Officer Services in Scotland*, Edinburgh: Scottish Government.

3 A journey from Belfast to London

Jim Campbell

I assume that most social workers, like me, often reflect upon the reasons why we joined the profession and think about how and why our careers followed certain paths. This sort of internal conversation takes place at different times in our lives, sometimes when we are stressed about the job, at other times when we can appreciate the value of social work as an affirmative and rewarding career. This is a good time for me to think about the topic of this book – 'becoming a social worker' – because after twenty years teaching social work at Queen's University Belfast, and some years of practice as a mental health social worker before then, I have recently been appointed as Professor of Social Work at Goldsmith's, University of London. So here is my story of how I became a social worker and how I see the profession through the lens of my experience. I also want to explore the issues that will face us as we look into the future.

Career choice

Like so many people who are attracted to a career in social work, I came to the profession in a roundabout way. I do remember, even though it was some time ago (in the mid-1970s), that I wanted to work in the public sector when I completed my undergraduate studies in philosophy and politics. In 1978, I had to make a decision whether to accept a place on a postgraduate diploma course that would eventually lead to a Master's in Social Work, or study for a Ph.D. Life as a student seemed so much easier then than it is today. Grants and subsidies were provided by the state for postgraduate study in the UK, and so, looking back, I feel very fortunate, and in some ways privileged, to have had these choices. I decided on the Ph.D. option and spent three full-time, and a number of part-time, years of study to complete my thesis. My Ph.D. focused on the concept of violence, as interpreted by a number of important late nineteenth- and twentieth-century political theorists. I have to say that my studies tended to drift along in a way that would not be allowed today in universities; Ph.D. students who may be reading this chapter will know what I am talking about, because there is now much greater pressure on students to complete their Ph.D.s in three or four years. I wanted to do something more pragmatic at the same time as my studies, something to do with 'the real world'. I therefore became involved in voluntary work with older people, and this experience helped me when I applied for my first full-time job as a social work assistant in the field of the psychiatry of old age, and later when I became a mental health social worker in Belfast.

My time as a social work assistant, however brief, was formative and has had a lasting impact upon me as a person, as a social worker and as a social work educator. It helped me to understand the nature of psychiatric institutions and the role social workers can play in multi-disciplinary approaches to delivering health and social care services. Most importantly, I realised the way that the concept of mental illness or mental ill-health is contested and contingent upon social as well as psychological and biological variables (see Rogers and Pilgrim 2010). Even if I didn't always recognise it at the time, it became apparent to me that social workers have a crucial part to play in making sense of such critical discourses in the work we carry out with clients and their families. After a few years in this post, I left to gain my professional qualification in social work at the University of Ulster, and around the same time completed my Ph.D. I was 32 years old, my son was 2 years old and my wife was already a social worker, so there was a lot to look forward to. For the next five years, I worked as a mental health social worker and Approved Social Worker (ASW) in Belfast in Northern Ireland. Eventually, I was employed as a lecturer in social work at Queen's University Belfast in the early 1990s.

So far, I have talked about my career choice in terms of individual decisions that I had made: good, bad or indifferent. Yet, as any good social worker will tell you, we need to take into account social, political and economic contexts when explaining why individuals make such decisions (see Hodkinson and Sparkes 1997; Paton 2007). I had come to social work a little late compared to some of my peers, but even by the early 1980s there was still a degree of optimism about the role the state could play in enhancing the lives of citizens; this established view has gradually been replaced by more pessimistic discourses that have challenged the post-war settlement on the welfare state (see Ferguson *et al.* 2002; Fook 2003). Thatcher governments and subsequent administrations made policy decisions that often adversely affected the lives of the clients whom social workers seek to help. In the twenty years that I spent at Queen's teaching social work students, there was a drift away from radical agendas towards more functional, controlling perspectives (see Ferguson and Woodward 2009). At times, it is gratifying that some students during these years were prepared to challenge and question this consensus; others were content to view social work education as simply an opportunity to gain a useful qualification for work.

On reflecting further, perhaps students, their lecturers and the wider social work community simply mirror the agendas and drivers that constrict and sometimes expand our views on social justice and wider political issues. Nowhere was that more evident than in the very place where I had lived and worked all my life – Northern Ireland. Early on in my career as a social work lecturer, I began to piece together, with colleagues, ideas about how we could develop the curriculum to reflect the challenges of living in a society that had suffered from many years of political conflict; the impact of sectarianism on social work practice and social work education has been a constant during these years. This project was difficult to contemplate twenty years ago when violence and political disagreement characterised Northern Irish society, but it is somewhat easier now that we have a political process that is gradually delivering peace. In my last few years at Queen's, I worked with colleagues and victims and survivors of 'the Troubles'[1] in Northern Ireland to deliver innovative approaches to social work education and learning with Bachelor of Social Work (BSW) students.

Current job

When I became a senior lecturer about a decade ago, I also became more involved in the management of social work education and research. I have recently been appointed as Professor of Social Work at Goldsmith's, University of London, and am looking forward to new and exciting challenges in these areas. What attracted me to Goldsmith's was its tradition of engaging with communities; I wanted to experience first hand how approaches to education and research can be applied to the problems associated with social exclusion and disadvantage. I hope that the practice, teaching and research experience that I have gained over the past quarter of a century will help me in my work with colleagues, students and social work agencies. I will therefore continue to pursue my interest in mental health social work, mental health law, and social work and political conflict.

MY TYPICAL WEEK

The job of a professor of social work can be described in a number of ways, and can vary from university to university. In my case, I have a particular role in enhancing the research culture in my department (which is cross-disciplinary and includes youth and community work and psychotherapeutic teaching programmes alongside social work) as well as representing and promoting the profession both inside and outside Goldsmith's. Every week is different and it is sometimes hard to plan. Quite a lot of my time is involved in meetings associated with the

---

management of the department and university. For example, every other Monday morning is spent with senior colleagues, making decisions about teaching and research policies on which the university expects us to deliver. With my research 'hat' on, I am involved in mentoring colleagues and helping them in terms of publications and research grant activity. I also attend a number of meetings that take place at the centre of the university which monitors such activity. Although professors of social work tend not to teach as much as they would have done during their lecturing career, I am happy to say that I still have some face-to-face contact with students, both in terms of tutoring, lecturing and the supervision of dissertations. I also have a number of Ph.D. students whom I supervise. In addition, I have meetings with social work and other agencies that are essential in ensuring that the high standards of the social work education and learning are maintained, particularly in the provision of practice learning opportunities.

Amidst these meetings and responsibilities I have to find time to pursue my own research and other interests. For the past few years, with my former colleague Professor John Pinkerton, I have been co-editor of the *British Journal of Social Work*. This is a prestigious journal published by Oxford University Press and owned by the British Association of Social Workers. It produces ten academic papers as well as critical commentaries and book reviews for each issue and there are eight issues in each yearly volume. As you can imagine, it does take a lot of time in terms of receiving papers, sending them out for peer review and eventually making decisions about whether to accept for publication or not. Often we can only find time in the evenings or weekends to attend to the constant ebb and flow of this work. As co-editors, we also have to respond to a variety of enquiries from authors, we chair editorial board meetings twice a year and represent the journal at international conferences. We are pleased to say that we encourage a wide variety of potential authors to submit papers, including academics, practitioners and service users and carers. We are also keen to internationalise the journal further in terms of a wider global readership and to publish material from people all over the world, especially those who are new to academic publishing. If you are reading this chapter, please think about getting published with us!

In this very busy life, I also have to make sure that I continue to publish and research in the areas I am interested in. I have recently completed a textbook for mental health social workers, with my former colleague Dr Gavin Davidson, *Post-Qualifying Mental Health Social Work Practice*, published by Sage. I am currently working on a few journal articles on social work and political conflict. Although academics often complain about the pressures of the job, pressures which undoubtedly increase year by year, I feel we should always remember that we are only one constituency among many in the world of social work, and that our colleagues, particularly those involved in everyday practice, also have difficult and challenging jobs. It is crucial that we find ways to make these worlds permeable; one way of doing this is for academics and practitioners to engage with each other, for example, through collaborative initiatives in education, training and development. This can be achieved through jointly run workshops and conferences or through jointly managed projects.

Reflection on the past and looking ahead

There seems little doubt that the social and political contexts within which social work is located have changed considerably in the past quarter of a century. It is, however, important to acknowledge that there are opportunities as well as challenges that have emerged as a result; we must not always look backwards and assume that there was a 'golden age', nor should we always complain that, with the passing of time, the profession has always been eroded and undermined (see Cree 2009). Our judgements about the past tend to be affected by quite subtle influences, the sort I described in my own biographical details. These reflections are conditioned by variables of age, gender, 'race' and ethnicity, sexual orientation, disability – yes, these affect social workers just as much as clients. I will now outline some of the key issues that have affected me in my career, before I go on to talk about where I feel the profession is going in the future.

I will start with the vexed issue that has challenged and frustrated social work since its inception in Victorian times: that of poverty and social exclusion. Social work's attitudes to the social problems faced by disadvantaged clients, families and communities have shifted in the face of political winds over the years. Where there have been opportunities to engage in radical politics and practice (this, in my view, has happened infrequently in the history of the profession), there is somehow more of an optimism of purpose and opportunity for meaningful change. Unfortunately, the readers of this book (and, even worse, many of the citizens who are in need of support and advice) are living through a period of prolonged austerity and significant challenges to the way society and social work is viewed by governments and powerful interests, local as well as international. We have generally occupied an uncomfortable space, having to attend to the demands of public opinion and policy makers, and yet hopefully maintaining our wish that interventions are progressive and enlightening (see Cree 2008; Parton and Kirk 2009). As we look into the future, managing this space will become ever more crucial. In this sense, I believe that the personal has also to be political, and to coin a simplistic parallel phrase, the professional must be more political as well. This can be achieved in different ways, through trade unions and professional organisations, by building alliances and activities with communities and by becoming more committed to politics and the life of the societies of which we are a part. Perhaps we need to re-examine the potential of class as an explanatory concept and embrace new social movements and ideas to help us along the way (see Eder 1993).

This concept of building alliances with disadvantaged constituencies appears at once appropriate but often difficult to conceive, given the position that the profession occupies, at least in developed societies. We would like to create opportunities for change, but something holds us back, governments, organisations and clients. At least this discourse about dealing with (if not challenging) disadvantage is denoted in social work education, training, policy and practice, but how real is it? We only have to reflect on the past to help us deconstruct the way in which these ideas and practices interplay. When I started social work, there was little acknowledgement of the rights of clients, let alone carers. Facilities were built to house citizens; they rarely had any say in the running of institutions and services. As social workers, we have to recognise that, however radical or enlightened the rhetoric of the profession, it often fails to view and identifying its place in society and the state, and confront the ways in which relationships of power adversely affect the work we share with clients. My difficulty with where we are now on this issue is that, in today's practice, we have new sets of conceptual difficulties to deal with in this area. We embrace the rhetoric of 'service user and carer empowerment', but all too often it becomes a clichéd mantra that hides inauthentic policies and practices, or it becomes a weapon to be used by the state to define and diminish the work of professions, while leaving clients even more vulnerable. We may be able to embrace the principles that underpin policies such as personalisation and the use of direct payments in adult services, but all too often the way these ideas are conceived and operationalised fails to match aspirations for social justice and integration. As we look into the future and consider the role of social workers in the lives of such vulnerable clients there has to be a better sense of engagement and debate about how services can be delivered in ways that meet the collective well-being of society and individuals without recourse to the marketisation of goods and services. Perhaps this means returning to some of the tenets of the post-war welfare state and translating these as a way to be used in future debates about these important relationships (see Ferguson and Woodward 2009).

I will complete this section by trying to connect the local with the global, using the experiences I described above. I am sure that most social workers who spent much of their careers in Northern Ireland over the past few decades would agree that the conflict tended to close down their appreciation of the wider national and international contexts of social work. It is really only in recent years, with the return of some sort of 'normality' to this society, that the 'common or garden' concerns of everyday life are understood, not just in terms of locality but also in the way globalisation affects us all. But the legacy of the conflict is an abiding reminder of the trauma of the past, so it must be resolved, even if it takes a generation to do so. One of my research interests is to explore the way in which our experience can be understood in other international contexts. I strongly believe that social workers in different countries and regions should be equipped to deal with past and present social and political conflicts if only because such conflicts are a continuing reality for so many citizens, both at home and internationally.

More generally, as social workers, we will be affected increasingly by global factors. These will create problems that need to be dealt with, but I believe there are many opportunities to effect change and engage with new constituencies. For example, the impact of different types of technologies and movements of capital and populations across national borders means the global has been pushed to the front of our consciousness as citizens and practitioners (see Bauman 2000). This means that our established understanding of knowledge of social problems and social work interventions will be tested. In my new job, for instance, some colleagues and agency staff are already using social network media to discuss and construct ideas and practices that are not in the public gaze (as traditionally framed by paradigms of modernity). And of course parallel experiences and processes must exist for the citizens who come into contact with social work services. I am sure that some of you who are reading this chapter are better placed than me to explain what all this will imply in terms of how the profession develops in the future, but it certainly means that I have a duty to figure out what I should be doing in these circumstances!

As we become increasingly aware of the international, it is important to contemplate how we relate to this wider world that such new technologies have revealed. As a result we seem to know more about other societies and social processes outside the boundaries of locality, and yet how much of this awareness translates into social work practice? This issue has certainly challenged me and my colleagues on the Editorial Board of the *British Journal of Social Work* as we strive to make sense of different forms of social work knowledge that are not always present within the covers of the journals. It is often the case that in the UK, we assume that our models of social work education, policy and practice are either unique or privileged. This assumption needs to be challenged, in particular by examining critically other social systems and social work methods across Europe and other continents. Two examples come to mind. In the UK, we seem to be fixated about casework approaches and, even when alternatives such as community development are available, this dominant paradigm is hard to shift. In some parts of Europe another tradition, that of social pedagogy, offers alternative perspectives where the relationships between social work and individuals, families and communities are mediated through the use of media, above and beyond the spoken word (see Smith 2009). And if we go beyond the narrow confines of these shores, then surely we can learn from some of the development approaches used in Latin America, Asia and Africa. I feel that an increasing understanding of these contexts will challenge and change the way in which social workers view their roles and responsibilities.

Conclusion

In concluding this chapter, a few thoughts come to mind. There is a richness of diversity in the biographical stories that we bring to the profession and yet there are so many commonalities in how we view the world and seek to change it. This mix of experience and knowledge, then shaped by organisational expectations and legal responsibilities, often pushes us in various directions which are sometimes hard to resist. None the less, we are not powerless in the face of these pressures. In becoming a social worker I embraced the opportunities to work with many interesting and engaging yet often powerless clients and I hope that that enthusiasm has lasted, despite the passage of time and movement away from practice towards education and research. There is a need for constant vigilance about how we think and feel when we are confronted with social injustice, and in the way we face a world which is often hostile. This will always be the case, so finding ways to deal with our anxieties and building alliances with colleagues, clients and social movements can help us feel less insecure and more able to effect change. These opportunities should not be confined to the minutiae of patch and locality working, however important these contexts are. We need to become more aware of our place, and that of the profession, in the wider world of international society and politics. In doing so, we can expand our understanding of the social work role and affirm all the reasons why we became social workers.

Note

1   Social work policy and practice in Northern Ireland have been shaped by decades of sectarian conflict that followed the partition of the island of Ireland in 1920 (Pinkerton and Campbell 2002). In recent years there has been evidence of growing opportunities for engagement with victims and survivors of the conflict which is changing the way in which social work is practised (Campbell and Duffy 2008).

References

Bauman, Z. (2000) *Globalization, the Human Consequences*, Oxford: Polity Press.

Campbell, J. and Duffy, J. (2008) 'Social Work, Political Violence and Citizenship in Northern Ireland', in Ramon, S. (ed.) *Social Work in Political Conflict*, Birmingham: Venture/BASW.

Cree, V.E. (2008) 'Social Work and Society', in Davies, M. (ed.) *Blackwell Companion to Social Work*, 3rd edn, Oxford: Blackwell.

Cree, V.E. (2009) 'The Changing Nature of Social Work', in Adams, R., Dominelli, L. and Payne, M. (eds) *Social Work. Themes, Issues and Critical Debates*, 3rd edn, Basingstoke: Palgrave Macmillan.

Eder, K. (1993) *The New Politics of Class: Social Movements and Cultural Dynamics in Advanced Societies*, London: Sage.

Fay, M.-T., Morrisey, M. and Smyth, M. (1999) *Northern Ireland's Troubles. The Human Costs*, London: Pluto Press.

Ferguson, I. and Woodward, R. (2009) *Radical Social Work: Making a Difference*, Bristol: The Policy Press.

Ferguson, I., Lavalette, M. and Mooney, G. (2002) *Rethinking Welfare: A Critical Perspective*, London: Sage.

Fook, J. (2003) 'Critical Social Work: The Current Issues', *Qualitative Social Work* 2(2): 123.

Hodkinson, P. and Sparkes, A. (1997) 'Careership: A Sociological Theory of Career Decision-making', *British Journal of Sociology of Education* 10(1): 23–35.

Parton, N. and Kirk, S. (2009) 'The Nature and Purposes of Social Work', in Shaw, I., Briar-Lawson, K., Orme, J. and Ruckdeschel, R. (eds) *The SAGE Handbook of Social Work Research*, London: Sage.

Paton, K. (2007) *Education and Career Decision-making: Challenging the Context of Choice*. Society for Research into Higher Education (SRHE) Annual Conference, Brighton, UK, 12 December.

Pinkerton, J. and Campbell, J. (2002) 'Social Work and Social Justice in Northern Ireland: Towards a New Occupational Space', *British Journal of Social Work*, 32(6): 723–737.

Rogers, A. and Pilgrim, D. (2010) *A Sociology of Mental Health and Illness*, 4th edn, Buckingham: Open University Press.

Smith, M. (2009) 'Social Work as Social Education: The Possibilities of Social Pedagogy in Scotland', *European Journal of Social Education* 16/17: 229–239.

4 Social work in Aotearoa New Zealand

An experience of cultural change

Marie Connolly

Curiously, it was my father who instilled the basics of my feminist thinking, which then influenced both the way I have lived my life and my approach to social work. I say 'curiously' because he was, in fact, something of a patriarch who thought little of the role of women and certainly left all things domestic to my mother. But he was a trade unionist of radical persuasion and he believed in fairness and the human right to fair treatment. A strongly opinionated but unequivocally rational man, for him the logic of fairness applied to everyone. Women's rights were nowhere near the forefront of his mind, but logic required that women be part of the equation. And so, in all kinds of ways, the messages of fair treatment and human rights filtered through my childhood, building a foundation that would later be influenced by social movements and my own experiences growing up as a young person in a working-class Liverpool family.

I was a teenager when my family emigrated from England in 1970. Supported passage basically provided three choices for the adventurous: Canada, a country my mother thought too cold; South Africa, where she predicted future troubles; and Australia, promoted in those days as an egalitarian paradise. It was no contest really and so we bid farewell to a large extended family and boarded an Italian ship to Australia, where my father was to work as a boilermaker for a large South Australian shipbuilding company. It was over 110° when we first arrived – 113° to be exact – an experience from which my parents never really recovered and one which ultimately influenced their move to Aotearoa New Zealand. For the rest of his life, my father saw New Zealand as the egalitarian paradise he had always imagined and my mother continues to live there happily, finding both cultural and climatic fit.

Becoming a social worker

Although I would like to say that my entry into social work was a result of careful career planning and reflective decision-making, this was far from the case. I don't think I really knew what a social worker was when my mother suggested I apply for a job in child welfare. Coming from a family of talkers, she was confident that a job based mostly around talking would be perfect for me! Somewhat uncertain about what it would involve, I applied for what was called a supernumerary position. (These were appointments that were over and above the established staffing level and were commonly available in government services during the 1970s. Supernumerary positions provided an entry into social work for people lacking formal social work qualifications.) I recall during the interview talking vaguely about helping people and, while I am sure my performance would not meet the criteria of contemporary expectations, it was enough to get through, and I so began my career in child welfare.

As I reflect on those early years, I appreciate the way in which supernumerary social workers were nurtured into the field of practice. Today so many child protection social workers have to 'hit the ground running', regardless of their experience. My first six weeks in the job involved reading the social work manual, and getting to know the community in which I would work. This was followed by several months of residential in-house training where I learned the basics of working with people – an interesting mixture of psychodynamic and behavioural approaches that were popular at the time. Only after this period of residential training was I able to talk to clients and assume casework responsibility for a small number of children in foster care. This limited entry into social work continued for twelve months, followed by a further long stint of residential training. Only after this was I considered ready to take on full casework responsibilities, and to be employed as a fully fledged social worker.

Child welfare social workers in New Zealand at that time were seconded to specialist teams. An intake team responded to enquiries and undertook short-term work with clients, usually up to three months. Then there was the foster team where I first began, looking after children in care. There was a court team and an adoptions team, and a team that did community development work. Over the next few years, I moved from one specialist team to another, building expertise and experience that later became invaluable when I took up an academic position. But before that I needed to become qualified.

The School of Social Science at the Victoria University of Wellington was the first to provide social work training in New Zealand in 1949 (Nash 2009). The curriculum was modelled on the British system combining social administration and casework. By the time I reached the institution, there was a healthy, if sometimes confusing mix of ideas that informed the kind of social work practised in the late 1970s and early 1980s. The behaviourists were still popular, along with the family therapists of the 1970s. Systems thinking embedded itself strongly within the social work psyche. But the book I found most intriguing was *Change: Principles of Problem Formation and Problem Resolution* published in 1974 by Paul Watzlawick and his colleagues. It was a fascinating exploration of what influences processes of change, how we end up perpetuating problems rather than resolving them, and how we can do things differently once we understand this.

Social work in Aotearoa New Zealand

When I look back now upon my training and my work within child welfare during those early years, I am struck by just how British it all was. New Zealand's child welfare system was based on developments in the UK, and I suspect that our conversations within the workplace would have resonated strongly with those across the UK, and probably other English-speaking jurisdictions. This would all change during the 1980s. Māori, the indigenous peoples of Aotearoa New Zealand, had long been over-represented in child welfare statistics. As a people, Māori had also been obstructed from the realisation of collective rights within a country that, ironically, saw itself as the epitome of the classless society. Not everyone, in fact, did receive a 'fair go'. During the 1980s, both Māori and non-Māori voiced concern about the alienating nature of child welfare practices that saw children being removed from their families and estranged from their cultural origins. By the end of the 1980s, in a critical convergence of ideas, childcare and protection responses in Aotearoa New Zealand were radically transformed. Family group conferencing was formally introduced into legislation. A model of family decision-making, the family group conference (FGC) became the key mechanism for responding to children at risk. As a practice, it fundamentally changed the nature of power relationships between the family and the state, and there wasn't a person involved in child and family services who was unaffected by this transformation. In a sweeping change, child welfare had adopted a practice based on traditional Māori processes of collective decision-making. For me, and for many social workers like me, social work practice had changed irrevocably. Child welfare in Aotearoa had shaken off its Britishness. At least that is how it seemed in 1989. As it turned out, during the 1990s, child protection services in Aotearoa did their utmost to emulate developing practices in England, the USA and Australia. Risk assessment discourses and investigative-focused practices swept across New Zealand with alacrity. The family-led practices that had flourished with the introduction of the FGC struggled to exist alongside this dominant forensic paradigm. And soon we were experiencing the very same problems that have challenged child protection services across international jurisdictions.

From practice to academia and back again

It was with some sense of alarm that I watched these changes that served to undermine family-led child protection processes in New Zealand. By then, I had moved to an academic role at the University of Canterbury where I was happily focusing my efforts on teaching social work theory and research. Being an early career academic at a time when social work was launching into strengths-based ideas was both an exciting and a privileged time for me, and offered a role I assumed I would never leave. But after almost fifteen years in academia, an opportunity presented itself – the Chief Social Worker position within the New Zealand government became available. The public face of social work in New Zealand, the Chief Social Worker's key responsibility was to support good practice and work towards the development of strong services for children. Advising government at the senior executive level, appearing before select committees and defending professional practice in the media was a daunting prospect. But having an opportunity to influence the future shape of child protection service delivery was irresistible. It was, nevertheless, with a sense of trepidation that I took up the role in 2005. Unexpectedly, the next five years proved to be the most rewarding of my professional career.

The Chief Social Worker's Office within the Ministry of Social Development was positioned outside the child welfare system and was directly responsible to the Chief Executive. Being positioned external to the statutory service created a degree of independence from direct practice that was important when undertaking child death and other serious case reviews, a particular responsibility of my office. Although outside the child protection system, we worked closely with the statutory service, developing new service delivery models, providing leadership in best practice, and working to develop policies and practices that supported the family-responsive legislation that we were fortunate enough to have. The work was immensely varied. In any one week I could be attending meetings in the Minister's office, talking to the media, presenting ideas at national events, undertaking practice research or policy-writing, and talking to practitioners across the country – an activity I enjoyed more than anything else. I was always inspired and humbled when I visited offices and listened to the stories and experiences of practitioners. They would often greet me with a waiata (song) and we would always celebrate with food. Almost without exception, their enthusiasm and commitment to the work of supporting children was palpable. While the intensity of their experiences was explicitly confronting, they invariably talked about the courage and strength of families and the need for perseverance when working through complex issues of child protection and youth justice. I always returned to Wellington feeling practice was in good heart despite the challenges.

MY TYPICAL WEEK

This is what a week in the Chief Social Worker's office might look like:

Monday   Review weekend media responses; prepare staff for new serious case review; operational policy review meeting; work with communications team on practice guide; make presentation to multi-disciplinary forum; prepare report for Minister.

Tuesday   Fly to Auckland and pick up rental car; drive to stakeholder meetings; present awards at Auckland site in afternoon; fly back late.

Wednesday   Weekly Senior Executive meeting (all day); regular meeting with Minister 5–6.30 p.m.

Thursday   Fly to Christchurch for three Southern Regional visits; drive to youth justice residence for workshop delivery; check in with CSW staff; stay overnight in Christchurch.

Friday   Drive to rural sites for site visits; return to Christchurch for Wellington flight.

Weekend   Catch up on reading and writing.

During my five years in the role, I worked with a talented group of people who were deeply committed to reforming the child welfare system in Aotearoa (see Connolly and Smith 2010). I was extremely fortunate to have been in that place at that time, as many good executive teams have applied effort yet struggled to facilitate reform that would strengthen child protection services. It is an area of work that is difficult to get right, both in practice and management, and there will always be incidents that will test the community's confidence and tolerance. An important lesson I learned, nevertheless, during my time in government is that change is possible, even within the most challenging of systems, and that committed people can make a positive difference to the lives of children and their families.

In 2010, I left the role of Chief Social Worker and returned to academic teaching and research at the University of Melbourne. Since that time, I am delighted to see that students are still excited about the prospect of entering the profession of social work. Being closely aligned with practice over the past five years has reinforced to me the importance of creating knowledge-building bridges that make logical sense to social work students and busy field practitioners. Responding to the demands of contemporary practice often leaves little time for trawling through research findings in the hope of identifying new practice ideas. Within this demanding environment, there is a danger that social workers will practise in a knowledge vacuum, developing initiatives that lack the benefit of an evidence base. Over time, we have established a body of knowledge that supports good social work practice, and research is constantly being undertaken that promises to strengthen practice further. Much of this new knowledge, however, remains out of reach of many practitioners; or at least is packaged in ways that make it difficult to assimilate in practice. If the gap between the interests of academic knowledge producers and practitioners becomes a chasm, we will run the risk of social work research becoming irrelevant to practice and practice development. Creating research and practice partnerships will help us to construct knowledge-building bridges. Increasingly ways are being found to strengthen the relevance of social work research and knowledge through academic and practice partnerships and practice frameworks that integrate empirical research, ethical principles and knowledge into easily accessible models that guide practice (see Connolly and Healy 2009). Academic/field partnerships that contribute to and support ongoing professional development are important, and so too were partnerships in practice-based practitioner research. Epstein (2010), for example, describes processes of clinical data-mining that focus primarily on practice-related questions and use practitioner-generated information to inform practice decision-making. Not surprisingly, this practice-based method builds a sense of joint ownership of the research and its outcomes, and there is evidence that direct changes in policy and practice have been facilitated through these research/practice partnerships.

Twenty-first-century social work

The demands of twenty-first-century social work require, perhaps now more than ever, a workforce that is strong ethically, academically and professionally. Over time, social work has searched for a unified knowledge base to support expertise and secure disciplinary identity. During the 1970s, professional credibility depended upon disciplines having a unified body of knowledge, and for a while it seemed that systems theory might provide this theoretical unification for social work. This was not to be, and as social work theorising and practice strengthened in confidence it became clear that we do not need a single representative theory; we can integrate theoretical frameworks in ways that are responsive to deeply held cultural and disciplinary values. Social work values provide an underpinning framework that strongly influences social work thinking and the application of practice knowledge in important ways. Interpretative lenses filter ideas and critically shape disciplinary responses. For example, concern for social justice has long been the hallmark of progressive social work. Even in the most difficult of practice environments it creates value-driven responses that reflect a deep disciplinary concern for marginalised populations. Social work also values critical reflection and the importance of reflective practice, a lens through which we can interrogate the impact we have on the people and systems we work with. It is the application of these, and other, interpretative lenses that support responses that are unmistakably social work in nature. For example, cognitive-behavioural therapy is practised by social workers and by other allied disciplines. Because the principles and interventions of cognitive-behavioural therapy are non-discipline-specific, we may conclude that a service user would experience the same practice response regardless of the practitioner's disciplinary background. An exploration of the clinical literature relating to cognitive-behavioural interventions would, however, challenge this. In the following quote, Sharon Berlin, an American social work theorist, adapts cognitive theory in ways that reflect social work concerns:

My work to revise more orthodox versions of cognitive therapy constitutes an attempt to pull what I think are a body of good ideas away from an excessive commitment to the 'ideology of an independent self' (Markus and Cross 1990: 601) and to increase the breadth of targets and the range of interventions to encompass social interventions for difficult social situations. These efforts are occurring at a time in which the life chances of many people are being systematically undercut as a result of shifts in popular sentiment and political leadership that emphasize the high costs of welfare benefits and adhere to the old belief that the good life is available to anyone who is willing to work for it. Especially in these times, it seems critical to have a cognitive perspective that acknowledges that willingness . . . is only a part of the social mobility/personal adaptation story.

(Berlin 2002: 31)

Here Berlin interprets theory through a social work lens and adapts it in ways that reflect social work concerns and values. Berlin's integrative treatment is very different from other, similar texts that have been written from a different disciplinary perspective (see, for example, a psychological treatment by Kazantzis *et al.* 2010). This is not to say that one is any better than the other. They are just different, reflecting unique disciplinary approaches.

Our interpretative disciplinary lenses also situate practice within particular cultural contexts. Theories and practices within human services can be colonising in ways that reflect dominant cultural values and norms. Countries have differing cultural imperatives and will develop responses that reflect particular cultural and societal fit. Social work as a discipline, and its supporting social work training, provide well for practice in a globalised world. Put simply, globalisation is about the movement of ideas, ideas that can create inter-dependencies across international boundaries. Some ideas have the capacity to positively change the face of social work practice, for example in the development of technological advances that bring people closer together. Globalised ideas can also, however, create disadvantaged communities when punitive economic policies have deleterious consequences for more vulnerable people in society. Social work as a profession fosters democratisation and supports human rights and fairness. It is a profession that my father was pleased to see me join. Social work as a discipline has matured in the decades since I completed my professional training, and, I believe, has become much more knowledgeable in the process. While some practice environments may undoubtedly be challenging, particularly when they impact upon and constrain personal freedom, social work's critical interpretative lens remains constant, creating advocacy imperatives that unify practitioners no matter where they may practise in the world.

References

Berlin, S.B. (2002) *Clinical Social Work Practice: A Cognitive-Integrative Perspective.* New York: Oxford University Press.

Connolly, M. and Healy, K. (2009) Social work practice theories and frameworks. In Connolly, M. and Harms, L. (eds) *Social Work: Contexts and Practice,* 2nd edn. Melbourne: Oxford University Press: 19–36.

Connolly, M. and Smith, R. (2010) Reforming child welfare: An integrated approach. *Child Welfare, 89* (3): 9–31.

Epstein, I. (2010) *Clinical Data-mining: Integrating Practice and Research.* New York: Oxford University Press.

Kazantzis, N., Reinecke, M.A. and Freeman, A. (2010) *Cognitive and Behavioural Theories in Clinical Practice.* New York: Guilford Press.

Markus, H. and Cross, S. (1990) The interpersonal self. In Pervin, L.A. (ed.) *Handbook of Personality: Theory and Research,* New York: Guilford Press: 576–608.

Nash, M. (2009) Histories of the social work profession. In Connolly, M. and Harms, L. (eds) *Social Work: Contexts and Practice,* 2nd edn. Melbourne: Oxford University Press: 363–377.

Watzlawick, P., Weakland, J. and Fisch, R. (1974) *Change: Principles of Problem Formation and Problem Resolution,* New York: W.W. Norton.

5 A very political social worker

Hilton Dawson

When I worked as a social worker, someone once said, 'As a social worker, you'd make a better politician.' Then, when I was a Member of Parliament, someone else said, 'As a politician, you'd make a pretty good social worker.' I think these people should probably mind their own business! However, reflecting further, I think they were talking about two sides of the same coin. As a Member of Parliament I used to wonder how my colleagues without social work experience could cope with the vast range of human problems and humanity which present daily at constituency 'surgeries'. As a social worker I was always acutely aware, not only that many of the problems we see are founded in bigger social issues, but that these problems would be better addressed if the people experiencing them and those trying to help them actually used the political power they/we have. But I am getting ahead of myself. . . .

Childhood and youth

I grew up in Newbiggin by the Sea, a fishing and mining village on the Northumbrian Coast, in the Northeast of England. My brother (also a social worker) and I were brought up by two loving, selfless, teacher parents in a wider family committed to Christian ethics and rooted in a working-class community within an inspiring natural environment. Although we haven't ever discussed this, I believe that our upbringing must have had a lot to do with the way we have both chosen to live our lives.

As a boy, my childhood was inevitably dominated by either fighting or football; for a big strong lad who was reluctant to get hit, the choice was obvious. I first began to learn for myself about life through the international language and lore of what is still called 'the beautiful game'. Bobby Charlton (of Manchester United and England fame) was born in the next village to mine, while Alfredo Di Stefano (the Argentine-Spanish striker) often appeared in the imagination of our back streets. With a strong sense of right and wrong, the lessons about teamwork and sporting fairness were particularly important to me. I believe that playing football every day, sometimes all day, has contributed to the fitness and energy I am lucky enough to enjoy today.

I became a rebel despite shyness. This may surprise some people, because I have always felt compelled to say what I am thinking and driven to play my part in whatever is going on around me. I was bored and disaffected at secondary school, and the first time I heard Bob Dylan I felt the thrill of recognition and understood that he had something I needed to learn. Desperate to join the student revolution, I headed off to Warwick University to study philosophy and politics. Shortly before I left university, my dad died, and within twelve months I had married my sixth-form sweetheart. (Two children and increasing grandchildren later, we are still together after almost forty years.) Love and family life came together in Karl Marx's eleventh thesis on Feurbach: 'The philosophers have only interpreted the world, in various ways; the point is to change it' (Marx and Engels 1970: 123). A university anarchist, I discovered books, music, art, ideas. Although only a moderate scholar, I began a lifelong fascination and struggle with the work of Martin Heidegger. Although Heidegger was capable of abysmal personal behaviour to the extent of espousing Nazism in the 1930s, his description of the human condition in *Being and Time* remains utterly profound for me and I believe that his depiction of what he refers to as 'care' and 'concern' and 'being toward others' provides a sure, existential foundation for our work. The other writer to whom I regularly return is the Irish novelist and poet James Joyce, who demonstrates the significance of all our ordinary lives in hugely complex but even more glorious prose.

Community work

Imbued with a collective spirit and a desire to see something of the world, my partner Sue and I went to live on a 'kibbutz' in Israel. Kibbutz Masada was an impressive and resilient community, but the experience of living next to a minefield with armed guards and warplanes flying overhead to Lebanon gave us a powerful desire to start a family and to bring up children in safety. We returned to England and home to Northumberland. Our first daughter was born ten months later, by which time I had started a new job as a community worker and the foundations of my becoming a social worker had been laid. As the Warden at the Choppington Miners Welfare in Northumberland, we lived in a community which was locally notorious for its social problems, and yet which contained some of the most capable, warm and thoroughly decent people it has ever been my privilege to know. I managed the building, ran the bar, stoked the boilers, compered functions, invited young people in, and worked with a group of women to develop a whole range of new community initiatives, including community theatre and community arts. I worked all hours, made loads of mistakes and learned how to work with people. For the first time,

I also came into contact with local Labour politicians. Impressed with their daily practical efforts to make politics work for people, I performed a massive political somersault by joining and immediately becoming active in the party that I had so despised in my radical, ineffectual youth.

Working at 'the Welfare', I also learned that social workers had much more influence than me, particularly over the big decisions about the young people with whom I worked. When a job as an unqualified social worker in the local team came along, I was invited to apply for it. Then, as soon as I was appointed, everything changed. Although I continued to live in the same house in the same community, to many people I had switched sides. The compensation was to become the youngest and only unqualified member of a team of exceptionally bright and committed social workers, presided over by a manager and seniors of great maturity and practice wisdom. This was generic work in a small mining town, and I was supported, challenged and helped to develop by managers, peers and the people we tried so hard to serve. I loved the work and devoured every moment of the twenty months I was there. The lessons and the experience have become part of me.

Studying social work

Sue and I still debate how we decided to uproot ourselves from job, home and extended family in the Northeast so that I could study for a social work qualification at the University of Lancaster, with one child of 3 years of age and another on the way. I clearly recall the clapped-out van with all our possessions struggling up the hill on the A69, and me sitting at the wheel, silently vowing that I would never, ever put our family in this position again. But in 1980, there was simply no other place to be! The University of Lancaster was the home of the Centre for Youth, Crime and Community, and the focus of radical thinking in social work. On our first day of the course, Norman Tutt, then Director, hailed us as the 'intellectual elite of the next generation of social workers'. I spent much of the next two years embraced in the diversion of young people from care and custody, collecting data under the guidance of David Thorpe and being the first student at a pioneering centre in Rochdale, set up to implement the new theories.[1] This was intoxicating stuff, and after qualifying I spent five years setting up two schemes in Preston and Lancaster, working directly with young people and key players in the police and magistracy to monitor and manage systems in what became a 'custody-free zone'. This might seem a rose-tinted world away from the current system in which young people are accelerated into the prison system. However, in my bleaker moments I question how well we actually served some young people by keeping them so zealously out of care, and how much the ideology of 'diversion' actually served the cost-cutting agendas of the 1980s, to the detriment of some good services for children.

Entering politics

Throughout this time, I was active in local politics and community activities, revelling in opposing Thatcherism through picketing and support for the miners' strike between 1984 and 1985 and involved in family events in the neighbourhood. I first stood for the local council for the 'unwinnable' ward where I lived in 1983 and then won it in 1987, largely because I was better known by this time and we had persuaded people who had never taken part in an election to come out and vote. In the late 1980s, I took on a new role managing residential care, fostering and adoption and services for under-8s in two districts of Lancashire, and by 1991, in my other life, I was Deputy Leader of Lancaster City Council. Interestingly, an attempt by a political opponent to have me disqualified from office as a councillor because of my grading as a local government officer foundered when my employers declared that I had 'no influence whatsoever on the policies of Lancashire County Council'! In fact, I did have enormous influence on the services I managed and on the lives of people who, hopefully, mainly benefited from them. I count these as my best years so far in social work. As a manager, I was supported and protected by my own managers so that we were able to introduce new systems which managed the care system better, change services for children with disabilities and obtain more resources for young children and their families. I also provided space and backing for some very talented people whom I managed and I was able to retain regular contact with children, young people and families. The best part for me was working with the Lancashire 'In Care' Group, supporting the development of local groups across the county to empower young people in care to ensure that services were driven by their needs and voices. I was learning all the time, from groups such as NAYPIC and Who Cares?,[2] as well as from dedicated social workers at all levels, and, above all, from young people themselves. At the same time, I was unashamedly using my influence at district level to ensure that all young people leaving care were provided with housing. I also used my contacts with the local media to get some positive news stories into the public domain.

By 1995 I had begun to withdraw from local politics, standing down from key positions with a view to leaving the council in 1999 and concentrating more on my career. Then one evening, a young man telephoned to say that he wanted to nominate me as the Labour candidate for Lancaster & Wyre at the next General Election. I knew that this would mean a colossal amount of work on top of everything else. I was uncertain whether I would even get the nomination, and there was a notional Conservative majority of 11,000 in a seat where the boundaries had been altered unfavourably. But the local MP was standing down and the 'Blair revolution' was under way, potentially making us more electable than ever before. Sitting at my kitchen table, I realised that this could be *the* day for me, and life-changing opportunities do not necessarily come at the most convenient time. The historic victory, when it came, was down to the Labour Party, to the hundreds of people who put their hearts and souls into the campaign, and to Tony Blair. But I believe that another reason we narrowly won rather than lost that day was because of my knowledge and experience of working with people.

Looking back on my time in Parliament, although I had great respect and personal liking for key individuals and was proud to have taken part in the detailed discussion and development of some important legislation, I always felt that the approach of New Labour to social policy was simplistic and authoritarian. This opinion did not endear me to my fellow politicians or provide me with much influence as a backbench MP. However, at least I tried, forming the All Party Group for Children and Young People in Care and thus bringing their voices to Parliament every month. I also introduced a

Private Member's Bill for a Children's Commissioner, and brought about some key amendments to a Housing Bill for people living in park homes.[3] The dripping water does eventually wear away the stone! Above all, representing and communicating with 80,000 people (the majority of whom had not voted for me), and aiming to serve them all well, has been perhaps the greatest privilege of my working life, as well as a unique way to roll casework, community work, group work and raw politics together into one.

Visits to Burundi, Angola and Sudan with Unicef[4] or at the behest of All Party Groups also exposed me to some of the most horrendous situations in the world. I was inspired by the work of so many people working to assist children and families in dangerous and desperate circumstances, yet I felt angry and impotent when I could only blather on in response to children dying before my eyes in Darfur. Closer to home, I was dismayed to observe the dismantling of systems which I had developed to support young people and utterly frustrated that, as an MP, I could only write a fruitless letter of protest, whereas as a social work manager, I might have been able to do something positive. After eight years and another narrow victory, I gave up politics to become a social worker once more.

Return to social work

Since 2005, successively and sometimes at the same time, I have worked for ChildLine,[5] been Chief Executive of Shaftesbury Young People, one of England's oldest children's charities, chaired the National Academy for Parenting Practitioners and worked as a consultant in the private sector before becoming Chief Executive of the British Association of Social Workers (BASW) in April 2009. Some say that this is the perfect job for me, and some days I agree. Basically, my job consists of standing up for the principles and practice of social work and the rights of social workers, engaging with governments and employers and media across the four countries of the UK. I spend a lot of time talking to social workers and expend a great deal of effort asserting that the values of social work and the skills of social workers are of great benefit to any society and should be valued and made central to the ongoing process of improvement and reform.

Looking ahead

Social work in England is in a particularly difficult position at the moment, but devolution seems likely to continue to provide opportunities for different and better models of social work to flourish in Scotland, Wales and Northern Ireland. Best of all, as an international profession recognised by the United Nations and with an international definition and ethical code, we can also look to the rest of the world. I have been fortunate enough to meet the man who is responsible for recruiting five million social workers in China; I have heard from the Brazil Association and the Russian Association about their critical engagement with presidents of two of the world's fastest developing countries; and I am

MY TYPICAL WEEK

Sunday   Evening – travel to Birmingham flat from home in Northumberland. Write my monthly article for PSW magazine on the train. Emails.

Monday   Start at 7.30 a.m. with an interview with local radio station about complaints of raised eligibility in adult services – set issues in national context.

Office – Management Team – monthly meeting to review finance, staffing, membership growth, latest on college negotiations.

Skype call to colleagues in Bulgaria, Armenia and Georgia – working on a project to glean information about the state of social work and social work associations across Europe on behalf of IFSW.[6]

Drive ninety miles to meeting with social workers.

Early evening meeting with social workers (members of BASW and SWU and non-members who work in children's services for an English local authority.

Drive back to the flat after the meeting – home about 10 p.m.

Emails throughout the day.

Tuesday   8.30 a.m. Flight to Belfast.

Summarise yesterday's meeting and send report from departure lounge.

Formal meeting with Northern Ireland Trade Union Certification Officer to discuss progress on the Social Workers Union (SWU); accompanied by SWU Northern Ireland trade union official.

Later, meet with NIASW (Northern Ireland Association of Social Workers) team to discuss various elements of their work-plan including an imminent appearance before the Health Committee of the Northern Ireland Assembly and the recent meeting with the Chief Social Worker. Supervision with our Northern Ireland Manager.

Discuss forthcoming meeting with Social Care Minister with social work specialist media and agree to take part in a webinar on 'the state of social work' early next week.

Called by our Press Officer and agree to do pre-record for BBC TV News responding to an embargoed report from a voluntary organisation on problems of recruiting foster care.

Back into Birmingham airport at 7.30 p.m. and by 8.15 p.m. I'm in deserted BBC studios at the Mailbox doing an interview.

Emails.

Wednesday
6.30 a.m. Make myself go to the gym.

Kent St – debating progress on current 'Speak Out' campaign linking key resources – BASW, SWU and committees. Receive membership update. Speak to a couple of members by phone.

The foster care issue from yesterday has started a mini-media 'feeding frenzy'. I do a couple of radio interviews from the office and have a lengthy conversation with regional TV about a live studio discussion as part of the early evening news. Then it all goes quiet. Something else has come up and the news has moved on.

6 p.m. Teleconference with Honorary Officers and the other members of the Management Team ahead of the next meeting with the College of Social Work.

Emails.

Thursday
Day in London; 9.30 a.m. train from Birmingham.

Meeting with a trade union.

Catch up with our Parliamentary Officer over lunch in Parliament.

Meeting with Department of Health civil servants on forthcoming 'Social Care' White Paper.

7.10 p.m. Return train from Euston.

Catch up with reading on the train. Emails.

Friday
Office morning, catching up on diary and plans for next week.

Discussions on forthcoming UK-wide staff meeting and AGM planning.

Talk about a couple of staff issues with senior managers. Emails.

Five-hour drive home today so the trick is to get out of Birmingham and beyond the M1 by 5 p.m. I have some emails and some writing to do at the weekend but am looking forward to a long run on the beach – trying to get ready for that marathon!

Phone rings – can I do a local radio interview at 7 a.m. tomorrow?

currently enjoying working with colleagues from across the IFSW (International Federation of Social Workers) on social work and social worker associations across Europe.

BASW is a growing organisation with record membership, an excellent staff team and a committed elected Council made up of social workers from a variety of backgrounds from across the UK. The current climate is not, however, a favourable one for social workers or for those who use our services. On a daily basis, BASW members draw attention to the impact of continuing cuts to services; to the raising of thresholds for support; and to the constant undermining of their ability to do their jobs. While the welcome Munro Report[7] has asserted the importance of social workers being freed from unnecessary bureaucracy and being allowed to 'do social work' in order to protect children, I see little sign of employers being prepared to take this on board. The beacons of excellent practice burn brightly but they are few and, sadly, far between. Meanwhile in many adult services, we are seeing a wholesale retreat from the use of social workers, with some of the most vulnerable people in our society left at risk. It is an absurd but financially convenient view that somehow 'personalisation' means that people will be able to direct their own support without 'interference' from precisely those professionals whose principles and skills they need to empower them. Social work roles are being undertaken by unqualified people without the experience or training to even recognise when they are out of their depth and some of the best public servants in our country are being cast aside, when there should be an effective career structure which keeps the most experienced and best-qualified social workers close to practice. All my life experience tells me that it is only social workers ourselves who can rescue our profession and that if we fail to stand up now, not only will our governments have cause to regret it, but the people who require and are entitled to excellent social work services will suffer. We all have a part to play in the future of social work – one thing I know is that I am still becoming a social worker. Someday, wherever I am, I will become the best social worker I can be.

Notes

1   For further information, see Tutt (1978), Thorpe (1978) and Thorpe *et al.* (1980).

2   National Association of Young People in Care (NAYPIC), an organisation run by and for young people looked after by the care system or who had left care, was first established in England in 1979. It ended and was replaced by A National Voice (ANV) in 1998. The *Who Cares?* magazine was first launched in 1985. The Who Cares? Trust was subsequently established as a charity in 1992 to improve the everyday lives and future life chances of children in care.

3   The parliamentary debates in 2003 and 2004 on the Housing Bill may be read at www.publications. parliament.uk/pa/cm200304/cmhansrd/vo040112/debtext/40112-26.htm.

4   Unicef describes itself as the world's leading organisation protecting the rights of children and young people. See www.unicef.org.uk/.

5   ChildLine is a confidential counselling service for children and young people which operates by telephone and email. See http://www.childline.org.uk/Pages/Home.aspx.

6   International Federation of Social Workers: see note 8 in Chapter 1 above, also www.ifsw.org.

7   Professor Eileen Munro's first report into child protection in England and Wales, published in October 2010, analysed why problems had come about in the child protection system and why previous reforms had unforeseen consequences. The second report, published in February 2011, considered the child's journey through the protection. The final report, 'A Child-Centred System', published in May 2011, highlights the importance of professional judgement in deciding how best to help children and their families. See www.education.gov.uk/munroreview/.

References

Heidegger, M. (1962) *Being and Time*, translated by J. McQuarrie and E. Robinson, Oxford: Blackwell.

Marx, K. and Engels, F. (1970) *The German Ideology*, edited and with introduction by C.J. Arthur, New York: International Publishers.

Thorpe, D. (1978) 'Intermediate Treatment', in N. Tutt (ed.) *Alternative Strategies for Coping with Crime*, Oxford: Blackwell & Martin Robertson: 64–81.

Thorpe, D.H., Smith, D., Green, C.J. and Paley, J.H. (1980) *Out of Care: The Community Support of Juvenile Offenders*, London: George Allen & Unwin.

Tutt, N. (ed.) (1978) *Alternative Strategies for Coping with Crime*, Oxford: Blackwell & Martin Robertson.

6 Social work

A profession that happened my way

Lena Dominelli

I grew up in the beautiful wilderness of British Columbia (BC), Canada. Surrounded by wildlife and the natural beauty of mountains, lakes and rivers, city life and urban realities did not encroach upon my consciousness. This is ironic given that my father had spent his early adult life organising working-class people to fight for social justice and decent housing with indoor toilets and running water. But I was not to learn this until much later after I had become involved in struggles for social justice in my own right and even left Canada for Britain. Living in remote countryside in a loving home and surrounded by caring neighbours taught me to appreciate supportive human relationships and the value of self-sufficiency. Life in those conditions was harsh – cold, snowy winters and poverty were part of everyday life. But we were happy, and my parents' aspirations for a better life were passed on to my brothers and sisters and me. Living in dignity, doing no harm to others, including the living things around us on which our livelihoods depended, were inculcated into our upbringing and have guided me as an activist scholar since. I will always remember my father going out hunting to catch our meat and my mother counting out the bullets when he left and when he returned. His biggest pride was to tell us, 'See, one bullet is missing, and here is dinner. And look where the bullet is – right between the eyes, so that death comes quickly and painlessly. You should respect animals. Never kill more than you can eat and always make their death swift and painless.' Although I don't hunt or fish, his words have meant that I have respected all living things on which our lives depend. That interdependency between living things was eventually to inform my writing *Green Social Work* decades later, but its foundations were laid years ago in childhood.

We left those pristine wilds to go to live on the outskirts of Vancouver before I reached my teens because my dad decided that we children needed to get a better education than he and mom had had. Education for both of my parents was our passport to a better future that included a decent standard of living. For me, education filled a natural curiosity about the world and I loved reading books, figuring out how things worked and why, and embarking on adventures (imaginary and real through various rides on the Canadian Pacific Railway that employed my dad on pittance wages and the trips the family took when dad purchased his first car – a beautiful 1948 Mercury which today would have been called his first banger). We children did not look forward to city life, but took it in our stride and adjusted to our new environment, making new friends and learning different things.

As we grew up, we learned about the social problems we had been spared from even hearing about in the secluded villages and small towns of the interior of BC. As typical Canadian teenagers, we started working part-time in a range of boring, low-paid jobs to buy 'extras' that included school books and to save up to pay for university. I did my share of baby-sitting (thank goodness I enjoyed caring for children and keeping them enthralled with wonderful stories that captured their imaginations); berry-picking and other low-grade agricultural work, routine factory labour; I worked as a retail clerk and as a waitress. Such work was hard to find in the late 1960s, but I remember trying to organise women in one of my workplaces and arguing that we should join a union to challenge our low pay (below the then minimum wage in Canada), being told 'No, we cannot do that, we would lose our jobs', and then being given a range of personal reasons as to why this was not possible for them. Although not particularly conscious of this fact, I guess I must have picked up working-class history and trade union struggles from my dad who was an active trade unionist. My mother was the strong woman who looked after the family and stayed at home until her youngest child was of school age, when she joined the paid labour force to supplement dad's income, help lift us out of poverty and stop dad working three shifts a day to make ends meet. I now tease my mom and tell her my capacity for getting a job done comes from the role model she set!

Undergraduate studies

For my undergraduate degree, when I finally decided that working in dead-end jobs was not for me, I went to a brand-new, local university called Simon Fraser University (SFU) because it promised to be an interesting and innovative institution with a vision that challenged established hierarchies in the academy. I had no desire to join 'stuffy' – as I saw it – UBC (University of British Columbia) and attending SFU also meant I could save money on food and accommodation by commuting from home. The competition between these two institutions to prove they were the best in the province was intense and remains so today. With a couple of exceptions, I enjoyed both school and university. I had talented, gifted teachers who inspired me to develop my curiosity and ask questions. At SFU, I was fortunate enough to be taught by brilliant scholars who went to teach in this fantastic university on the top of Burnaby Mountain and engage with students as equals – a radical thought in those days. Although I started off in the natural sciences doing chemistry, biology, physics and mathematics – subjects I loved – what I would now call 'sexual harassment' led me to drop those subjects and switch to the social sciences and humanities. In addition, as someone who had always 'served' in various student governance structures, I did likewise at SFU. However, my natural radicalism was developed further here by both the political and the hippy movements of the late 1960s. As a student leader, I had my first lessons in power politics and the limitations of institutional structures when it comes to social change that enhances people's lives: demonstrations, sit-ins and creative protests, including my introducing Michelle (alias Michael who sported a beard and wore clothes made out of newspaper cuttings) during the Miss SFU contest. Much to our astonishment, he was a big hit and the audience thought his antics were hilarious. I hadn't heard the term 'gender-bending' then, but that critical, creative urge continues to inspire my activism.

However, in this radical mix, social work, or applied sociology as it was called then, was not a discipline favoured by the sociologists, political scientists and anthropologists with whom I mixed. Indeed, my questions about what it was and what its practitioners did were always shrugged off with 'I wouldn't worry about going there if I were you, it is all about controlling people'. So, I completed my double honours in PSA (political science, sociology and anthropology) and English (literature and linguistics), and obtained first-class marks that resulted in my getting a highly coveted scholarship to study in either England or the USA. For me, there was no doubt – I was going to an idealised England where amazing things happened, and which in my mind's eye was full of brilliant intellectuals, wonderful opportunities to learn, and nice houses with gardens.

Coming to England

My first shock to this idealistic picture of the country occurred while I was still in Canada. Like all Canadians, I was told to go to Oxford or Cambridge, or, for social sciences, the LSE (London School of Economics). By this time I had decided to do an MA in sociology. My naivety knew no bounds, and after a co-educational experience I was non-comprehending when I received my acceptance letter from Oxford only to be told that I had to choose one of three women's colleges. I had no idea that gender discrimination existed in these hallowed halls of learning. I turned down the offer, and subsequently also the LSE when I discovered it was a dull, dark building right on the streets of central London. After this point I discovered Sussex, a fairly new, award-winning university set in beautiful grounds and with a radical reputation. I decided this would be the place for me, and was lucky enough to have Tom Bottomore as a tutor, and, when I registered for my Ph.D., as my supervisor. I was truly privileged: he knew intellectuals throughout the world, and I had no difficulty in being introduced to the best minds of the day, and going to meet them – including Pierre Bourdieu. And, of course, I became involved in the student politics and activism of the UK. I maintained my friendship with Tom until he passed away soon after his retirement, as I did with Kathleen Aberle Gough who sadly died young of cancer. I also keep in irregular touch with 'Tony' (to his friends) Giddens.

My second shock came when I reached Britain, at Heathrow Airport's Terminal 3, finally arriving after fog diverted the plane to Prestwick and then returned to London. I had been sent letters warning me that I was coming to a highly industrialised country, and yet I was shocked by its shabbiness, and the tenements that lined the roads into London. Swinging London, contrary to what I had been led to believe, also closed its doors early. It was with relief that we (a close friend had come to meet me at Heathrow) reached the beautiful South Downs. Eventually, I settled in Woodingdean and lived in 'digs' (lodgings) for six years. From there, I explored the UK's length and breadth with my new-found friends.

For my Ph.D. studies, my interest in new models of social development resulted in my focusing on workers' control and the trade union movement in Algeria. As part of my research, I spent time exploring similar developments in the then Yugoslavia, Poland and the Soviet Union. I also studied China, but this was one place I did not visit until my Ph.D. was finished. This meant that I acquired an interesting list of countries visited, leading to many questions about what happened when I was there and who approached me – presumably to recruit me to communist ways. The idea that I would be remotely interested in supporting an authoritarian political group that eschewed independent thinking, especially among women, was always amusing to me. Obviously my interrogators had never read what happened to Alexandra Kollontai or Rosa Luxemburg for dissenting from communist orthodoxies (see Daniels 1993).

My critical reaction to the developments in these communist countries was disappointment. Liberation for marginalised peoples seemed as distant as ever, despite their pretences to the contrary and the minor gains achieved by women as workers in waged work and maternal health care. However, the knowledge and experiences accumulated through these visits resulted in my being appointed to work in the then Commission on Industrial Relations (CIR), arguing for trade union recognition and undertaking research on workers' control in Europe (facilitated by my knowledge of several European languages).

I rejected a job offer in the newly formed ACAS (Arbitration and Conciliation Services) that replaced CIR to join the radical Community Development Projects programme (CDPs) where I became a team leader and sought to improve housing and employment opportunities among working-class people experiencing industrial decline, and supporting Gujerati Muslims to adapt to life in Northern English cities.[1] When I discovered that I was being paid less than my male colleagues, I asked the union to take up my case and end this anomaly. Imagine my chagrin when I was left outside the door to await the decision made by an all-male group. The thin walls next to where I was seated meant that I could overhear their words and their mirth as they decided that as a woman who would soon be married, I did not need a raise in pay that reflected either the responsibilities I carried or the qualifications I brought to the post! I felt humiliated by the process and couldn't believe that the male union representative who was supposed to be looking after my interests colluded with the employer, despite my having read Gramsci's pessimistic view of trade unions as part of the hegemonic power structures in capitalist societies (see Ackers and Payne 1998). However, as I was to find out, this was the first of many humiliations for daring to think 'outside the box' or stand up for my rights or those of others, throughout my professional life.

The end of the CDPs meant that I moved into social work, initially as a community work lecturer at Warwick University, where Peter Leonard was inspiring radical social workers to think about class. Besides critiquing *Social Work Practice Under Capitalism* (Corrigan and Leonard 1978), I was working with students and black activists from a grass-roots perspective, adding what became known as feminist social work and anti-racist social work to the classroom repertoire. From there, I became involved in more mainstream social work. I eventually trained and qualified as a social worker, and worked in probation offices, social services departments and residential establishments so that I could understand better the pressures social workers were under and try to see how far radical ideas could be implemented in practice. I loved this work because in those days practitioners could be imaginative and experimental in trying to develop new ideas for practice and innovative interventions in practice. My community work, international and radical sociological perspectives were always there, guiding my unique reflections and analyses of the profession's theories and practices. These are also visible in my contributions to radical social work, feminist social work, anti-racist social work, anti-oppressive social work, and now, green social work. My commitment to being an activist scholar meant that theory and practice were constantly appraised and reappraised; I have always devoted time and effort to doing research and being grounded in practice in order to ensure that whatever I developed resonated with service users at the grass-roots level to whom I feel accountable (often at great personal cost). This model has served me well and is continuing to do so currently through my work within the Gilesgate Energy Project, which aims to address fuel poverty and generate job opportunities through renewable green energy technologies.[2]

MY TYPICAL WEEK

I have no regular pattern to my working week except that I spend it teaching students individually or in classes, meeting with colleagues, doing research, doing voluntary work, spending time with my family, and when I can create space, writing. To fit all this in, I work long hours. But I am also lucky enough to spend time overseas, which I see as my staff development time because that is where I learn about what is happening outside the UK and I get inspired to think differently about what we do here. Overseas travel is a great morale booster as well as broadening my horizons, and I feel as a person with multiple heritages that I represent that type of intellectual who feels equally at home wherever they are, and whose curiosity about people and the world is unending. I am, in that sense, a perpetual student. My constantly asking questions, taking nothing for granted, can sometimes be experienced as irritating, and sometimes I get told that I should 'know my place'. At other times, people in Britain enquire of me, 'When will you go back to your country?' I have got beyond being annoyed by such questions and can see the funny side of it, especially when I ask 'Which country do you mean?' and they retort, 'You know, where you originally came from?' During one of these conversations when recently quizzed in this way in Durham, I replied, much to the questioner's consternation, 'Do you mean Southampton?' (I had worked previously at the University of Southampton.)

My vision for social work

My concerns with realising social justice, eradicating structural inequalities across all social divisions, my commitment to validating people's insistence on the realisation of their human and citizenship rights and attempts to develop new fields for theory and practice can be explored in my writings and practice initiatives aimed at improving practice with women, children, older people, black and minority ethnic groups and offenders since the mid-1970s. This has culminated in my most recent publication, *Green Social Work* (Dominelli 2012). This book brings together issues of social justice with human rights, global citizenship-based and environmental justice in a critique of economic and social development models that produce profits for the few, hardship for the many and the degradation of the world's resources, including its air, waters, lands, oceans, flora and fauna.

I argue here that holistic practices expose the structural inequalities that hold back poor people's capacity for realising their talents to the full. Moreover, they enable practitioners to work across disciplinary (and other) divides to mobilise alongside people, in ways that develop alternative development models that care about both people and the physical world in which their lives are embedded. This vision raises a number of questions for social work practice as the twenty-first century unfolds. Crucial among these questions are addressing people's needs to be prepared for the three phases of extreme weather events: before they strike, while they are unfolding and in the reconstruction period afterwards. Developing preventive strategies that thread through these different stages becomes a major way in which social workers can help people survive better the potential tragedies that follow in the wake of extreme hazards caused by climate change. Rising to this challenge requires that practitioners learn about the science behind climate change, engage in debates about its likely impact on people's livelihoods and their habitats, assist in developing environmentally friendly policies, and help people develop alternative ways of living that will reduce pressure on the earth's ecosystem and biosphere. This needs to be done while still demanding that poor and marginalised people living in the Global South rise out of poverty and obtain their fair share of the earth's resources. I have been promoting such endeavours at a policy level by participating in discussions on climate change at the UNFCCC[3] meetings in Copenhagen, Cancun and Durban.

For social workers in the UK, my critiques have demanded an end to bureaucratised, competence-based approaches to the profession that service only the interests of neoliberalism and corporate management. Although I have been protesting about these developments since the mid-1990s, I am delighted that Lord Laming (2009) and Eileen Munro (2012) have also recommended change and have encouraged practitioners to use their knowledge, skills and professional judgement in making decisions about what would best meet the needs of a particular service user or family. However, I would also add that this development has to go hand-in-hand with analyses of structural inequalities and insisting that individual service users take responsibility for their particular behaviour. It is unhelpful to confuse structural barriers with personal ones in complex cases, as has often happened when social workers fail to engage effectively with anti-oppressive practice. In addition, social workers have to learn how to handle the media and get their 'good news' stories (of which there are many) into its discourses, rather than accept being the scapegoat for much wider professional failings involving both health practitioners and the police. They must also argue for the resources that they need to motivate people to change their behaviour at the personal level, engage with institutional and cultural change, and develop new approaches to practice. This often means accessing labour-intensive and more expensive, skilled social work professionals.

Notes

1   For more information on the Community Development Projects programme, see Smith (1996, 2006).

2   For more information, see http://www.dur.ac.uk/ihrr/vulnerabilityresearch/transcendingrisk/gilesgateproject/.

3   United Nations Framework Convention on Climate Change, see unfccc.int/.

References

Ackers, P. and Payne, J. (1998) 'British trade unions and social partnership: Rhetoric, reality and strategy', *The International Journal of Human Resource Management* 9 (3): 339–360.

Corrigan, P. and Leonard, P. (1978) *Social Work Practice Under Capitalism: A Marxist Approach*, Basingstoke: Palgrave Macmillan.

Daniels, R.V. (1993) *A Documentary History of Communism in Russia. From Lenin to Gorbachev*, Lebanon, NH: University Press of New Hampshire.

Dominelli, L. (2012) *Green Social Work*. Cambridge: Polity Press.

Laming, W. (2009) *The Protection of Children in England: A Progress Report*. London: DCSF.

Munro, E. (2012) *Munro Review of Child Protection: Final Report – A Child-centred System*. London: DoE.

Smith, M.K. (1996, 2006) 'Community work', *The Encyclopaedia of Informal Education*, www.infed.org/community/b-comwrk.htm.

7 Diverse strokes in social work

Coping with a multi-textured canvas

Merlyn D'Souza

When I think 'social work', my thoughts and memories rewind to my parents, John and Teresa D'Souza, and my grandmother, Natalie Saldanha, whose lives embodied the values upon which the discipline of social work is built. Through their words and deeds they role-modelled hospitality, generosity, a deep respect and strong concern for socially and economically disadvantaged people. Even though we were raised in a small house in Mahim, Mumbai, we always made room for and shared our meals with families who visited us and needed nurture and support. We categorised our guests informally as 'temporary' and 'permanent' and welcomed them all – family, neighbours and strangers alike. Both my parents were loving and caring. They gave to others in times of plenty and in times of scarcity.

My exposure to the socially disadvantaged began as a toddler, through our domestic help. I enjoyed sitting with her to have breakfast and basked in the love she showered on me as would a family member. I recall a more formal experience of social service when I was in the seventh grade in a church ministry called the Legion of Mary. We visited abandoned and lonely patients in nearby hospitals. The older visitors who accompanied us trained us in the art of listening. I continued to volunteer with other groups of people during my school and college years at Canossa Convent School and Sophia College. The summer rural camps organised by the nuns were the highlight of my teenage years, and brought me closer to the realities of rural life. During the camps, we lived in villages for two weeks to a month at a time, helping the local people to build roads, teaching their children English, and socialising with fellow volunteers. In retrospect, I wonder if the villagers gained as much as we did. It was truly a life-changing experience for me.

Social work training into practice

In 1984, I pursued my Master's degree in Social Work (MSW) at the College of Social Work, Nirmala Niketan. Our curriculum was based on a generalist model. According to Timberlake, a generalist practice model has a 'multidimensional conceptual framework that reflects an open selection of theories and intervention' (Timberlake *et al.* 2002: 4). The grounded exposure that we received in theory, fieldwork, thesis writing and co-curricular activities set the foundation for our future work as professional social workers. One of the highlights of our training was a survey that we conducted of the victims in Bhopal who were affected by the gas leak from the Union Carbide factory.[1] Even though the survey attempted to assess the losses of victims, only a few of them have received compensation to date.

I began my professional social work career at the Family Service Centre, a family welfare agency that provided services such as foster care, adoption and financial sponsorship of poor students. My next job was in school social work involving a broad spectrum of activities ranging from counselling to sensitivity training programmes to help raise students' awareness about social realities. Freire (1970) argued that the value of a good-quality and holistic education is reflected by its ripple-effect in the lives of students, as well as those of their families and the larger community. One of our goals was to advocate a reflective education system as he had proposed. Freire cautioned that students should not be regarded as containers in which knowledge is deposited as one might deposit cash in in a bank; instead, they should be encouraged to understand and analyse content for themselves. Freire introduced the concept of 'praxis': reflection–action–reflection, where reflection leads to action which, in turn, is analysed and reflected upon. In St Xavier's School, Mumbai, we initiated a street club in 1987 that served as a temporary day shelter for street children. The school provided these children with shelter, a midday snack/meal, functional literacy and other recreational activities. This unique concept of a street club in a regular school helped us sow the seeds for future clubs in urban Mumbai and rural Maharashtra, a state in Western India.

Praxis continues

From 1990 to 1993, I worked in the College of Social Work, Nirmala Niketan, as a faculty member. I taught group work and sociology, and supervised students placed in slum communities and institutional care settings. During my tenure, the college conducted a survey of slum and pavement dwellers in Mumbai (then called 'Bombay'). A year later, we were involved in rehabilitating victims of the December 1992 communal riots in the city.[2] I recall vividly meeting a group of women who had escaped the riots and sought shelter in a rehabilitation camp. After spending nearly a month sheltering from the riots, some of them longed to revisit their homes. I volunteered to accompany them. When we arrived, we discovered that their homes had been completely destroyed. I observed one woman desperately searching for something and I assumed she was looking for her gold ornaments or money. A little later, I saw her devotedly clasping her treasure, her Sacred Scriptures. Upon returning to the rehabilitation camp, we stopped at a roadside cart to eat 'vada-pav' (spiced potato with bread) and drink tea, and as we ate and drank, we shared our collective grief and pain. Soon after the communal riots had come to an end, the city was further torn apart by bomb blasts in March 1993. The image of 'Bombay' as a safe, 'easygoing' and friendly city was shattered. It took several months for the city to limp back to normal. Since then, 'Mumbai', as it is now known, has been the target of a spate of terrorist attacks by different groups. The latest attack took place on 13 July 2011. However, Mumbai, known for its resilience and a 'never-say-die' attitude, has since bounced back into action.

In 1995, I completed a Master's degree in Pastoral Studies (MAPS) at the Catholic Theological Union (CTU) in Chicago. Pastoral counselling and spiritual direction were my areas of focus. The CTU, with its rich cultural diversity and thrust on social justice, triggered a paradigm shift in my thinking. I felt empowered to think globally and act locally. The spiritual direction programme at the Claret Center, Chicago helped me process my own life story as I prepared myself spiritually and emotionally to journey with others.

From 1996 to 1999, I worked as a school counsellor at Bombay International School, and later in 2002 as the Community Action and Service (CAS) coordinator for the American School in Mumbai. Both schools encouraged me to experiment with creative and innovative curriculum ideas. I helped students gain exposure to a wide range of issues, from communal harmony to children traumatised by various crises, to personality development and leadership building.

From 1999 to 2001, I completed Ph.D. course work at the University of Houston. Initially, I had planned to do my thesis on the status of single women in India. However, during the second year of my studies, I felt inspired to explore the issue of minors forced into prostitution. I was appalled to learn that the city I came from, Mumbai, was deeply entrenched in the coils of this heinous crime. By the spring of 2001, I decided to return to India for a year; one of the triggering factors was my father's deteriorating health. On 17 July 2001, my father passed away. A few months later, I started working with the International Justice Mission (IJM) and later moved on to work at different non-governmental organisations (NGOs) like Oasis, Saksham and, currently, Justice and Care. The work is extremely taxing and time-consuming and I have not yet had the leisure I need to complete my Ph.D.

Rescue work

When trafficked persons are first rescued by the police from a place where they have been kept captive (with or without the assistance of an NGO), they initially tend to be hostile. Their experience of being duped, coerced and cheated teaches them not to trust anyone. Besides their own personal experience of betrayal, they are brainwashed by pimps and brothel managers into distrusting the police and rescue teams. They are further made to believe that they are 'criminals' rather than victims, and are told that they will have to work to repay their 'debts' for the money loaned to their families. Most often the girls earn Rs. 120–300 per hour, depending on the geographic area in which they are working, their age and their skin colour (younger and paler-skinned girls are paid more). If the girl is a virgin, she can be bought for Rs. 10,000 to Rs. 50,000 for the first night of her service. According to informal practice, half the money goes to the brothel manager and the other half into the girl's account. However, during rescue operations, we discovered that most of the girls do not have any money of their own. Their money is snatched by the brothel owner on the pretext of expenses incurred on food, clothes and other personal items. As a result, very few girls/women in prostitution are able to save any money.

Rescued girls are brought to the police station to file a FIR (first information report) and then sent to a government shelter home. The day after the rescue, the girls/women are brought before the magistrate and a court order is passed for verification of their age and medical status. They are segregated according to their ages; minors and majors are placed in different shelter homes. Social workers, caseworkers, counsellors and lawyers regularly follow up with the rescued girls/women. The goal is to ensure that they are safe, have enough mental and emotional space for their recovery process and are then gradually reintegrated into society. Efforts are made to transfer the rescued women from the government shelter homes to private shelter homes within the city or to a home from their state of origin. The shelter homes are selected according to available vacancies and the interests of the rescued person. For example, those interested in pursuing their education are sent to homes that assign priority to education. We support rescued people, especially minors, as long as they need our help; however, our focus is always to make them independent. Through the home investigation reports, if we are able to ascertain that their families are supportive and safe, we encourage them to return home. Most rescued women are interested in finding a job to support themselves. Nevertheless, it is difficult for them to sustain a job while trying to resist the lure of easy and fast money through returning to a life of prostitution. It is extremely satisfying when rescued women are open to the recovery process and are willing to examine different options in their lives. But it is also the case that survivors of trafficking face a long and arduous journey as they travel from the brothel/place from where they were rescued towards their healing, transformation and reintegration into society. During their time of recovery at the shelter homes, they undergo different levels of training and receive various types of support to help them become economically, socially and emotionally strong.

'Nina'

I wish to share vignettes from the life of a trafficked girl, 'Nina', a young, innocent girl from rural Maharashtra. When Nina was in her early teens, her father sold her into prostitution. When I first met Nina in the shelter home she was hostile. As I continued to work with her, her trust in me slowly began to increase. Nevertheless, she could not accept the fact that her father had been involved in selling her into prostitution. One day during a regular visit, I discovered that Nina was not in the shelter home. I was advised that her father had recently arrived from her village with a local politician as guarantor and demanded to take her home; the child welfare committee had agreed. We eventually located Nina again after a couple of months in a brothel, physically and emotionally shattered, and took her back to the shelter home. She was withdrawn and quiet. She now had clear evidence of her father's complicity in selling her to brothels, and yet she continued to remain in denial and refused to testify against him. For a second time, her father used a loophole in the system and took Nina back to her village. This time we were able to track her down immediately and rescue her before she was sold to another brothel. Nina's health soon started to deteriorate and medical investigation confirmed that she was HIV positive. She refused to take any medication and her condition worsened. Until the very end, Nina refused to testify against her father. We had intended to move her from the shelter home to a hospice in Mumbai, but she stated that she wished to return to her village. She believed that one way of punishing her father was for him to witness her suffering and pain. When she was escorted to her village, her father refused to take her into his home, and so her sister who lived next door took care of her. Nina died of AIDS on 17 March 2005. Her smile, caring ways and her wry humour will always stay with us. In her cohort, three other girls died of AIDS between the ages of 18 and 21. How different their lives would have been had they not been sold or duped into the sex trade.

Theories that inform social work with trafficked women

Social case work, cognitive-behavioural therapy, social advocacy and empowerment theory are some of the theories that have informed my work. Helen Perlman has been one of my role-models. According to her, 'the essence of social case work is that it aims to facilitate the individual's social adaptation, to restore, reshape or reinforce his/(her) functioning as a social being' (Perlman 1974: 7). Our main goals are to restore, empower and reintegrate trafficked people back into society. At the micro level we look at their restoration, healing and empowerment; while at the macro level we seek systemic changes through social advocacy that will help generate a revival in our law enforcement system. The conviction of a single perpetrator in a court of law sends a strong message to traffickers and other perpetrators of human trafficking and reinforces the work on an individual level.

Albert Ellis' (1994) work on rational emotive behaviour therapy (REBT) has influenced our work with trafficked people profoundly. According to REBT, psychological distress or trauma is due not just to an adversity or activating event, but also to what people think or believe about the adversity or event they have experienced. A change in their thinking pattern will therefore bring about changes in their affect and behaviour (Corey 2012).

After a rescue, it may take three to six months and sometimes even a year before trafficked persons begin to trust the people who reach out to them. In a majority of cases, their family members have been directly or indirectly involved in selling or duping them into the sex trade or other forms of 'slavery'. Despite evidence of family involvement, they typically refuse to testify against their families, as Nina's case demonstrates. Victims who are removed from the control of their perpetrators have first to be freed from their negative thinking. While working with people forced into prostitution, we encounter several irrational beliefs: for example, 'once a prostitute, always a prostitute'; 'I have to pay off my debts to my brothel manager'; 'there are no working options to prostitution'; 'I am no good and hence I am trapped into prostitution'; 'the only asset a girl has is her body which has to be used'. The daunting process of re-educating trafficked persons eventually helps to transform their lives. Elizabeth Johnson, an American therapist, has trained several aftercare professionals in Mumbai to provide trauma-focused behaviour therapy to the victims of trafficking (see also Butler *et al.* 2006). Her training has proved especially useful in helping us to reach out to trafficked persons in their recovery process.

One of the challenges in working with trafficked victims is that they find it very difficult to forgive themselves. They blame themselves for what has happened, despite the existence of rational evidence to the contrary. In my work with hurting people, I stress the importance of forgiving oneself. Sr. Usha (2007), in her teachings on inner healing, specifies the importance of forgiveness in living a deep, authentic life. According to Sr. Usha, 'when we harbour negative feelings in our hearts towards others, we are out of harmony with the whole of creation' (2007: 107). Lobo states further that the main goal of forgiveness therapy is 'to evacuate the hurt feelings lying within yourself, followed by forgiving the person/s concerned' (2010: 227). In his retreats and books, he recommends two basic principles: the first is recall, which means 'to remember all details possible'; the second is relive, that is, 'allow the hurt feelings to surface. Get in touch with them' (2010: 228). The trafficked person's decision during therapy to forgive his/her perpetrator should, of course, in no way detract from the crucial task of prosecuting those who have harmed them. Social workers and lawyers empower the victim to fight for justice and live interdependently in society. They are made aware that when those who have done wrong to them are charged, other innocent lives are saved. However, the decision whether or not to testify in court lies solely with the individual.

Alliance

One of the key elements in the empowerment process of social work is the practitioner/worker/client relationship. This relationship is viewed as an 'alliance', a reciprocal exchange of learning with an emphasis on the value of self-determination (Robbins *et al.* 1999). The key to effective social work is therefore the relationship we establish with our clients, as well as our openness to change; it leads to our own healing and restoration and to that of the people with whom we work. Once we arrive at a healthy level of mutual trust, those with whom we are working feel encouraged to share their experiences in a safe environment along with others in recovery. This process helps reduce self-blame from past events and fosters a sense of personal freedom.

In our work with trafficked people, we engage constantly with various systems including the government, judiciary, police and NGOs. Half the battle against trafficking is won when we are able to establish at least one or two trusting relationships within each system. Practice needs to be further 'embedded in a partnership rooted in the principles of solidarity and reciprocity to link individual growth with social support and development' (Dominelli 2004: 2). If we are to win the battle against traffickers, NGOs, government and other stakeholders must work in close collaboration with one another. The thrust of an 'embedded partnership' would be to link survivors of trafficking to available resources, support systems and opportunities that would give them a fresh start in life.

MY TYPICAL WEEK: BEING A CHANGE AGENT

In the initial years I was involved in the rescue, rehabilitation and reintegration of trafficked persons while simultaneously coordinating with lawyers to seek the prosecution of traffickers. However, in the last couple of years my goal has been centred on enhancing the quality of rehabilitation and restoration programmes for rescued people. This includes counselling rescued persons, networking with shelter homes, implementing life-skill programmes in the shelter homes, managing and training a team of social workers/student social workers/volunteers, and working towards a growth-oriented future plan with and for the reintegration of trafficked people.

The work is exciting and no two working days are alike. Every month there are new developments in trafficking, new twists emerge in existing cases, and slow yet deliberate systemic changes begin to evolve. One of our future goals is to train and dialogue with various stakeholders to strengthen and create new systems, procedures and protocols to combat human trafficking.

Conclusion

The past twenty-six years in the field of social work have been exciting yet difficult, fulfilling yet frustrating, but overall, immensely satisfying. The most joyous outcome is when hurting people become open to the process of transformation and are willing to make life-enhancing choices. My aim in working with victims of trauma is to bring restoration and healing into the lives of hurting and broken persons. In my experience I have found that whether the suffering person is a trafficked child, or a child from a broken home, or a school student chasing drugs, they all yearn to connect with someone who believes in them, loves them, someone whom they can trust and to whom they can communicate their life story. Rescued girls and women fondly call us 'Didhi' which means sister. As these girls/women move on in life, we delight in hearing their voice on the phone, saying 'Didhi (sister), I have got a job' or 'I am safe', or 'Happy Birthday' or 'Happy Christmas'. Yes, they remember the major milestones in our lives, and so do we.

It is my privilege to work in a multicultural environment in India. The different nuances, shades and strokes within the Indian culture fascinate me, just as if I was a painter immersed in a work of art. My heart is filled with gratitude for this opportunity to serve, be attentive to people, listen to their stories as they unfold – a sacred journey which shapes and moulds my life in the process.

Notes

1   In December 1984, a leak of Methyl Isocyanate gas and other chemicals from the Union Carbide India Limited pesticide plant in Bhopal, Madhya Pradesh, India, resulted in the exposure of hundreds of thousands of people. Estimates vary on the death-toll; the government of Madhya Pradesh has confirmed a total of 3,787 deaths related to the gas release. Many others have died since, and the land remains contaminated (see http://www.mp.gov.in/bgtrrdmp/relief.htm).

2   It is estimated that over 1,000 Muslims and Hindus were killed during the communal riots which took place between December 1992 and January 1993; the riots were followed by bombings in March 1993 in which another 250 people, mostly Hindus, died. See *Frontline* 20 (14), 5–18 July 2003.

References

Butler, A.C., Chapman, J.E., Forman, E.M. and Beck, A.T. (2006) 'The empirical status of cognitive-behavioral therapy: A review of meta-analyses', *Clinical Psychology Review* 26 (1): 17–31.

Corey, G. (2012) *Theory and Practice of Counseling and Psychotherapy*, 9th edn, Belmont, CA: Wadsworth Publishing.

Dominelli, L. (2004) *Social Work Theory and Practice for a Changing Profession,* Cambridge: Polity Press.

Ellis, A. (1994) *Reason and Emotion in Psychotherapy: Comprehensive Method of Treating Human Disturbances: Revised and Updated*, New York: Citadel Press.

Freire, P. (1970) *Pedagogy of the Oppressed*, New York: Continuum International Publishing Group.

Guttierez, L. and Lewis, E. (1999) *Empowering People of Colour*, New York: Columbia University Press.

Lobo, A. (2010) *Unmasking the Lie,* Mumbai: St Paul's Press.

Perlman, H. (1974) *Social Case Work: A Problem Solving Process,* Chicago, IL: University of Chicago Press.

Robbins, S., Chatterjee, P. and Canda, E. (1999) *Contemporary Human Behaviour Theory. A Critical Perspective for Social Work*, Boston, MA: Allyn and Bacon.

Timberlake, E.M., Farber, M.Z. and Sabatino, C.A. (2002) *The General Method of Social Work Practice. McMahon's Generalist Perspective*, Boston, MA: Allyn and Bacon.

Sr. Usha, M. (SND) (2007) *The Way to Peace*, Gujarat: Gujarat Sahitya Prakash.

8 They call me 'mum'

Gudrun Elvhage and
Pernilla Liedgren Dobronravoff

This chapter is unlike all the other chapters in this book because, instead of telling the stories of our own lives and social work practice, we have chosen instead to introduce our work with Beyan, an Iraqi Kurdish woman who manages a women's centre in Erbil. Beyan was interviewed for this chapter. The name 'Beyan' is a pseudonym, a very common Kurdish name, to protect her identity. Development of the social work programme in Iraqi Kurdistan began in 2009, following an invitation by the Iraqi Kurdish government to Ersta Sköndal University College in Sweden to work together with a university in Iraqi Kurdistan. Nearly eighty students have already begun to read a corresponding European Bachelor degree in Social Work (180 ECTS).[1] The work is funded as a joint project by UNICEF and the Kurdish Regional Government (KRG). The project involves building a new department of social work as well as a new degree course at one of the largest universities in northern Iraq.

We are two social workers and lecturers in social work who have been involved in the project since its outset. Gudrun taught during the first semester and, together, Gudrun and Pernilla worked with the students. Pernilla also conducted a study about teaching styles during our stay in Iraqi Kurdistan. We will begin by setting the scene, socially and culturally, before going on to describe Beyan's work in more detail.

As the title of this chapter indicates, the social worker in question is called 'mum' by the women with whom she works.[2] As the reader will understand when the text is unravelled, being called 'mum' as a social worker in Iraqi Kurdistan is very prestigious.

Iraqi Kurdistan

The northern part of Iraq, including the provinces of Dohuk, Erbil and Sulimania, has been the independent region of Iraqi Kurdistan since 1991. The region's population is 4.7 million; the majority of people are Kurds but other ethnic groups are also represented, including Assyrians, Chaldeans, Turkmen, Armenians and Arabs. The population is young, with about 50 per cent under the age of 20.[3]

During the government of Saddam Hussein, the Baath regime implemented an Act of Social Welfare which, compared to other countries in the Middle East, could be considered secular, liberal and equal, which in practice did not make any difference. Besides the empty words on equality, the regime during Saddam's government encouraged informers, which made people insecure about whom they might trust (Yildiz 2007). The Kurdish people were especially vulnerable in Saddam Hussein's Iraq. It is widely accepted that the Saddam government used the Kurds for experiments with chemical weapons, and the genocide during the Anfal campaigns in the late 1980s broke up many families.[4] Many children in Kurdistan have subsequently been reported as having post-traumatic stress syndrome (see Ahmad *et al.* 2000, 2007).

Iraqi Kurdistan is, in many ways, a fragile democracy. Corruption has been known to be a great problem in society but has only recently been acknowledged by the government as a problem that needs to be overcome.[5] Meanwhile, there have been reports of protests in Sulimania against the KRG and corruption.[6] The future will tell the outcome, but there is at least a hope that movements and protests in the broader region might support the development of democracy in Iraqi Kurdistan. Landmines are also an issue in Iraqi Kurdistan where 3,512 minefields are registered in an area of 788 square kilometres. Between 1991 and 2008, 8,174 people were injured by landmines, resulting in a great many physically disabled citizens.[7]

Beyan's story

The women's centre is situated about ten minutes away from the city. We travel by car and the traffic is as usual very busy. When we first heard about the centre, we wondered what it would be like to work there. Is it safe for women staying there and is it safe for social workers working there? What kinds of difficulties do the women experience, and how and in what ways can social work help them?

The centre looks just like a typical Kurdish house: it is big, grey, with two floors and a small balcony, set behind a front wall; there are trees and flowers around the house. The only different thing, to our eyes, is the two guards standing outside the house, two men in green military clothes carrying machine-guns. The manager told us they have four guards in all, two working the day shift and two at night. The house has two main purposes. First, it is a house for women in danger. Women arrive in fear and have no other place to go, so the centre provides a temporary home for them while they work out what to do next. Second, the centre works as a meeting place and place of dialogue. Women drop in, just for a couple of hours, for a conversation with a social worker. Sometimes their problems with parents or husbands can be resolved quickly and a woman feels able to go home again.

Over the course of each month, the centre provides support for between fifteen and twenty women and non-residential support for about ten women. The women come from all over Kurdistan, from other cities and also from other countries, some from as far away as Syria, hundreds of miles away. The manager of the centre welcomes us at the door and we are invited inside. This is Beyan, a middle-aged woman wearing a clear green long dress, looking strong and confident, with a straight posture. She speaks with a warm, clear voice and offers us some thirst-quenching tea to drink. We are served our tea and are seated on each side of an enormous desk. One of the other social worker staff members interrupts during the interview to ask something and then returns to her job. She is one of four female employees in the centre.

Beyan is very passionate when she talks about her work. Her eyes sparkle when she says that being a social worker was a childhood dream of hers. She tells us she had always wanted to be involved in this field, 'from the very beginning of my educational path, specifically at high school'. Being a successful student, she had a variety of 'majors' (main subjects) to choose from, but decided to study psychology, since social work was her goal, and there was no social work training available at this time. After graduation, Beyan worked as a teacher in a college, teaching psychology for seven years, and then worked with schoolchildren with social problems for the next eight years. While teaching, she became involved in setting up a new centre for family counselling, and started to volunteer part-time there. Her motivation for doing this was the pressing need she had observed: the enormous problems women were experiencing because of relatives' ignorance and lack of knowledge. Her role in the centre was mainly to work with women's issues. Beyan went on to resign from teaching and begin work at the women's centre, where she works today. The women's centre has been sponsored by the Kurdish Regional Government since 2007; it is one of few centres in Erbil financed by the government.

Why the need for a women's centre?

During the later years of Saddam's regime, so-called 'honour' crimes (acts of violence perpetrated against individuals, usually women, by male members of their community in order to restore family honour) were condoned (Yildiz 2007).[8] The Kurdish Parliament decided in 2002 to instigate a new Family Act which moved away from Sharia law and made honour murder illegal (Yildiz 2007: 60). The Parliament actively supports women's rights, but resistance remains in society, especially in areas dominated by tribes. Domestic violence is common and women sometimes suffer so much in marriage that they choose to take their own lives by setting themselves on fire (Yildiz 2007; Vian Nissan and Abdulgaghi 2009). According to Kurdish Women's Rights Watch, forty-nine suspected honour murders were reported during the period from May until December 2008.[9] This number does not include suicide through self-burning that may be done independently or through pressure from male relatives. The situation for some women is unbearable; even being a victim of violence or murder is enough to raise suspicions that something dishonourable has taken place. Not only are women threatened with violence, they are also in fear of losing their children. If a husband decides to divorce his wife, the children automatically stay with him or his family. Sometimes, the new wife (or wives; men are allowed to have three wives) does not want the children and they end up as street children. Women are controlled in many ways. Besides violence, it is believed that female genital mutilation is widespread. According to a report from Human Rights Watch, between 23 and 78 per cent of girls and women are circumcised; the level varies according to age, area and education.[10]

Now that the political situation seems to be settling down in the area, migrants who fled during the years of oppression have started to return. Some return as temporary visitors but others come back to stay. Research has shown that home-coming migrants are important bearers of culture (Christou and King 2006; King and Christou 2010). They often bring new values, for example a new shared interest in child rearing. Some migrant men take greater responsibility for their children even though this will be perceived as effeminate. There is also a growing group of guest workers arriving in Iraqi Kurdistan from the Philippines, Ethiopia, Somalia, Indonesia and Bangladesh as well as increasing numbers of internal refugees from Iraq, trying to settle in the safer zone of Iraqi Kurdistan.[11] All of these suggest the possibilities for challenges in the future to old ways of thinking.

Legally, there have been great strides during recent years. The Constitution, adopted as a permanent Constitution in 2005 and ratified in the same year, gives men and women equal status before the law and prohibits discrimination based on sex. But there are contradictions in the legislation. In reality, there are no judgments that contradict Islamic rules. This means that the Supreme Court and federal courts (that is, judges and experts in Sharia law) have considerable scope to interpret the laws. Women's rights must therefore be justified within the Muslim religious framework. Citizens of Iraq can choose religious or secular courts in family law cases; this again weakens the position of women. Sharia courts weigh the woman's testimony as half that of a man's.[12]

Returning to Beyan's story

When we ask Beyan if there are any specific episodes that stand out for her in her decision to become a social worker, she says there is nothing specific, except for an overall sense of solidarity with women in need. She says:

> I'm a woman and I have a family and I live within a family. I've seen women who have been in urgent need of professional help and even if what I do would be a drop in the sea, I would do anything to help. In Iraqi Kurdistan you are very vulnerable as a woman, since most of the power is ascribed to men and their benevolence. In the end, we are all human and we all face problems and need to help and be there for each other.

What Beyan found most important in her education was the practical training. She explains that the reality of the job, for her, is not possible to transmit in the classroom and the theories only made sense when confronted with the practice. The first year of her education had been spent studying theory and doing some research as well as visiting other universities and workplaces. The second year of study focused on practical work. Beyan spent a lot of time in psychiatric settings, working on psychological issues. She felt that this had given her good experience and a strong foundation for later professional practice.

If she hadn't been a social worker, Beyan thinks she would have tried to do something similar which was supportive to vulnerable women; maybe she would have opened a cafeteria as a meeting point for these women. But changing profession is not something she thinks about, because she cannot see herself changing direction now.

A TYPICAL WEEK AT THE CENTRE

Beyan tells us that her work at the centre is unpredictable; however, predictably so. Asked to describe a week, she chooses instead to describe one day and says each and every day is similar. During the day, she has a lot of paperwork to do concerning the women staying at the centre. This relates to forms and reports for police and courts about different issues, very often mistreatments, beatings and violations. The centre attempts to solve most of the matters on the basis of dialogue and discussion between all sides involved in the confrontation. This means that social workers try to get husbands, parents or other persons involved to meet and talk together. The centre also coordinates with other organisations to take matters further in order to continue providing assistance and ensure women's safety.

At four o'clock in the afternoon, Beyan officially finishes for the day but is 'on call' at home. A day with regular office hours would be, she suggests, more an exception than something she would expect. Usually work goes on long after office hours and she must always be ready to take time from family and social life to give to these women and their families. She often works an eighteen-hour day. The previous day, for example, she received a new case at 6 p.m.; then, at 9.30 p.m. a second case came in. The third and last case arrived at 1.45 a.m. Besides women arriving during the night (this is the usual pattern), a group of women also stay for more long-term care at the centre. In one particularly difficult case, the centre has supported a woman for the past three years.

Beyan explains:

> If you work with social issues, you can never abandon your clients. Their lives depend on you. I always have to be prepared for something to happen. My job requires my full attention since this centre is for those women who are threatened with death. One little mistake or ignorance on my part might jeopardise their lives. If you work with a clear conscience in this field you can be very successful, but if you do this job only for economic reasons it won't give you much and you can't be successful.

Reviewing the social work task with women in Iraqi Kurdistan

Beyan tells us that her first priority is to protect women's lives. The issues that women face are often severe, and she must begin by looking at death threats. When an immediate problem is resolved, other issues can then be dealt with, such as providing a woman with enough knowledge and self-esteem to be able to protect herself outside the centre. Beyan is not willing to send women back to their families unless there has been significant change in the situation. If this is not achieved, there are good chances, she believes, that women will be locked up and stigmatised, possibly even worse than before. She says that the most difficult part of her job is communicating with and finding understanding with some families. This may not, of course, just be the family's problem. In some cases the problem lies with cultural mores and society, which do not allow people to behave outside the norm and put pressure on families. She also finds it difficult when a woman leaves the centre to go back to her family due to a court decision, without anything in the situation having changed, and she knows that this woman will not survive. She is not able to do anything but wait. 'These things are very hard', she says.

Nevertheless, there are successful cases, when everything turns out for the best. Beyan describes a woman who had earlier been placed at the centre who later came back to volunteer; and another whose family brought their daughters to work at the centre, because they know that the centre does such a good job. The biggest success in Beyan's work is, she says, the trust and love she receives from people. Many of the women call her 'mum', which she considers to be a great honour, because it is so difficult to call anyone else this except your own mother.

Looking ahead

If the trust and the love of people are her greatest success, Beyan sees the physical standard of the centre as her biggest failure. She would like the centre to be larger and more comfortable, and of a higher standard. She would also like to be able to provide a better service for her clients. For the future, she hopes to be able to expand and to become the leading centre in the region. There is a need for more space because the needs of women are so great. Beyan looks back three years and recalls people initially being quite negative about the centre, an opinion, which has, in many ways, changed. That makes her optimistic for the future. If she won a million American dollars, she tells us she would buy her two daughters some small presents but put the rest into the centre. We have no difficulty in believing her.

Notes

1 Under the European Credit Transfer System (ECTS), a Bachelor's (undergraduate) degree is equivalent to 180 credits.

2 A similar issue is discussed in Cree (2011), an article on supervising international Ph.D. students in social work.

3 See UNDP (2004) *Iraq Living Conditions Survey 2004*, Volume 1 Tabulation Report, table 1.6: Age in broad groups, mean and median age (electronic). Retrieved 15 July 2011: http://cosit.gov.iq/english/pdf/english_tabulation.pdf.

  KRG (2011) *The People of the Kurdistan Region* (electronic). Retrieved 14 March 2011: http://www.krg.org/articles/detail.asp?rnr=141&lngnr=12&smap=03010400&anr=18657.

  Save the Kurdistan Children (2010) *What is Iraqi Kurdistan?* (electronic). Retrieved 15 July 2011: http://www.ksc-kcf.com/About_K.asp.

4 Human Right Watch's report *Genocide in Iraq – The Anfal Campaign Against the Kurds*, first published in July 1993, details the systematic murder of between 50,000 and 100,000 Kurds. The killings (of primarily 'battle-aged' men) occurred between February and September 1988. See http://www.cfr.org/iran/hrw-genocide-iraq-anfal-campaign-against-kurds/p11654.

5 KRG (2010) *The KRG's Programme: Renewal and Reconstruction* (electronic). Retrieved 15 July 2011: http://krg.org/articles/detail.asp?anr=32349&lngnr=12&rnr=93&smap=04020000.

6 Kardozi , K. (2011) *Day Twenty Three of Protest in Sulaimaniyah, Iraqi Kurdistan, A Brighter Day, the 11th of March 2011*. Kurdnet (electronic). Retrieved 15 July 2011: http://ekurd.net/mismas/articles/misc2011/3/state4820.htm.

7 UNDP (2010) *UNDP Helps Mine Victims in Iraqi Kurdistan Become Independent* (electronic). Retrieved 15 July 2011: http://content.undp.org/go/newsroom/2009/december/undp-helps-mine-victims-in-iraqi-kurdistan-become-independent.en.

8 'Honour' crimes are pervasive in Iraq and other countries in the region. If a woman is raped, instead of receiving help she may become a double victim, ostracised by her family, or worse, killed, and the stigma against reporting any form of sex crime in Iraq is exacerbated and perpetuated in legislation. See http://www.globaljusticecenter.net/projects/iraq/honor-killings.html.

9 Kurdish Women's Rights Watch (2010) Roundup of media reports on honour-based violence and violent incidents involving women in Iraqi Kurdistan Region, May to December 2008 (electronic). Retrieved 15 July 2011: www.kwrw.org/index.asp?id=152.

10 See WHO (2008) *Eliminating Female Genital Mutilation. An Interagency Statement.* UNAIDS, UNDP, UNECA,

UNESCO, UNFPA, UNHCHR, UNHCR, *UNICEF, UNIFEM, WHO* (electronic). Retrieved 15 July 2011: http://whqlibdoc.who.int/publications/2008/9789241596442_eng.pdf.

Gabar, C. (2009) *The Situation in Southern Kurdistan 'Iraqi Kurdistan Region', the 19th of October 2009. Kurdnet* (electronic). Retrieved 15 July 2011: http://www.ekurd.net/mismas/articles/misc2009/10/independentstate3241.htm.

Human Rights Watch (2010) *They Took Me and Told Me Nothing. Female Genital Mutilation in Iraqi Kurdistan* (electronic). Retrieved 15 July 2011: http://www.hrw.org/en/node/90862/section/2.

11 Peyamner (2006) *National Shame of Imported Labor in Kurdish North of Iraq* (electonic). Retrieved 15 July 2011: http://peyamner.com/details.aspx?l=4&tid=40677.

12 See Hagberg, Jonegård (2010) *Risk och säkerhet –för kvinnor i irakiska Kurdistan.* Rapport genomförd januari 2010. http://minmedia.minheder.nu/2011/05/risksakerhetkurdistan.pdf.

References

Ahmad, A., Sofi, M., Sundelin-Wahlsten, A. and von Knorring, A.L. (2000) Post Traumatic Stress Disorder in Children After the Military Operation 'Anfal' in Iraqi Kurdistan, *European Child & Adolescent Psychiatry* 9(4): 235–243.

Ahmad, A., Abdul-Majeed, A.M., Siddiq, A., Jabar, F., Qahar, J., Rasheed, J. and von Knorring, A.L. (2007) Reporting Questionnaire for Children as a Screening Instrument for Child Mental Health Problems in Iraqi Kurdistan, *Transcultural Psychiatry* 44(1): 5–26.

Christou, A. and King, R. (2006) Migrants Encounter Migrants in the City: The Changing Context of Home for Second-generation Greek-American Return Migrants, *International Journal of Urban Regional Research* 20(4): 816–835.

Cree, V. (2011) 'I'd Like to Call You My Mother'. Reflections on Supervising International Ph.D. Students in Social Work, *Social Work Education* 1: 1–14.

King, R. and Christou, A. (2010) Cultural Geographies of Counter-diasporic Migration: Perspectives from the Study of Second-generation Returnees to Greece, *Population, Space and Place* 16(2): 103–119.

Vian Nissan, H. and Abdulgaghi, A. (2009) Suicide in the Kurdistan Region of Iraq, State of the Art, *Nordic Journal of Psychiatry* 63(4): 280–284.

Yildiz, K. (2007) *The Kurds in Iraq*, London: Pluto Press.

9 An indigenous social work experience in Aotearoa New Zealand

Moana Eruera

Ehara taku toa i te toa takitahi, Engari he toa takitini
[My strength is not that of the individual but that of many]

These words of wisdom are well known to our Māori people (Māori are the indigenous people of Aotearoa New Zealand) and are used to express the sentiments of my journey into social work. These words have their source within a Māori worldview and are part of our transmission of knowledge and values which can guide us in our lives and within our work. I have chosen this 'whakatauki' (saying or proverb), as it acknowledges the contributions of all those people who have helped to shape my practice and from whom I have learned so much. I continue to be inspired and motivated by the valuable work of Māori and indigenous practitioners in the reclaiming and evolution of indigenous frameworks, practice and literature. It is hoped that sharing this story will give insights and a perspective to be considered in social work with other cultures.

Ko tōku whānau, ko au [I am my family, past, present and future]

My 'whakapapa'[1] defines me, and has shaped my values, beliefs and the strength of my connection with those in my life both personally and professionally; it is therefore the starting point for my story.

I am the 'mataamua' (first-born child) and have two younger sisters. My dad is Māori and my mum is of Scottish and Irish heritage, born here in Aotearoa New Zealand. Their marriage in the 1960s was accepted, but was a union of two very different cultures. My mum entered into Dad's 'whanau' (extended family) whose members had very little contact with non-Māori people, none if they could avoid it, and spoke Māori as their first language. My dad was welcomed into the Scottish/Irish family and was socialised into their ways of doing things which, although very different from his experiences, he learned to enjoy.

While I was growing up, it wasn't 'cool' to be Māori and until I was about 10 years old I didn't realise that I was any different to other children, although our mum worked hard to protect us from any racist negativity. My first recollection of being different was at our small, rural primary school where my sister and I were two of only four Māori children. Children at the school, who were probably just repeating the words of the adults around them, would sometimes refer to Māori in derogatory ways and, although not directing this at us, we began to feel different. As I grew older, I was to realise and learn to manage the negative stereotypes about Māori.

My parents were always involved in voluntary and community work, and ran a social welfare family home for six long-term foster children who lived with us while we were growing up. At the time, I didn't understand some of their behaviour, but it included stealing or hoarding food and hiding it under their mattresses for later, or eating until they made themselves sick. I made the connection later in my social work training that this behaviour was the effect of severe abuse and neglect that they had suffered in their families before coming to live with us. My parents were always attentive and committed to these children being an integrated part of our whanau and they were always treated the same as us. This experience modelled and taught me lots about empathy, giving, caring and sharing for others, understanding and tolerance. After about five years with us, to the dismay of our parents, these children were all placed back with their families. For several of these children, nothing had improved or changed at home; however, despite our parents advocating strongly against them being returned home that's what happened, and for at least one child this led to traumatic events later in her life. This held a social work lesson for me that I often reflect upon about the importance and long-term effects of every decision made for children in statutory care.

Learning has been an important factor throughout my life, and our parents valued education and created opportunities for us that they didn't have themselves when growing up. My mum was committed to us learning about our Māori language and culture; it was normal to our dad. So mum persuaded dad to send us to a Māori girls' boarding-school for our secondary schooling. Living away from home at 12 years old with 300 other Māori girls was initially overwhelming and challenging, a real change from living with my family in a small country town. For the first year I struggled, was homesick, and appealed to anyone who would listen about how much I hated it there and to get me out. However, my parents were confident that they had made the right decision and so made me stick it out and, after a while, I adapted; I realise now looking back that the experience gave me a grounding that I appreciate. Although Māori is my dad's first language, it was at secondary school that we were immersed in Māori language and culture, and our environment taught us that it was great to be Māori, something to be proud of. It shaped our identity as strong Māori women, taught us to engage and sustain meaningful relationships, passed on cultural traditions and protocols, and set the foundation for our lifetime of work contributing to self-determination for Māori and indigenous peoples.

Upon finishing secondary school, I had absolutely no idea about what I wanted to do as a job and so followed my friends into university, mostly to have fun, go flatting and meet boys after having been at an all-girls' boarding-school. But I chose to continue my study of Māori language and culture. I surrounded myself with people who were like me, mostly other Māori, who loved, lived and promoted everything about our people, language and culture that made us unique.

1 Personal reflections and learning for social work

- The importance of identity, culture and practices

- The nature and quality of relationships

- Empathy, caring and service to others

- The critical role of life experiences and learning

- The role of family in shaping our values

'Na tōu rourou, na tāku rourou ka ora ai te iwi' [From your contribution and my contribution our people will flourish]

Looking back, growing up in a family where voluntary and community work were an everyday part of our life, it isn't surprising that I moved into social work.

At 21, I had tried a few jobs, mostly things like working in a cheese factory, picking apples, working in a pub, sorting wool in the sheep-shearing sheds and other things that gave me some income while I was studying. Then, after completing my degree, an opportunity arose that I hadn't really considered as a pathway for me, and that was through the Department of Social Welfare. It was implementing an employment strategy to increase the number of Māori statutory social workers to work with the high numbers of Māori children in statutory care. It had made a commitment to employ a number of Māori social workers on a trial basis, for one year, with a view to making them permanent staff. I was ambivalent but sent in a job application, strongly influenced by my mum who really wanted me to get a permanent paid job. I was both surprised and fortunate to be offered one of these positions. The surprise was because of my age. At 21, I was younger than the considered norm for social workers accepted into statutory social work and I was very conscious (and a little nervous) of that as I moved into the new position.

So this was to be my first social work role, a statutory social worker for the Department of Social Welfare. I was a young Māori woman with a university qualification but little life experience and was paired to work alongside a mature Māori woman with a wealth of life experience and a community work background but no qualification. She was to become significant as the first of many female Māori mentors throughout my social work career. We connected straight away and, between us, started to learn about and experience some of the tensions and philosophical differences of working with Māori families and communities within the constraints of a statutory organisation. Unknown to me, at the time it was to be the start of ten years' work in statutory child protection and youth offending.

There were many significant learning experiences while working in statutory roles; however, there are two that stand out. The first and most exciting as a Māori practitioner was being a part of the introduction and application of a report called *Puao te Atatu*[2] which marked a milestone for Māori and social work practice in Aotearoa New Zealand. The report made recommendations on 'the most appropriate means to achieve the goal of an approach which would meet the needs of Māori in policy, planning and service delivery in the Department of Social Welfare' (Department of Social Welfare 1988: 5). It acknowledged Māori as 'tangata whenua'[3] and formally recognised Māori cultural values and customary practices as important in the policies and practices for fostering and care of Māori children and family case work for Māori clients. The second was the introduction of the Children, Young Persons and their Families Act of 1989 which ensured that extended families and tribes contributed to decision-making processes for children in care (see Connolly 1994). The Act also created a legal pathway for tribal social services where I was to work later in my career.

While I was working within statutory services, I began postgraduate social work study which was another enlightening, although often challenging, time for me. I had been working for about six years predominantly with Māori youth and their families, and had been an avid advocate for Māori families to be worked 'with, not on' in a way that recognised and responded to cultural values, beliefs and practices. As a result, I was often perceived as a troublemaker within the statutory social work

Moana Eruera

environment, someone who constantly challenged and just wouldn't accept and follow the processes that treated everyone 'the same', except that everyone isn't the same.

I entered into postgraduate studies sponsored by the Department of Social Welfare and found myself in an institution where much of the knowledge was Eurocentric and, in many cases, was in conflict with my reality, experiences, values, beliefs and practices. There was a distinct gap in information about Māori worldviews and practices. Within Aotearoa New Zealand, Māori are acknowledged through the Treaty of Waitangi as the indigenous people of the country and have specific rights defined by the principles of protection, participation and partnership. This Treaty is a foundation document of the country and is to be practised and applied within all Crown activities. As such, it informs and guides social work practices within this Aotearoa New Zealand context. A disproportionate percentage of Māori engage with social work services compared to non-Māori and therefore it is critical that all social workers are able to practise with cultural safety when working with Māori. It seemed that again I was to advocate for Māori inclusion and was often treated as the 'Māori activist' in the class. This did not change the fact that I still had to learn and work with much information and curriculum that I did not believe in, since much of it was, in my mind, a tool of colonisation which did not recognise Māori knowledge base and practices as valid. Somehow, I managed to reconcile these tensions in order to pass the course by regurgitating the information required by my tutors or by critiquing the appropriateness of Eurocentric practices when working with Māori people and other indigenous or minority cultures. I felt quite battle-worn when I successfully completed my qualification and I didn't attend my graduation ceremony.

I often consider my time as a social work student and later, as I moved away from front-line social work and into the role of tutor and facilitator of social and community work education, I am constantly reminded of the importance of validating knowledge and experiences for learners.

2 Personal reflections and learning for social work

- The significant role of mentors who featured and continued to support me throughout my professional career
- The importance of strong advocacy in social work
- Being open to the many different pathways into social work
- Creating space for the validation of knowledge and practices, particularly those of indigenous and minority groups

'Taku mahi' [My current work]

My social work practice developed and changed over the years, and eventually I reached a point where I realised I wanted to refocus. After more than twenty years in social work, beginning in statutory roles, then moving to community work and into tribal social service delivery, I reached a point where I wanted to shift my focus from front-line work supporting users of social work. This was influenced by a number of factors.

For the whole of my working career, I had been living and working away from my own tribal area and I had a strong desire to move our family home to our 'whenua' (literally, land) so that we could strengthen our connection with our extended family and make a direct contribution to tribal development. My husband, who is from a different tribe and part of the country, supported this and so we moved to Northland region.

I wanted to work with a more prevention educational focus and was still committed to the development of services to support practitioners. Especially after seeing many of my social work colleagues go through stress and burn-out (and having experienced it myself), I decided that I wanted to be able to actively support practitioners. The maintenance of well-being for Māori working in social work and more broadly social services, and effective work with 'whānau' Māori (family members) is becoming more complex, and therefore the processes used to support this work, such as supervision, professional development and training, and social and community research are also critically important. As Māori, there is a distinct cultural overlap between professional and personal accountabilities, collective and individual obligations, cultural and clinical interventions and others whom we encounter in our work. Supervision, practice development and training can help us to work through these issues and maintain good health, safety and accountability so that we can be effective with those we are working with and for. With the rapid increase in the delivery of tribal social services and the reclaiming and development of Māori frameworks and models of practice within Aotearoa New Zealand, it is imperative that we have good processes in place to support practitioners. The practice issues that Māori practitioners face when working with our own people are complex, whether they are located within a statutory, community or tribal organisation. Examples of these may include: meeting the needs of whānau Māori as well as mainstream accountabilities; provision of effective services for Māori who are at varied and diverse stages in their cultural development; and achieving a balance between the expectations of paid employment and the expectations and collective responsibilities evident within Māori communities (see also Eruera and Stevens 2010).

I decided that my skills were best utilised by supporting practitioners and in practice development; I am now in my seventh year working as a social and community work consultant where I am contracted to assist in a range of projects, some of which include training design and delivery, community research, supervision, family violence prevention and others. Most commonly, the projects seek specific knowledge, skills and practices for working with Māori communities, families or tribes.

More recently, over the past five years I have been involved in two projects that I am very passionate about. The first project focused on working for the Amokura Family Violence Prevention Consortium, an integrated community change initiative to promote whānau well-being and violence prevention in Northland, Aotearoa New Zealand, led by the chief executive officers of seven tribal authorities for the region. The aims were to provide strategic leadership and build 'whānau' violence primary prevention, early intervention, and community action capacity within families, tribes, community and service providers within the region. The consortium activities were guided by a Māori framework called 'Mauri Ora',[4] which provides a Māori analysis and tasks for addressing 'whānau' violence.

The project worked towards the goal of individual and collective well-being and aimed to:

- *dispel the illusion* (at individual and collective levels) that family violence is normal, acceptable and culturally valid;

- *remove opportunities* for family violence to take place;

- *teach transformative practices* based on Māori cultural imperatives that provide alternatives to violence.

Amokura strategic directions and activities were implemented through four work streams to advance this important 'kaupapa'.[5] They were advocacy, provider development and training, research, community awareness and education. My role within this project was to coordinate the provider development and training activities throughout the region. It was exciting work and implemented a workforce development strategy across sectors for the prevention of violence within Māori families by up-skilling practitioners to use Māori cultural frameworks to prevent, recognise and respond to violence appropriately, employing a range of strategies with families.

The second project is called 'Whānau Ora', a whānau-centred approach for the design, transformation and delivery of existing government-funded services and initiatives to whānau that build on the aspirations, strengths and capabilities of whānau to improve economic, cultural and social development. The Whānau Ora Taskforce constructed a framework which identified a philosophy, core principles and key elements for government-funded services to deliver whānau-centred initiatives.[6] The Whānau Ora policy framework is another milestone for Māori and indigenous development, in that it transposes Māori values into government policy, uses a strengths-based, not deficit, approach, has an integrated view of 'well-ness' working across sectors, particularly social services and health, and builds the capability of service provision to improve outcomes for Māori families. I have been involved in supporting a range of projects for Whānau Ora in the field of practice development, service provider transformation of services and research.

Since returning home ten years ago, I have also committed a huge amount of time in a voluntary capacity to the development of our 'marae' (tribal gathering place) and enjoy achievements which benefit our extended family and tribe.

3 Personal reflections and learning for social work

- Using our knowledge and skills for those things we are most passionate about

- The importance of continuing to contribute to voluntary work

• The range of different ways we can participate in social work, for example through research, practice development and training, supervision and others

Looking forward

I celebrate the many achievements of Māori reclamation which have occurred over the past twenty-five years that represent the commitment, determination and hard work of many Māori for the well-being of our people. Sometimes as we continue to work towards self-determination for Māori, we forget how much we have already achieved. These achievements include things such as our children being fortunate to attend a total immersion Māori-speaking school, and Māori being recognised as an official language with many words and greetings adopted and used in everyday conversations by all New Zealanders. We have Māori media nationwide, which means we can watch programmes in our own language. These television channels are popular with Māori and non-Māori viewers alike. We have two Māori political parties which hold significant portfolios and influence in the government arena. Our culture and arts are becoming world-renowned, for example the 'haka' and Māori tattoo known as 'tamoko'.

I am still committed and passionate about Māori and indigenous practice development, and see this work as important and beneficial for *all* people in Aotearoa New Zealand, as well as making a contribution to the progress of indigenous people.

Finally, in the words of our elders:

> He aha te mea nui o tenei ao?
> He tangata, he tangata, he tangata.

> [If you ask me, what is the most important thing in the world?
> I will reply, it is People! It is People! It is People!]

(see Metge 1995)

Notes

1 'Whakapapa' is literally translated as 'genealogy' but reflects the belief in relationships with the creator, with people and with the environment.

2 See *Puao te Atatu, The Report of the Ministerial Advisory Committee on a Maori Perspective for the Department of Social Welfare*, Wellington, September 1988 (see http://www.msd.govt.nz/documents/about-msd-and-our-work/publications-resources/archive/1988-puaoteatatu.pdf).

3 'Tangata whenua' literally translated means 'people of the land', and refers to indigenous peoples and Māori within the context of Aotearoa New Zealand.

4   See *Transforming Whanau Violence – A Conceptual Framework*, Ministry of Maori Development, 2004.

5   Kaupapa Māori is the conceptualisation of Māori knowledge that has been developed through oral tradition.

6   See *Whanau Ora: Report of the Taskforce on Whanau-Centred Initiatives*, Wellington, 2010 (http://www.msd. govt.nz/documents/about-msd-and-our-work/publications-resources/planning-strategy/whanau-ora/ whanau-ora-taskforce-report.pdf).

References

Connolly, M. (1994) 'An Act of Empowerment: The Children, Young Persons and their Families Act (1989)', *British Journal of Social Work* 24 (1): 87–100.

Department of Social Welfare (1988) *Puao te Atatu, The Report of the Ministerial Advisory Committee on a Maori Perspective for the Department of Social Welfare*, Wellington, September.

Eruera, M. and Stevens, G. (2010) 'Te Whiriwhiringa o te Kete. Weaving the Past into the Present for the Future', Presentation for Supervision Conference held at the University of Auckland, May.

Metge, J. (1995) *New Growth from Old: The Whānau in the Modern World*, Wellington: Victoria University Press.

10 Working with HIV

Bill Foley

I have been a social worker for sixteen years. I am now 54 years old, and I came to social work late in life through a circuitous route. Yet in retrospect, the seeds of interest in social work, in its broadest form, were present from much earlier on in life.

I was born and grew up in a working-class area of Dublin in a post-war local authority housing estate. I was a mild-mannered boy in a sometimes tough neighbourhood. I was called names at school and tended to avoid team sports, engaging in the more solitary field sports when pressed into compulsory physical education. I gravitated towards the 'geeky' intellectual types in secondary school. Against the norm and expectation in the area, I actively sought to carry on education to Leaving Certificate Standard (completed at aged 17 or 18 years). I was the only one to go to this level in my family, and one of only a handful of my peer group from my estate. While the appeal of a college education beckoned, at that time it was not possible for my family to afford to support me through college. I entered the labour market in a variety of office jobs, rather than the trades that my brothers had followed. Eventually, I settled in a law firm as a para-legal and began further education through various evening classes, culminating in a Legal Diploma.

I had been drawn to religion at school. This was partly related to the strong Catholic faith of my father but also because I saw it as a way of getting actively involved in helping people. I joined the Society of St Vincent De Paul (www.svp.ie/) and was a volunteer there for most of my time at secondary school.

I mostly did fundraising and visiting the sick and elderly of the community and helping out with some practical chores such as shopping. It was a training ground for building awareness of the way some sectors of society could be marginalised. In retrospect, it was the beginning of my politicisation and awareness of issues of equality, fairness and social justice.

As the time approached to leave school and enter the workforce I became increasingly aware of my own difference from many of my peers. I was shy in social settings, particularly in mixed company. While I developed friendships with girls there was no real attraction. Gradually I realised I was gay. It was a pivotal moment for me. It forced me to reflect on my beliefs. I felt let down by the Church and my faith fell away very rapidly. I left school and began to get involved in the gay and lesbian community. Initially, I volunteered on a minor level, helping out with social functions and running clubs. It was the early days of the gay and lesbian movement in Ireland and gay male sexuality was still criminalised.[1] Self-help and consciousness-raising groups were being formed and I joined in, thus strengthening my burgeoning awareness of social injustice and discrimination issues. By the late 1970s, I was helping out with the production of a newsletter for gay and lesbian people with the National (Lesbian and) Gay Federation and writing regular contributory articles. I met many interesting people (many friends – including my partner) during that time, and later joined a small group of people who came together as the Dublin Lesbian and Gay Men's Collective. We were a mixed bag of socialists and communists, some with republican leanings, so debates about politics and strategies could be intense at times. We set about an activist agenda focusing on gay and lesbian liberation, and were centrally involved in organising some of the earliest gay and lesbian pride marches in Dublin. We also published a regular newsletter outlining our politics and our place in the struggle for a socialist republican anti-discriminatory Ireland. When a man was murdered in a park in Dublin city in 1982, the assailants were found to be a group of local youths. They had been 'queer-bashing' men in the park for some time. The 'Declan Flynn case' was notorious in Dublin at the time, not least because the judge gave suspended sentences on the basis that being approached by a gay man was provocation enough for young men to respond violently. Our collective arranged a protest march to the park where the murder had been committed; the march attracted a record number of people for a public demonstration on a gay and lesbian issue in Ireland.

The collective also became involved in the wider political movement. We consciously made connections with the Labour and trade union movements, seeing them as natural allies to our cause. We were responsible for contributing to the development and formation of anti-discriminatory policies for gay and lesbian members of many of the public sector trade unions. We also played an active role in national referendums in the 1980s about abortion and divorce. The visibility of the gay and lesbian collective members within these campaigns was high and we developed a considerable amount of respect among left-leaning political activists. For many, it was the first time they had come into contact with gay and lesbian people who were prepared to talk about issues of sexuality on both a personal and political level. While we lost the two abortion referendums, we won the one on divorce. It was one of the defining periods of the development of modern Ireland. The debates brought subjects such as sexuality, fertility control, relationships and women's right to choose to the fore and there was considerable advancement of the issues as a result. Women's rights within the collectives also came to be central, with awareness of the double oppression of lesbians as women and as a result of their sexuality. This crystallising awareness led to a split, with the men's and women's collective meeting separately, only coming together for joint projects. We had been working on a project to build awareness of the lives of Irish lesbians and gay men for some years. This culminated in the publication of a book *Out for Ourselves* in 1986, of which I was a contributing editor. The publication of the book was effectively the last action of the collectives and they gradually dissipated.

HIV in Ireland

Following the split in the collectives in the early 1980s, the men's and women's groups began to focus separately on issues of concern to them. As part of the men's group, we became aware of a growing amount of publicity in the USA about what was being referred to as a 'gay cancer'. When it emerged that the likely cause was a sexually transmissible infection, the gay community was targeted for a lot of media and public health abuse. In Ireland, this issue seemed a long way away, but we quickly realised that it would only be a matter of time before it arrived. We began meeting to discuss possible responses and formally launched our response organisation, 'Gay Health Action', in 1985. Our first information leaflet was published in 1985 and widely distributed. It was the first leaflet for the gay community funded publicly by a government agency (at a time when gay male sexuality was still criminalised). By now, it was clear that this was a virus and that the disease was not confined to the gay community. The development of an antibody test in 1985 for HIV (or HTLV III as it was then called) meant that those infected could be identified for possible treatment and prevention interventions. Initial scepticism from some quarters soon changed to serious acknowledgement and praise for our efforts when later in 1985 information emerged about patients in Ireland being diagnosed with the disease as early as 1982. From this beginning, there was considerable effort put into making alliances with others initially associated with the disease (drug treatment agencies and the haemophilia society). A range of organisations was established to address the issues from a preventive perspective. This was at a time when there was no treatment available and the only option was education about methods to avoid infection. I was centrally involved in the work of Gay Health Action and helped to found associated organisations including AIDS Action Alliance (now Dublin AIDS Alliance) and CAIRDE (a buddying and support group for people affected by AIDS/HIV). Both organisations still exist but the latter organisation has since changed its focus of operation to provide support for migrant women with HIV.

I continued my involvement in the developing services and campaigns throughout the 1980s and 1990s. In 1988, the Irish AIDS Initiative Conference brought together those working on the ground in the voluntary and statutory sector with people living with HIV. I was a member of the organising committee and chair of the conference that set an agenda of shared concerns and highlighted service development needs. Subsequently, the AIDS Liaison Forum invited the Department of Health to jointly run a conference on the World AIDS Day theme of 'Sharing the Challenge' in 1991. This conference launched the National Aids Strategy Committee, a partnership of statutory and voluntary personnel charged with responsibility for developing a national strategy. The NASC reported twice, in 1992 and 2000: the 1992 report raised concerns about the potential exponential epidemic spread of the disease and its impact on society and health budgets; by 2000, the scenario had changed significantly with the advent of medical treatment and the focus was now on managing people with a chronic disease (DOHC 1992, 2000).

While the gay community responded early to the HIV crisis, the official response was slow. The Irish Department of Health first provided funding for the appointment of two counsellors in the social work department of a large Dublin teaching hospital in 1989. In the 1990s, the services were expanded and departments of infectious diseases or genito-urinary medicine addressing HIV/AIDS were opened in a number of hospitals in Ireland. There was also the development of methadone treatment clinics and needle exchange programmes for intravenous drug users. Social workers were part of the development of these services. The Irish Association of Social Workers formed a special-interest HIV counsellors' group in the early 1990s and published an information and resource pack in 1992. The Health Services Executive established a specialist service for gay men, the Gay Men's Health Project, in Dublin in 1992. This organisation founded the Gay Health Network that brought together services from all over Ireland to share resources, ideas and experiences of working with people with HIV. I was a volunteer with the Network for almost ten years until early 2001 and contributed to the 2000 GHN Survey.

All of my activities at this time were conducted in a voluntary capacity. I was heavily involved in volunteering my 'free' hours to the organisations and spent most of my time when not in work at some meeting or other, or drafting leaflets for distribution and reports for funding submissions. It amounted to a full-time job on top of the one I had to earn money. This pace of work continued for about seven years when I realised I needed some rationalisation of the time I was spending at work – either paid or voluntary. The motivation behind involvement remained strong; predictions about the future, with HIV in it, were bleak when anticipated numbers of infected and likely mortality rates were taken into account.

The move to social work

As will be clear already, I was juggling a lot of things in the late 1970s and early 1980s. I was in a full-time job. I was attending part-time education to enhance my career opportunities in the legal profession. I was volunteering a huge amount of time to various civil rights/gay lesbian and HIV/AIDS campaigns. Therefore 'leisure time' was limited. Looking back, I don't know how I did it! It was certainly an exciting time that gave satisfaction in dealing with life-and-death issues in a way that could make a difference, but it was also exhausting. By the late 1980s, I began to reflect on where my future career path lay. It seemed I had two clear options. One was to continue with legal studies and qualify as a lawyer. This would also fulfil a long-term ambition of completing a degree course in college. There were now also a range of service developments for people with HIV/AIDS. As I had enjoyed my work with

HIV/AIDS, I began to consider a possible change of career that would enable me to focus on this issue in a full-time paid post. Having considered the options, I set upon social work as the most likely achievable career path that would enable me to work with people with HIV/AIDS. I applied to Trinity College Dublin and began the full-time, four-year degree course in Social Work and Social Studies in 1995. Just as I was completing my degree, a post became available in a large inner-city Dublin teaching hospital in its newly developed Infectious Diseases Unit. I applied for and was lucky enough to get the job.

The changing role of social work in HIV

By the time I entered social work as a professional, there had been some advances in the development of treatment for HIV. Nevertheless, it was still regarded as a life-threatening illness and there continued to be many fatalities. Prevention and education continued to be key components of the responses by medical clinics; my job was to provide social work services and counselling to patients. Pre-test counselling was the norm for those considering HIV testing and counselling was also standard for those with a diagnosis. Clients were offered help in disclosure to partners. For those at high risk who routinely tested, there was an important role of education of the risks involved and ways of risk reduction. Frequent hospital admissions were the norm for many. The client profile spanned the range of those affected by HIV including gay men, injecting drug users, immigrant populations, particularly from sub-Saharan countries or areas where HIV was more prevalent, and increasingly some heterosexual contacts. Clients presented with concerns about many issues in the face of their diagnosis. Most felt a high sense of stigma associated with their diagnosis. There was considerable fear for their future prognosis with no ability to know when they might become vulnerable to a life-threatening opportunistic infection. Many clients had multiple social problems, from drug and alcohol addiction to issues concerning social welfare, homelessness and mental health. It was a challenging and rewarding and stimulating environment to work in. I became part of an HIV counsellors' group that comprised social workers from the Dublin hospitals and counsellors from drug treatment clinics. This helped to set standards for practice as well as identifying issues that could benefit from campaigning input. We made several submissions to the National AIDS Task Force (a Department of Health government programme to tackle AIDS/HIV). We also arranged a series of educational workshops for doctors and other professionals on the topic of disclosure. These workshops were helpful in clarifying issues relating to disclosure of the HIV status of patients to their partners where the patient consistently declined to do so. From this, a series of guidelines that are still used today were published under the auspices of the Department of Health.

When a new generation of treatment drugs were developed in 1998 called protease inhibitors, it signalled a significant change in the services for people with HIV/AIDS. Some even heralded the new combination drugs as a cure. Unfortunately, this was not to be the case. However, the new treatments had a significant effect on the health and lives of people with HIV. They had the effect of suppressing HIV in the body and boosting the immune system. Many people recovered healthy immune systems. Many were also able to return to work. Further refinements in the available treatments and the emergence of new drugs have made the treatment even more effective. As a result, the numbers now admitted to hospitals for treatment with an HIV-related illness are few. Most of those who are admitted are people who had not been diagnosed and who developed symptoms of HIV/AIDS before they could seek treatment. Some are from a drug-using (IVDU) background whose main health concern comes from persistent drug use rather than HIV. This change has had a significant effect on the nature of my work and the role of social work in medical services for people with HIV/AIDS. Doctors now provide a pre-test discussion for those taking the HIV test. This tends to emphasise the benefits of early diagnosis and access to treatment. It has also led to doctors comparing HIV to diabetes, in that it is a lifelong infection that can be managed by medication.

Some statistics

When the first cases of HIV began to be diagnosed in Ireland, the numbers involved were very small – in the single and double digits per year – with 60 per cent of those diagnosed being intravenous drug users. Gradually, over the late 1980s and 1990s, this pattern began to change. The numbers of newly diagnosed HIV cases per main risk category (MSM, IVDU[2] and heterosexual) remained under fifty cases, but the trend was rising. In 2001, the numbers of newly diagnosed heterosexual cases rose dramatically to a peak of just under 230. This was partly due to the rise in immigration of people from regions of the world where there is a high prevalence of HIV. From 2006 to 2010, the pattern changed again. The rate of newly diagnosed IVDU cases fell significantly, with only twenty-two new cases diagnosed in 2010. For MSM, the pattern has been on the rise since 2006, with 134 new diagnoses in 2010. The heterosexual rate of new diagnoses per year has been falling again so that MSM now comprise the largest group of new diagnosis in Ireland (O'Donnell et al. 2011). These figures reflect the changing face of HIV in Ireland, with the range of groups affected bringing with them their own associated social problems and concerns.

MY TYPICAL WEEK

I work with the infectious diseases team of a Dublin teaching hospital specialising in acute diseases. There are three consultants who lead the team, made up of five registrars, three senior house officers and two interns (junior doctors) as well as one pharmacist and one social worker (me). The team works on a multi-disciplinary basis within the medical model and the constraints of the demands of an acute medical setting. We have access to occupational therapy and physiotherapy departments. We have a specialist twelve-bedded ward (including six isolation rooms with negative pressure for treatment of TB) and highly trained nursing staff with special interest in infectious diseases and HIV. The team is 'on call' in our Emergency Department every six days. All patients admitted on call are provided with a medical and multi-disciplinary service. Patients admitted reflect the demographics of the catchment area of the hospital. It is a poor area with one of the highest rates of elderly and drug-using populations in the city. The patients therefore tend to be a mix of the elderly, people with addiction problems and homeless people. The team also has special responsibility for treating those with infectious diseases and we regularly take over the care of patients admitted with these conditions. This includes those with HIV as well as TB, hepatitis and other tropical infections. Any patient admitted can be referred to me for social work assessment and service provision. In addition, we run HIV and sexually transmitted infections (STI) clinics. There are three infectious diseases clinics per week where those with HIV attend regularly for treatment and monitoring of their condition. These clinics also deal with those attending for hepatitis or TB treatments, or those seeking HIV testing. There are five STI clinics per week that test and treat infections and also provide HIV testing. Referrals can be made to me from any of the clinics at any time. The current pattern of referrals gives priority to those who are diagnosed HIV positive, or if particular social concerns arise, such as those patients attending the STI clinic as a result of sexual assault. Any of the HIV-diagnosed patients can seek social work input in relation to counselling support or help with practical concerns such as social welfare issues or accommodation.

Monday a.m.: Team meeting to review all inpatients currently in hospital under the care of our team. Each patient's case is individually assessed and issues of concern identified. My role is to conduct a social assessment of the client and identify any supports they may require and any potential gaps in their ability to manage.

Senior social work meeting to address administrative, operational and strategic issues of concern for the social work department.

p.m.: Check computer system for new referrals. (Typically two or three new referrals to be seen.) I carry out an initial assessment interview with the new clients on the wards. Review any patients who have been previously assessed and for whom a discharge plan was unclear or incomplete.

Tuesday a.m.: Visit our outpatient clinic to provide counselling support to a newly diagnosed HIV positive client.

p.m.: Inpatient reviews and administration follow-up.

Wednesday a.m.: Administrative work/writing letters and records. Family meetings and client interviews.

p.m.: Cover for referrals from STI clinics.

Thursday	a.m.: Social work main meeting held three Thursdays per month.
	p.m.: Review inpatients and develop and refine discharge plans.
Friday	Administrative tasks; telephone contacts with community services and assess new referrals.
Weekend	My weekends are now for pleasure and relaxing. (I have not carried out any significant voluntary work since about 2001.) My partner is involved with a Gay Law and Social Reform group and I have frequent contact and informal discussions with members regarding ongoing actions and policy (e.g. campaigns for civil partnership and civil marriage for gay and lesbian people).

Looking ahead

Over the years, the type of work I do at the hospital has changed considerably. With improved treatments for HIV, outpatient clients make fewer demands on counselling services and are more likely to request interventions at times of life crisis. Inpatient work today is more likely to involve working with an elderly person in relation to needs for community supports or nursing home care, rather than HIV-related issues. Thus, overall, the amount of specialist HIV work in my role has reduced. Nevertheless, the post continues to provide a wide range of social work challenges and satisfaction. Any other profession would be hard pressed to match it. I think that it is this variety that keeps me engaged in the work.

Notes

1   The Gay and Lesbian Equality Network was founded in 1990 with the aim of addressing law reform for the gay and lesbian communities. Thanks to its efforts, gay male consensual sexual activity was finally decriminalised in 1993.

2   Men who have sex with men (MSM) and IVDU (intravenous drug users).

References

Department of Health and Children (DOHC) (1992) *Report of the National AIDS Strategy Committee*, Dublin: The Stationery Office.

Department of Health and Children (DOHC) (2000) *Report of the National AIDS Strategy Committee,* Dublin: The Stationery Office.

Dublin Lesbian and Gay Men's Collectives (1986) *Out for Ourselves: The Lives of Irish Lesbians and Gay Men,* Dublin: Women's Community Press.

O'Donnell, K., Jackson, S., Moran, J. and O'Hora, A. (2011) *HIV and AIDS in Ireland 2010,* Dublin: Health Protection and Surveillance Centre.

11 The accidental social worker

Jan Fook

'Choosing' social work? I wish I could say that I actively chose social work as a career, but alas, this is far from the truth.

I grew up in Australia, in suburban Sydney, in the 1960s, the daughter of a dynamic woman who would have been a feminist (if she had been white and middle class) and of a man who would have been a church minister (if he had been white). As it was, my parents were of Chinese descent, from a line of families who had lived in Australia for several generations. Their parents had been rural small business owners, and, disappointingly for my parents, this is what they also became, despite valiant efforts to become more socially mobile. My mother constantly craved an education (she had to leave school in her third year of high school in order to housekeep for the family). My father, despite parental disapproval, studied for four years to become a church minister, yet was unable to gain employment as such. The suspicion was that Australia was not ready for a Chinese minister in that particular religion.

There were therefore high hopes for my generation. University education was taken for granted, and, as is usual for Chinese families, professional education was preferred. I can remember the limited range of choices put to me by my parents at the time: social work or teaching. I wanted to be a teacher. My mother wanted me to be a social worker. To cut a long story short, I became a social worker.

Luckily, I was easily able to gain entrance to what was regarded as one of the best social work programmes in Australia at the time. I had attained good grades for my high school leaving, and so

96

competed successfully for a highly prized place. But my first year of studying social work was mixed, and my ambivalence grew as I progressed through the four years of the course. To be honest, I enjoyed the more 'foundational' disciplines. My most enduring positive memories of my social work study are encountering *The Sociological Imagination* by C. Wright Mills (1959), and Tolkein's (1954) work (in a subject called, enticingly, The Literature of Fantasy). I struggled with the more social work-oriented subjects, as I could not understand their disciplinary base, and found it difficult to engage with the content. I seriously contemplated transferring to an Arts degree. My grades were consistently disappointing – usually only a pass, or just above pass level. I confess to either not understanding, or not being particularly interested in, most of the subjects which were required. My experience with placements was OK – I found I could talk comfortably with people, and of course the activities were much more pleasant than the factory jobs I did in my holidays to earn some spare cash. However, I do not recall feeling a special connection with the work or any sort of 'calling' to the profession. Why did I persevere? Probably because I was a diligent soul, who felt I should finish something I had started.

I am aware that this is an entirely unprepossessing start to a career in social work. Throughout my four years of undergraduate study, and the first two years of practice as a social worker, I had secretly harboured the ambition of becoming an academic. I assumed, however, since my grades were so unremarkable, that such a door would always remain closed. But I was (and still am) fortunate to be blessed with a very vigilant and supportive partner who was always alert to my needs. When a lecturing position was advertised at our local college, he urged me to apply.

You might say I have since never looked back.

Becoming a lecturer

I took to teaching, to use a cliché, like a duck to water. What was it that engaged me? For one thing, there was the challenge of reading up on topics which were absolutely central to the social work and welfare professions – the welfare state, the ideologies which informed it, and the basic philosophies and humanitarian impulses behind the welfare movement. These topics had been covered in my undergraduate training, but it felt as if I had passed through their coverage as if in a grey fog. I was forced to reconnect with these topics in a way which enabled me to make them relevant for first-year students from very mixed backgrounds. Thus my interest was finally kindled in the crucial foundations of social work.

The second challenge was that all the people I was teaching were of mature age (mid-twenties upwards) and mostly from working-class backgrounds. I should mention that this was an industrial city to the north of Sydney. I had moved there immediately after my graduation from my social work degree, as I could not obtain work in Sydney. There was quite a degree of politics involved in the Australian social work and welfare professional community at the time. The college where I taught was not well regarded, and I was not teaching social work (a four-year degree), but rather social welfare (a two-year associate diploma). At the time, in the early 1980s, there were significant tensions regarding whether those with social welfare qualifications (and therefore social welfare workers) should be recognised as social workers. There was concern that the standards of social work and its education (involving a four-year professionally accredited degree programme at an established university) would be diluted if lesser qualifications from lesser higher education institutions were accepted. In some cases there was even opposition to developing better access pathways for people with welfare qualifications to upgrade to social work study. Therefore, teaching at the sort of institution I was at, and the sorts of students I taught, was not regarded as very prestigious. In social work circles it was also seen as problematic.

This backdrop, however, was significant in my professional development. I really liked the challenge of connecting with people who themselves felt and were marginalised, and who had often come to study welfare as a second or third occupation. They had made clear choices about why they wanted to be welfare workers, and had often been through bitter experiences which had brought them to this point. I actually enjoyed translating difficult academic material so that they could integrate its meaning directly with the specifics of their lives. Many of them, when they first met me, wondered if I had come directly off 'the boat'. (The term 'boat people' was coined at the time to refer to the many boatloads of Vietnamese refugees arriving regularly on Australian shores during this period.) As well, I looked young to them (I guess I was – I began lecturing at the age of 24). I clearly remember one outgoing young man, Terry, aged in his late thirties, who confronted me at the beginning of a lecture and asked what I could possibly know. I can't remember what I replied (probably something about what was important being not what I knew, but how I could get them to learn) but it didn't phase me. It put me on my mettle to make the educational experience worthwhile, with this group of people who were most evidently not of my class, ethnic background or age. Terry actually belonged to a local family of butchers, so I also saw him every Saturday when I did my weekly grocery shopping. I particularly liked the sausages and meatloaf he made (still the best I've ever had in my life) and I was chuffed to think that I taught welfare to this man who was such a good butcher!

These were the sorts of satisfactions I gained from my first teaching position, and I am happy to report that I was also greatly appreciated by my students. However, it was impressed upon me, quite soon after taking up this lecturing position, that teaching well was not enough – I needed to gain a higher degree. I therefore enrolled in a Master's degree at the University of Sydney. This was a research degree involving a 50,000-word thesis. (Such degrees have since become outmoded, but at the time it was seen as sufficient for research credibility, in the same way that the Ph.D. is now regarded.)

I took to this work, again, like a duck to water. I revelled in the intellectual autonomy and creativity this afforded me, and whittled away contentedly at developing a model for the practice of radical casework. This was my response to the big intellectual problem of the 'radical' period in social work, when individual casework methods became devalued and criticised. I had begun to gain a sense of the excitement of being able to contribute to the social work profession through intellectual means. Although I was aware of the need for academics to publish at this time, it was some years before I successfully managed this with my Master's thesis. Unhappily, I must report that there were several people who actively hindered its publication. This was in an era when there was very little locally produced academic social work literature – we relied heavily on British (and, to a lesser extent,

American) material. I suppose professional jealousy may have been a factor. There may also have been political opposition to the idea of a 'radical' casework. This was, of course, one of my introductions to what can be a very cut-throat world in academia. My Master's thesis was, however, finally published in 1993 (Fook 1993), and was widely used in Australian social work programmes throughout the next decade. This small taste of interest in my work set me on the path to making further academic contributions.

I had caught the academic bug, and over the next few decades became completely dedicated to carving out the distinctive nature of social work as an academic discipline, and hence its place in the academy, and the rightful role of social work academics. My own background as a young lower middle-class woman of Chinese descent in a White Australia, working in less than prestigious programmes in marginal institutions, gave me a sturdy platform from which to champion new and alternative perspectives for a young profession, still seeking to gain legitimacy in the academy. I am very much committed to developing the distinctive 'person-in-situation' orientation of social work (Hamilton 1951) as an intellectual foundation for practice and research, and for developing methods and approaches to research and practice which integrate this vision. This flows on to establishing the legitimacy of such approaches in the established academy. This vision has sustained my clear idea of my own contribution and sense of mission in my profession, and makes me proud of my profession, and proud to be a member of it. In this sense, I feel that I have now actively chosen social work as my profession, but this has been only after I was able to envisage my own distinctive place in it. I am, from this point of view, very much an accidental social worker, and I am aware that I have to keep carving out my place.

What am I doing now?

After my initial teaching post, I moved around Australia for a variety of reasons. I still sought mostly academic positions. I lived in both rural and urban settings. From the mid-1990s I held two major positions. In the first, I was responsible for designing, writing and establishing a new social work programme which was innovative, as it was both reflective and taught by distance. However, while in this role I also felt I had made a major contribution to social work education in Australia, and was ready to move on.

I had begun to develop my model of critical reflection so that it could be taught in workshop format to practising professionals. I therefore accepted a position, in the early 2000s, which involved providing continuing professional education across many health and welfare professions. I was very energised by the potential to develop a sort of 'person-in-situation' approach to critical reflection, thus making a social work perspective on critical reflection relevant to many different professions. Policy makers, researchers, counsellors, teachers, managers, health professionals, social workers and social care workers from many fields of work were among those with whom I conducted workshops. This approach to critical reflection was subsequently published (Fook and Gardner 2007) and is currently used quite extensively around the world. I greatly enjoyed this work, but continued to feel the need to be challenged by new contexts.

In 2006, my partner and I decided to move to the UK. I had about twenty-five years' academic experience by this time, and when I came to the UK I returned to a conventional social work academic position. I headed a department of social work at a major university with a very good reputation for its social work programmes. This was the perfect introduction to UK social work for me, and I came to understand a lot more about contextuality – how the context frames and creates the social work which is practised within it. I was also able to gain a better understanding of Australian social work from this new UK vantage point.

These comments are pertinent to an understanding of social work in an international context. Some years before I moved from Australia, I had begun to travel fairly widely delivering talks and workshops, and had made many cursory observations about the differences in social work between different countries. Doing professional work internationally for me is a slightly surreal experience, as I often feel I am parachuting in, and cannot really engage in-depth with how my ideas might be interpreted in that context. My ideas are always treated with respect because I am an invited guest, but I often feel that having such a position to some extent inhibits the development of my ideas in a manner which may be more appropriate to that context.

However, I was aware, from both reading and observations, that there were some reasonably distinctive features of Australian social work, and that its standards of education and practice were held in high regard across the world. It was also known as professionally rather than bureaucratically driven, and had a clear critical tradition. Other than that, distinctions were more blurred, since common literature from across the Western world was used, meaning that often similar discourses would pertain, whether or not practices and policies were different. Quite often we Australian social work academics would refer to British social work literature as if it was our own, on the unspoken assumption that everything was automatically transferable. I think the colonial tradition still lives on in social work.

When I began to settle in the UK, I came to understand important cultural differences between the two countries and how these impinged upon social work. British social work seems to be far more integrated into the social fabric than Australian. I would regularly be surprised to see UK news items reporting on welfare matters, policies affecting social work practice, and criticisms (lots of these) of social workers. The 'person on the street' seemed to have an awareness of social work and furthermore strong opinions about it. In Australia, most people do not even seem to know what social workers are, let alone what they do! This level of interest in social work has both up- and down-sides. The up-side is that social work feels important, backed by a long history. The down-side is that it is regularly open to criticism and public pressure, in a way that I feel is out of proportion to the effective levels of power which social workers actually can exercise.

Given that the UK is a highly bureaucratised country compared to Australia, in Britain changes in policy seem led by crises and reviews, or are, rather, a response to these. Changes in policy do not tend to attract high media attention, and policies feel as if they can be created from a more positive basis due to consideration of a range of factors, rather than in a more reactionary way in response to critical events. There is thus a different attitude towards change. In Britain, change seems difficult, because there is a mountain of past traditions and practices to take into account before moving on. In Australia, change is easier, because apart from anything else, there may well be no policy or protocol in place to address newly discovered issues. Very little has to be trawled through or criticised before new directions can be proposed.

I thus came to understand how in the UK, concerns about the control dimensions of social work could dominate, and how anti-oppressive practice (AOP) approaches to social work might be seen as vital in addressing this. In Australia, by contrast, AOP is much less widespread as an approach. In fact, it is easily arguable that critical approaches to social work are more dominant (e.g. Allan *et al.* 2009). These approaches tend to be developed from a more explicit theoretical base, and hence are potentially more complex in their application and interpretation. These differences tie in with the idea that it feels much harder to exercise personal discretion and creativity in the British social work context, which has more of a modernist feel. In Australia, there appears to be more of a base of optimism in the individual professional's own agency. I have sometimes seen the latter comment directed at my own work (Fook 2002), while questioning whether its approach is relevant for the British context, with its overlay of control.

Realising what seemed to be quite fundamental differences between Australian and British social work led me to question my own capacity to provide professional leadership in the UK context, and I began to wonder whether I could make a better contribution by broadening my reach beyond social work. I was lucky enough to see my current job advertised (again my partner found it and urged me to apply).

My current position involves working in a partnership between three higher education institutions (HEIs). My role is to seed and develop collaborative projects between the three. The projects are loosely in the area of interprofessionalism (health and social care) and can involve teaching, research or enterprise projects. In doing this, I try to develop projects which involve staff from each institution, and are also cross-professional and cross-disciplinary. Typically, I will work with someone from social work or health (physiotherapy, midwifery, nursing or medicine) and also from disciplines such as sociology, criminology, psychology or management. For example, some of the projects I have been involved with include: developing an interprofessional doctorate programme in health and social care (across the three HEIs); seeding research projects in cultural competence, the development of interprofessional education, professionalism, reflective practice teaching across the professions; establishing a Centre for Critical Reflection in the Professions (conducting continuing professional education workshops for practitioners); establishing a network of social science academics in health; and assisting with projects in developing user involvement in research. I have employed some research assistants (using outside earnings) to assist staff from the three HEIs to develop research grant applications.

I do a little consultancy work overseas, and to this end I have been employed in Norway to assist with practice research in a national programme to develop social services through partnerships between practitioners and researchers.

I also have some more conventional academic responsibilities. I supervise Ph.D. students, and I assist in reviews for numerous others. I do this across the HEIs, so it is interesting trying to differentiate between the various requirements and research cultures of each. I also do a small amount of teaching in two of the social work programmes offered between the three HEIs, and I do a little research development for social work staff. Other than this I also continue to do my own academic work, writing and researching mostly on critical reflection. To this end I have obtained (with some co-applicants) a UK Economic and Social Research Council grant to run a series of interdisciplinary seminars on critical reflection. I hope this series will allow us to establish an international interdisciplinary network, which will give further profile to research with critical reflection.

MY TYPICAL WEEK

Here is a typical week, in fact, the week when I am actually writing this chapter:

Monday   a.m.: Emails (involving work on the professional doctorate; and editing work on a number of book proposals).

Lunch with one of the Deans of the Faculties with whom I work – discussion re the professional doctorate and possible future activities.

p.m.: More emails, preparing for a critical reflection workshop to be delivered on Wednesday.

Tuesday   a.m.: Preparation for a critical reflection workshop to be delivered in June; read and approve ethics application from social work student for dissertation research.

p.m.: Travel by train from Salisbury to Plymouth for workshop on Wednesday – work on train reading Ph.D. student material for international teleconference to be held on Friday.

Evening: Dinner with colleague in Plymouth.

Wednesday   All day: Conduct critical reflection workshop for University of Plymouth with forty participants (teaching staff as well as practice assessors and teachers).

Early evening: Train back home. Work on train – read material on cultural competence research and prepare draft programme for focus group to be held the following week; read material in preparation for writing this chapter. Arrive home at 9.30 p.m. Answer emails from the previous day and a half.

Thursday   a.m.: Skype conference re cultural competence focus group; more emails (involving professional doctorate and planning for launch of some research materials, and ESRC seminar series).

Friday	p.m.: Begin writing book chapter.
	a.m.: Skype meeting for supervision session for Ph.D. student.
	Rest of day: Continue writing chapter.
	5–6 p.m.: International teleconference for supervision of Ph.D. student in Canada.

I find my work quite energising, as I tend to work with people from each of the HEIs. They are usually exceptional because they themselves see beyond the bounds of one institution or one discipline/profession. Such work is potentially liberating, as we see each other as individuals first and members of different professions second. The people I work with have usually volunteered to work on projects with me, or have themselves initiated them, so they are highly motivated. On the whole, the projects that have been developed are innovative, so there is much room for creativity. Working across three different sets of academic cultures, with different traditions, has provided stimulating opportunities to learn about the nature of contextuality. The diversity of people I work with continually challenges me, and reminds me that I cannot always take particular professional approaches for granted either. Common meanings and frameworks have to be developed in a collegiate way.

Looking ahead

I am currently really enjoying my professional life and also the opportunities to live and work in different countries. Although this chapter was written while I lived and worked in the UK, in August of 2011 I moved to Canada. I now hold the position of Director of the School of Social Work at Dalhousie University, Nova Scotia. I am currently really enjoying my professional work, and also the opportunities to live and work in different countries. In the latter part of my career, I plan to consolidate my academic contribution in whatever job or country I am in. This is about developing my model of critical reflection as a research method for better understanding experience. My hope is that this method will allow not just social workers but all professionals who work from a social science base, and indeed social scientists themselves, to come to more complex understandings of people's experience through dialoguing about it in a collaborative way. To do this, I believe a systematic academic base needs to be laid out, delving into how we see the nature of experience, our developing approaches to representing it, and the sorts of methodologies that are currently in vogue. This then needs to be fleshed out empirically. This is all work which will take me to the end of my career. I hope, in the end, to be seen as a social worker but also as a social scientist – a social scientist who has come through the path of social work, and has used unique social work expertise to make a contribution to social science.

References

Allan, J., Briskman, L. and Pease, B. (eds) (2009) *Critical Social Work*, Sydney: Allen & Unwin.

Fook, J. (1993) *Radical Social Casework: A Theory of Practice*, Sydney: Allen & Unwin.

Fook, J. (2002) *Social Work: Critical Theory and Practice*, London: Sage.

Fook, J. and Gardner, F. (2007) *Practising Critical Reflection: A Resource Handbook*, Maidenhead: Open University Press.

Hamilton, G. (1951) *The Theory and Practice of Social Casework*, New York: Columbia University Press.

Mills, C.W. (1959) *The Sociological Imagination*, New York: Free Press.

Tolkein, J.R.R. (1954) *The Lord of the Rings*, London: George Allen & Unwin.

12 From London to California

A journey in social work education

Mekada J. Graham

My journey into social work was beset with many twists, turns and challenges. In fact, social work was not my immediate career choice as a young woman. I applied several times for entry into an undergraduate teaching programme. However, before I say more about this, my journey into higher education seems improbable given my background.

I was born in East London and spent my early years living with my young parents in Cable Street in Whitechapel. My parents moved to North London to live first with my grandfather and aunt and her family for several years, and then in a prefabricated council house.[1] The primary school I attended introduced me to the local library which became an important place to me. This is where I discovered my love of books and wonderful stories, often about children living in boarding-schools and having exciting lives. I made weekly visits on my own or with my siblings, reading mostly fiction, and then to the Saturday morning cinema which was almost next door.

I grew up in a working-class area, where lack of finances was a fact of life, although this was something I became more aware of as I grew older. My grandfather supported our family in so many different ways. He had managed to secure a permanent job as a chauffeur in the government in post-war Britain and although he had left school at the age of 14, he had a love of reading, education and politics generally which I think fuelled his ongoing upbeat optimism about the future we would inherit. He had sets of encyclopaedias and subscribed to *Reader's Digest*.[2]

As a child of mixed parentage, I experienced racism throughout my school years. My mother was white English and my father black born in the Caribbean. My father came to London during the mid-1940s. He was a seaman and spent some time in the army, then undertook manual work and experienced some years of unemployment. As a child, people would often ask me which country I was from and seemed perplexed when I replied I was born in London and lived down the road! My experiences at school were very mixed. I made some great friends but, on the other hand, in the rough and tumble of the school playground I was frequently the butt of hurtful and bullying behaviour from my classmates. I sometimes found these experiences very distressing and remember running home one time during the school day and my mother accompanying me back to school the following day. The headmistress came into the classroom and she expressed her concern about the bullying behaviour of some of the pupils. This intervention was short-lived and the taunting 'you look like a golliwog' from some classmates continued.

I now see that the education I received was less than adequate. I failed the '11-plus' exam[3] and was placed in a secondary modern school where I was supposed to be destined for a life working in a factory, manual employment or just filling in time before marriage and children, but my life took a different turn. I worked hard at school and I remember answering all the maths questions correctly in one particular exam and expected to move into the 'A' stream of pupils, but instead, I stayed in the same place and started to lose heart and motivation. I left school before my sixteenth birthday without any qualifications.

I managed to secure a job as an office junior in a publishing house on a magazine about parenting and young children. Acquiring this job was littered with experiences of discrimination. After my interview, the editor said she wanted me to start the following week. She told me to go to the Personnel Department and wrote 'hired' on the form I had given her. When I told Personnel that I had been offered the job and would start the following week, I was told this was obviously a mistake. I was asked to wait, and had to listen while I heard the phone call expressing concerns about employing a young black woman. Some months later, I came across a memo sent by the editor to the Personnel Department supporting her decision to employ a young black woman in the office; this included information about my parents' racial background.

In spite of such a difficult start, this job helped to set me on a path to higher education, as the editor took me under her wing. She saw me copying words from a book I was reading during my lunch break and was impressed by my thirst for learning. She was a middle-class young woman, educated at the University of Cambridge, and she introduced me to the world of theatre, posh restaurants and good conversation. She arranged for my tuition to be paid at evening classes. We worked together for several years and I became her personal assistant. I took up her offer to assist me in my educational goals and

I enrolled at evening classes in O-level English and shorthand. I went on to take A levels in sociology and English literature, and applied to enter a degree course in teaching. Although my applications and interviews were unsuccessful on several occasions, I was determined to pursue a degree in higher education. During this period, I met a fellow student who worked at the university in the Department of Social Work. Thanks to her encouragement, I applied and was accepted for the four-year degree and qualification in Social Sciences and Social Work.

Into higher education

My first year at Middlesex University was full of challenges, excitement and empowering experiences. I read many books and soaked up the lectures and enjoyed the grounding in the social sciences, including philosophy taught during the first two years of the degree course. As I moved through the degree and social work qualification, I developed more confidence and enjoyed university life, particularly discussion and debate. In the late 1970s there were few black students in social work programmes and in my cohort there were six students of colour, and we supported each other through the four years of study. Some students became lifelong friends, and I am grateful for their love and friendship and this experience in my life. At this time, assimilation was the prevailing model for social work and there was little attention paid to racism and discrimination in the social welfare system and the profession of social work.

Many students including myself turned to the USA to find literature which addressed the issues and concerns of black families and communities. One of the important texts which helped filled this void for me and other students was Barbara Solomon's *Black Empowerment: Social Work in Oppressed Communities* published in 1976. Solomon was critical of prevailing models of social work which seemed to focus on individual failings and adaptation, driving structural and social barriers to the periphery. A model of empowerment was proposed, drawing together multiple experiences of oppression to develop sets of strategies orientated towards social transformation and social change. I became more aware of social class and gender in British life at this time, and of the way in which inequalities are so entrenched and shape opportunities in education and subsequent life chances. Social class was the mainstay of British academic study and the focus of discussion and debate among students and professors; issues of 'race' were marginalised and placed within models of 'race relations'.[4] I wanted to know more about the histories and experiences of black people in Britain; however, this area of study was either neglected or ignored. Students were involved in an array of political and union activities and these concerns about social class and gender filtered through to social work, energising its possibilities to transform society.

My first placement in a local school was intriguing and a useful experience where I learned about social work in school settings from an experienced social worker. This was a positive introduction to social work and over the years I kept in touch with my practice teacher and worked with him in offering therapeutic services to young people in the care system. My second placement was more demanding, with limited support from my supervisor in what was a difficult and on occasion hostile environment. I had to deal with unpleasant, overt racism from clients, with little support or concern from practice teachers or colleagues in social services. These experiences shaped my stark realisation that social workers are members of society and bring with them ideas, prejudices and sometimes racism to their practice, despite their overall commitments to social justice and equality.

Social working in inner city London

My first two jobs in social work in the early 1980s were in the London boroughs of Newham and Hackney. I worked in the children and families departments; I enjoyed the work and the team approach to dealing with difficult and complex casework. During this period, I was active in the Association of Black Social Workers and Allied Professions (ABSWAP), a group which emerged to advocate for the social rights of black children and sought to address the over-representation of black children in the public care system. Meetings were held in Brixton in South London, and professionals came together to discuss concerns about social work practice with black communities and the plight of many black children who were drifting through the social welfare system away from their communities devoid of any long-term plans for their future. This England-wide organisation challenged prevailing myths and stereotypes about black families and communities, and went on to play a pivotal role in shifting the ideological base of social work practice. John Small, the first president of ABSWAP, set up New Black Families in Lambeth Social Services, and following these successful initiatives, ABSWAP provided evidence to the House of Commons Select Committee in 1983, which was later incorporated into the Children Act 1989.

There was an upsurge of activity in the early 1980s which also initiated the formation of Black Workers' Groups in many social work departments. These groups formulated strategies to challenge policy and practice and to initiate new directions. Gloria Barnes, a friend and colleague, spearheaded a new foster care team in the London Borough of Hackney dedicated to recruiting black foster carers, bringing a new approach to family finding which valued the experience and competence of black families as child rearers. Looking back, these were challenging and important times in social work which brought about significant changes in practice and approaches in working with minority communities. It is easy to forget that many changes were spearheaded by black professionals and community activists.

As time went on, I became interested in social work education and I moved to the training department in Hackney Social Services. I also taught on the qualifying social work course as a part-time lecturer at various colleges. I designed training programmes for local authorities with a focus on child protection and working with black children and families. I was particularly interested in identity issues and the needs of minority children in the care system. I developed resources for integrating identity issues into life story work and acted as a consultant in advising social workers and working with children in long-term care. After many years working in different agencies (including a short period in a developing country), I began to think about going back into education myself, and enrolled on a part-time Masters in Social Work programme at the University of Hertfordshire. I again loved the experience of discussion, debate with my fellow students and writing papers, and as I completed my degree, I began to teach part time in social policy. I decided to try to write a journal article to disseminate my ideas about social work in black communities, and after many rewrites and discussions with the editor, my article was finally published in 1999 in the *British Journal of Social Work*, in a special issue on minority perspectives. This achievement set me on a journey into academia and I started work on a Ph.D. in Social Welfare Policy at the University of Hertfordshire. I experienced institutional barriers along the way, but I enjoyed the experience of research and intellectual pursuits, and I am grateful for the mentoring and support I received from my two supervisors at this time.

Moving to California

Upon completion of my Ph.D., I started my search for full-time employment, while continuing as an adjunct professor/lecturer. I found my job search disappointing and difficult, as I had few interviews although submitting many applications. Rather than becoming disheartened, I began to think about wider horizons, and in conversations with academics in the USA I was encouraged to apply for positions offered (through the internet) at various universities. I went ahead and submitted applications to schools of Social Work, and after many months in which I had almost forgotten about my applications, I received an email from two universities in Wisconsin and California. The following year, I began my new job in California State University. The first year was a complete culture shock; the culture in the USA is very different, even though the language is the same! I appreciated the experience of social work in another part of the world, and here the history of social work has taken two very divergent pathways of practice, namely clinical social work (counselling and psychotherapy), and community practice (including policy advocacy and macro practice). Professional social work in the USA deals with a wide range of human and social issues in a vast array of contexts. Social workers are found in the criminal justice system (sometimes working in local jails); in universities and community colleges; in companies (usually in the employee assistance programmes); in 'non-profit' (voluntary) organisations as chief executive officers (CEOs); in government working on social policy; in political parties working as policy advocates; in hospitals, clinics and public health in administration and therapy settings; and in community organising. Applicants for health care under the Obama reforms[5] are now being assessed by the social work profession, as new careers are opening up in behavioural health with an emphasis on community-based clinics.

Social welfare shapes the nature of social work in societies, and in the USA welfare is based upon a residual perspective which provides short-term, stop-gap welfare measures on a temporary basis. The philosophy of individualism is paramount and the state intervenes only as a last resort, and because of this, living on social welfare benefits is highly stigmatised. However, every state has its own approach to social welfare, some more progressive than others. The major criterion for benefits is means-testing, and although organisations have different eligibility levels or standards of need, they are usually based on some relationship to the federal poverty level. As the recession over several years has taken grip, there is a high rate of poverty and homelessness in California and this situation is replicated in many other states. One of the responses to the financial crisis and increased poverty is the rise of food banks and shelters. New groups of individuals and families are joining the needy who are dependent upon the food banks for weekly food shopping. Many academics have written about the lack of social welfare benefits and the precarious nature of life for an increasing number of working families.

Moving from London to California, I began to see first hand the global context of social work and its importance in social development and humanising the world. The social work profession in the USA is subject to professional accreditation from the Council of Social Work Education and the practice of social work is regulated across the USA through licensing boards. To practise as an independent licensed social worker in California, you are required to have a graduate degree from an accredited programme in social work. I was welcomed by my colleagues and one colleague in particular came to my office to tell me how pleased he was that I was working in the department; he said he was currently using one of my publications in courses he was teaching. As time moved on, I became more comfortable with my job and my life in California. Being a black woman in the academy is not an unusual event here (unlike in the UK), and I have learned to appreciate my talents in writing and publishing, which have grown from strength to strength. At last, I have found an environment which seems more conducive to research and academic pursuits.

I have taught courses in social policy and research in both undergraduate and graduate programmes in social work. Some of my anxieties about teaching social policy were allayed when I became aware that the social welfare system here is based on the English Poor Laws, a subject I was well versed in from courses I had taught in the UK. I had also taught gender studies in the UK and I was able to integrate this knowledge into social work studies in California. Social work courses here are much broader and include subjects which would have been rejected as 'unnecessary' in the UK. My own education and particularly my Ph.D. had prepared me well for teaching in the USA, adding international experiences which bring together a unique understanding of social work and social welfare.

Since coming to California, I have made contact with other black academics from the UK (or they have contacted me) to share similar stories of our difficult experiences of trying to break through the 'glass ceiling' into academia. It appears that having the necessary qualifications and publications is not enough and discrimination is rife in UK universities. These experiences have been documented in various publications in recent years (see Wright *et al.* 2007). A recent UK survey by the Higher Education Statistics Agency (HESA) showed that out of 14,000 professors in 2010, there were only fifty black professors and only ten of these were black women.[6] It is a slow process of change and there is a new generation of minority lecturers making demands for equality in employment and an opening up of the academy in the UK.

My current job

I have recently taken the position as Director/Chair (Head of Department) of the Department of Social Work at California State University. I must admit that this is a new direction for me, as my main interest has been in research, writing and teaching. I have just finished my first year in this role and I am still 'finding my feet', although there have been enjoyable times during this period. My role as Director can be difficult, juggling with a range of issues and, in particular, dealing with administrative issues in a climate of stringent financial cutbacks. At the same time, there is an increase of students submitting applications to enter the graduate course in social work. Financial problems in the State of California mean that there has been an increase in student tuition fees and a freeze on faculty recruitment, as well as cuts in all areas of university life. Ours is a relatively new graduate social work programme; it was accredited by the Council of Social Work Education only a few years ago. Since then, social work education under the auspices of CSWE has changed its framework, and is now using practice behaviours and competences as measures in organising and shaping the curriculum.[7] This requires major changes to be made to our programme, followed by a re-accreditation by CSWE.

As Director, I have responsibility for the department as a whole, including managing the department's budget; supervision and evaluation of staff; leadership in ongoing curriculum review; scheduling faculty to courses; managing teaching loads across the department; providing reports to the Dean; providing support and mentoring to probationary faculty working for tenure; consulting with faculty; advising and meeting with students and outside agencies; and attending state and national directors' forums. I am also responsible for state grants in child welfare and mental health and managing these resources within the department. My job also involves some travelling across California and beyond.

The university serves a range of minority students, with many coming from working-class backgrounds. I feel a great deal of energy and enthusiasm for learning in this institution and a sense of friendship and collegiality among faculty and staff. I enjoy going to the office and there are different challenges and successes every day; there is certainly no boredom here! I am a member of the Deans' and Directors' Forums from all the universities teaching social work across California, where mentoring and support are available and where new directions and innovations in social work education are created and implemented.

MY TYPICAL WEEK

Monday   a.m.: Office. I greet and talk with faculty when I arrive before I open up the computer to read and catch up on emails and telephone messages. Meeting with Claudia, my administrative assistant, to discuss upcoming meetings within the university and outside agencies. Check in with the Director of Field and Director of Student Services to deal with student issues.

---

p.m.: Work on next semester's schedule and allocation of classes. Deal with student issues and make phone calls. Work on the administration of mental health stipend programme.

Tuesday 9 a.m.: Office greeting faculty. Preparation for meeting with Dean and Associate Dean to discuss financial issues – trying to maintain quality service with less – development of strategies. Deal with student issues, class scheduling and progress in our re-accreditation.

p.m.: Respond to emails and telephone messages. Meeting with adjunct professors. Meeting with Financial Director to discuss grant programmes and plans for the coming year. Meeting with students.

Wednesday 9 a.m.: Office, answering emails and telephone messages. Faculty meeting.

p.m.: Senate meeting.

Thursday a.m.: Preparation for mental health course this evening.

p.m.: Office, responding to emails and telephone calls. Meeting with student. Meeting with faculty. Teaching class – finish at 9.30 p.m.

Friday Research day, working on book or journal article. Work on re-accreditation documents.

Social work futures

There is growing interest in social work as a global profession where interdependence is palpable, as information highways bring the social realities of people's lives into public and private spaces. I believe that social work has an important part to play in bringing the world's communities together to foster harmonious relationships. New partnerships are being forged through social work's international institutions and federations to cultivate cooperation in the global community. I believe there is strong leadership and determination among social work educators to promote social work as a meaningful profession in all regions of the world. In my career, I have seen at first hand the contribution that the profession can make in social development within broad contexts, including changing individual lives on multiple levels. I am optimistic about the social work profession in the future; even in the face of many challenges ahead, there are so many successes which we should celebrate. I am thankful to have had the opportunity to engage in social work education across the world, and I would encourage student social workers wherever they are based to consider the opportunities that working abroad might bring to their ideas and their practice.

Acknowledgement

I dedicate this chapter to my mother, Norah, who passed away many years ago.

Notes

1   Prefabicated houses (often called 'prefabs') were modular homes which were built after the Second World War in the UK as a way of coping with a desperate housing shortage. They were aimed at families, and had two bedrooms and an inside toilet and separate bathroom.

2   This hugely popular, general interest magazine was first published in the USA in 1922; its first international edition was published in the UK in 1938. It provided news and education to many who had no access to more formal education.

3   The 11-plus examination was formerly administered to school students in their final year of primary education across the UK, and governed admission to various types of secondary school.

4   The 1976 Race Relations Act had made it unlawful for an employer to discriminate on racial grounds, where race was said to include colour, nationality and ethnic or national origins. Although the passing of this legislation was broadly welcomed, its focus was on individuals and it did nothing to address institutional racism.

5   The Patient Protection and Affordable Care Act 2010 provided for the phased introduction over four years of a comprehensive system of mandated health insurance.

6   Statistics are available from http://hesa.ac.uk/. See also report in the *Guardian* newspaper, available online at: http://www.guardian.co.uk/education/2011/may/27/only-50-black-british-professors.

7   See http://www.cswe.org/Accreditation/Handbook.aspx.

References

Solomon, B. (1976) *Black Empowerment, Social Work in Oppressed Communities*, New York: Columbia University Press.

Wright, C., Thompson, S. and Channer, Y. (2007) 'Out of Place – Black Women Academics in British Universities', *Women's History Review* 16 (2): 145–162.

13 Becoming a careful gardener

Md. Tuhinul Islam

I never thought in my wildest imagination that I would become a social worker. My father, being a practical man, wanted his son to be an army officer while my mother wanted me to be a doctor. Both jobs provide a person with security and prestige. Yet fate had something else in store. For as long as I can remember I wanted to support others and make their lives better. When I saw a plane flying over our home, I would point at it and tell those around me that one day I would become a pilot and take them on a holiday to distant lands. At other times I wanted to become an engineer and build bridges over the umpteen rivers in Bangladesh, so that no one would ever drown again. If any of my friends became sick I would dream of becoming a doctor to cure them of all ills. I wanted to solve everyone's problems and make the world a better place. Then I was offered a place at Khulna University to do forestry. . . .

Entry ticket

While at university, I volunteered at a local NGO (non-governmental organisation) offering educational classes to slum dwellers and street children. I tried to inspire the children towards learning. I helped them with their school homework, and organised fun activities such as singing and dancing sessions. I got involved with the NGO's safe drinking water and sanitation, health and hygiene and adult literacy programmes for slum dwellers. All this gave me a sense of achievement. My middle-class prejudice was amazed to see that such children were able to learn their lessons with minimum guidance, appreciate the benefits they received and make maximum use of them. I found them active, creative and fun-loving. Moreover, I noted that the members of the whole slum-dwelling community supported each other, even though they had many problems. This experience created in me a desire to help alleviate some of the hardships of such marginalised groups.

Something that had a profound effect on me was a painting drawn by a young girl at an education centre I visited for the first time. The painting was not brightly coloured, yet it stood out from all the paintings done by the children. I asked the girl to explain it to me, and she told me it was a reflection of her life and her family's story of poverty. The picture contained many sections: where her family members slept, what they did when it rained, the relationship between her family and the wider community. There was a section showing how her elder brother had died. It also showed her aspirations for the future: she wanted to be 'rich and a specialist doctor' – to help others by saving lives. Everyone in the centre was silent as she explained her picture, and I could not help but become emotional. As I was about to leave the centre, a young boy of 7 or 8 years came up to me and said, 'Many people come to visit our centre and our homes in the slum. They too cry like you, but their tears do not change our lives. . . . If we were your sons or daughters, nephews or nieces, what would you do for us? You live in the city, earn lots of money and enjoy life. You don't have time for us except to look and take pity. People like you come and go, again and again.'

I was moved by the frankness of this child and heard the seriousness with which he spoke. I felt embarrassed and shocked, and could give no reply. I was both touched and disturbed by the whole experience: the girl's painting and the boy's questioning. I could not sleep over the next few nights. I wanted to do something for these children but did not know what. I shared my thoughts with family and friends but could not reach any decision. Although life carried on, the feelings of that day remained locked in my heart.

After graduating, I worked for several years in the forestry, development and environmental sector, but my enthusiasm for it began to wane and I resigned. During a period of unemployment a friend, who worked in child welfare, informed me of a vacancy at a project working with the children of sex workers. I was intrigued, but told my friend that I had never worked with such a group before and that my educational background was completely different. He encouraged me nonetheless, and set up a meeting with the Executive Director of the organisation. After initial introductions, I talked about my interest and passion to work with marginalised children. The Director explained why he had set up the organisation, the values that drove him to work with disadvantaged peoples, the professional ethics he followed and his dreams for the future of such children. I found him inspiring and felt that he was talking 'my language'. At the end of our discussion, he asked me to visit some of the agency's children's projects before meeting him again. One of the NGO staff, Tareq, acted as my guide, taking me first to a primary school for 'harijan' ('untouchable', low-caste) children, and to the harijan community itself, and then to a pre-school for sex workers' children. I was impressed by the educational materials and the way teachers presented their lessons; these children were being offered a vastly superior educational experience to the average child in Bangladesh. Then we visited a brothel. Tareq asked me if I had ever visited a brothel before. I was shocked that he asked me such a question; after all, I was from a decent and respectable family! Tareq noticed my discriminatory tone and went on to explain how women become 'sex workers'. He talked about their life situation, how children grew up in a brothel environment and the risks that this posed. At the brothel, many women, including young girls, were 'dolled up' with strange face paint. Some were 'pulling' clients; others were bargaining with the clients they had already 'pulled'. I remember entering the brothel full of excitement, even a bit of romance, like a scene out of *Pakeezah*, a Bollywood film about the life of courtesans. But I left feeling really shocked. I had never experienced such a depressing scene in my life. Our final destination was a residential home for the children of sex workers. I saw the contrast between the children living in the brothel and the children staying in the home. The children living in the home were clean, and appeared confident and happy. I was much impressed by the contrast and wanted to be involved in such life-changing activity.

I met the Executive Director the following day and said I wanted to work for him. He offered me a fixed term post as coordinator of the Prevention and Protection of Sexual Abuse for the Children of Sex Workers project. He asked me to think carefully before making any decision, and to talk it over with my family, because he understood the stigma that would ensue from working with such a community.[1] Sure enough, my family did not approve. They did not understand my desire to work with such marginalised children. They felt their social position and prestige would be undermined by my working in such a field. I reflected on what the Executive Director had said, and then, listening to my heart, decided to go for it.

This was how I entered the world of child and social welfare work. At that time, I had little idea of what social work was really about, but it was the beginning of working towards answering the question posed by that young boy from the children's centre many years before, when he had asked me what I could do for children like him to make their lives better.

My journey continues

Although I was initially responsible for one project, I was always encouraged to get involved with other projects, and over time, I began to supervise those too. This was the beginning of my learning curve. I learned from experiences, training courses, colleagues and the Head of Programmes. When my contract ended, the organisation offered me the post of permanent Associate Programme Manager on its Education and Child Development Programme. Under this programme there were several projects for disadvantaged children and their families: for example, protection of children from tobacco hazards; education and health care facilities for working, street and domestic children; development projects for ethnic minorities as well as the residential home for the children of sex workers.

I enjoyed working with the children, seeing the tangible results of my efforts and the impact they had on the lives of the young people and their families. It was rewarding to see the lives of children and their families improve. Moreover, it was not solely a desk-based job; rather every day was different, full of diversity and challenges. I visited children and their families, as well as being directly involved from a strategic viewpoint at the implementation level of the project. This involvement with different projects, training and administrative work increased significantly and I was continuously learning new skills. I was asked to represent the organisation to various groups, including government officials, funding agencies and academics. I quickly realised that my own experience and the small amount of training I had undergone were not enough to explain the many dynamics of child welfare and their families. It was hard to convince others of the good work we were doing, especially when asked about the theoretical aspects of our work. I found talking about such issues 'heavy', as I barely understood what they were asking me. I decided I needed to go back to school, to learn 'academic-speak'.

I applied and was accepted on a Master's of International Child Welfare course at a British university. For my dissertation, with the encouragement of my supervisor, I considered the experiences of children leaving residential care; my dissertation was called 'The Rehabilitation of Sex Workers' Children: Reality and Challenges in Bangladesh'. During my studies, I attended as many seminars, workshops and training events as I could in addition to my regular lessons, in order to explore the dynamics and discourse of child welfare from as many angles as possible, enabling me to think more critically, and to 'hear the story behind the story'. One example: it had been our policy at our NGO to discourage mothers (the sex workers) from visiting their children in the residential home. We would even deny them entry if they arrived, because we felt that allowing them to visit their children would have a negative impact on their child's development and socialisation. We also discouraged the children from visiting their mothers in the brothel, for fear that they might be sexually exploited. Needless to say, many children ran away. Before doing my Master's, I had little understanding of why this might be happening; I had never heard of the term 'attachment'. On completion of my degree, I returned home and changed the policy, allowing mothers to visit their children whenever they wished. The result was unbelievable: children's running-away rate dropped significantly, children seemed happier and staff felt less stressed. I knew the time I had spent on my higher education was not wasted.

Once home, I continued to work for the same NGO, but with renewed energy, vigour and knowledge. We were better able to meet our donors' expectations of ensuring that the 'rights of children' were being met. Gradually, my experience and understanding of child welfare matured, and I began training others in the skills I had learned during my time in the UK. A few years later, I was promoted to Programme Manager, then to Assistant Director heading the Education and Child Development Programme. My responsibilities increased, I was required to spend more time on policy development, monitoring, supervision and the assessment of programmes. Yet my heart was still drawn towards the children's home. Perhaps, deep down, I felt that these children were more vulnerable than others, or that I saw their problems and progress more easily. Anyhow, I thought the children's home was our best project and I wanted to keep it that way.

I had two key concerns at this time. First, why were so many children evicted from the children's home because of their behaviour; and second, what happened to them when they left? (We did not know what became of them, except through piecemeal information from colleagues working in the brothel areas.) It seemed that we had given them a good start, better than other poor children in Bangladesh, but what was this for, if they simply returned to the lives they had come from? I decided I needed to spend some time in the children's home to get a clearer picture about what was going on. I also wanted to find out how other residential institutions were dealing with difficult behaviour. I visited childcare institutions run by both the government and the religious/madrasah communities to see how they did things. The government institutions appeared to have similar regimes and eviction rates to ours. In contrast, in one madrasah I visited, children seemed happy and were being offered an education, although there was little food and the quality of the lodgings was poor. This raised a question for me: What *is* important to a growing child? I decided I needed to learn more.

I applied to do a Ph.D. at another UK university in order to investigate further the experiences of young people leaving residential care in different institutions: the faith-based community, NGOs and the government. My fieldwork involved participant observation and interviews in different residential homes in Bangladesh. My findings suggested that young people from faith-based (madrasah) institutions were better prepared than those from the other institutions when they left care, in spite of poor-quality food, accommodation and health care support as compared to the NGO and government institution children. Madrasah outcomes in terms of children's educational qualifications, employment opportunities and positive mental health were also better. Young people in the madrasah seemed happier, calmer and healthier. They had developed resilience through their religious education and faith practices. This had a positive effect on their physical and mental well-being, affecting their entire lives. The 'soul food' they received from the madrasah was as a protection from life's knocks; something which the other institutions had failed to inculcate. Moreover, the madrasah did not evict its children. Since the madrasah was run on community donations, the whole community (both inside and outside the madrasah) felt part of it. Thus preparing the children for life-skills was not restricted only to staff; rather the whole community got involved. It was assumed that learning should influence every aspect of one's life. Children were also taught responsibility towards others. In his study, Sattar (2004) found that madrasah-educated children were more respectful and responsible towards the needs of their families, neighbourhood and society at large and involvement in criminal activity was less. His findings resonate with my own. One could say that madrasah staff are 'conscious gardeners', in comparison to staff in other institutions, as Cleave *et al.* (1982: 195) state:

> When a seedling is transplanted from one place to another, the transplantation may be a stimulus or a shock. The careful gardener seeks to minimise shock so that the plant is re-established as [easily] as possible.

I found life hard as an international student when I came to study in the UK. I felt lost on the sea of academia! Then a fellow student 'built me a bridge' to a member of staff who helped me to sorts things out. This person helped me to settle and 'fit into' the academic environment around me. Without her initial nurturing I might have drowned.

MY TYPICAL WEEK

At the time of writing this chapter, I am in the last throes of my Ph.D. During my studies, I have had the opportunity to attend seminars and workshops as well as volunteer with children's projects and charities working with vulnerable adults. My experience of the UK social work scene is that it is hugely desk-based. Management hardly has time to spend with service users. There is a climate of fear generated by funding concerns. Getting the paperwork right seems to be the priority. Faith and spirituality appear to play little or no part. The essence of looking out for one another and taking care of each other seems to be missing. We have not yet reached that level of secularity in Bangladesh.

Hopes, fears and challenges in the future

Throughout my Ph.D. years, I have continued to share my research findings and thoughts of service improvements with my Executive Director and staff involved in the children's home. The home has introduced religious education along with other subjects into its curriculum. Teachers and students are encouraged to attend prayers in the local mosque and community people are invited to cultural events organised in the home. This has had a positive impact on the lives of both children and staff. Children are calmer; fellow feelings have increased, attitudes towards life and future have improved. Moreover, confidence levels have increased. All this will have a positive impact on the children's future lives. Having said this, we have had some issues with certain international donor agencies who are against the teaching of religious education, complaining that it is against their ethical policy. We have tried to explain our purpose in teaching the Qu'ran and Hadith to the children, stressing the positive impact this has on their development. Unfortunately, some funding agencies have refused to listen and so we have had to terminate our relationship with them.

This leads to an important general point. My Ph.D. studies have highlighted that some strategies intended to promote child welfare may actually have a negative impact on children's lives, conflicting as they do with their religious values and cultural practices. I believe that Bangladesh should not be made to go down the road of Western secularism; that secularism has damaged family connections in the UK, leaving vulnerable members of society to fend for themselves or to seek state support. This might be acceptable in the UK with its developed welfare system, but Bangladesh cannot support this – we need our families; they are our welfare system, and I believe strongly that faith and spirituality keep families together. I also believe that the madrasahs and NGOs would greatly benefit from each other's skills and talents, building from the United Nations Convention on the Rights of the Child (UNCRC), which states that children should not be treated differently due to their religious beliefs. The UNCRC also states that children should be treated as children, irrespective of their background or birth identity. It is estimated that there are around 1,200 to 1,500 sex worker children in Bangladesh at present (Alam 2005). International NGOs provide a wealth of funds for the safety and protection of such children; however, they often neglect to see the conditions of children living in the madrasahs. A little sector-wide support could produce a proliferation of quality human resources, contributing to the development of the whole country.

I believe, in conclusion, that the developed and developing worlds can learn from each other. The developing world can teach about the benefits of religion and native culture. The developed world can teach about the importance of democracy and 'minority' rights. We need to accept individual countries' practices as different, and not impose our own understandings and beliefs upon others. My own research has shown that faith matters. This is something that the West can take on board and use to improve the outcomes of its own work.

Global social work is changing constantly. There are many more social workers from developing countries coming to practise within the UK and other developed countries, as well as many UK-trained social workers practising abroad. Thus it is essential to learn from the practices and understandings of others to see what works best in particular contexts. As human beings, we are meant to share and learn from each other. The present learns from the past to improve the future. The goal of social work should be about improving the lives of people; that should be the goal of social workers too.

Note

1   This reflects Goffman's early (1963) ideas about 'courtesy stigma'; he argued that we can be stigmatised simply through contact with stigmatised others. See also Cree *et al.* (2004) and Cree and Sidhva (2011) on stigma surrounding HIV.

References

Alam, R. (2005) *Brothel-based Sex Workers in Bangladesh: Living Conditions and Socio-economic Status*. Dhaka: Tdh Italy Foundation.

Cleave, S., Jowett, S. and Bate, M. (1982) *And so to School. A Study of Continuity from Preschool to Infant School*. London: NFER-Nelson.

Cree, V.E. and Sidhva, D. (2011) 'Children and HIV in Scotland. Findings from a cross-sector needs assessment of children and young people infected and affected by HIV in Scotland', *British Journal of Social Work*, Advance Access published 5 April 2011, doi:10.1093/bjsw/bcr036.

Cree, V.E., Kay, H., Tisdall, K. and Wallace, J. (2004) 'Stigma and parental HIV', *Qualitative Social Work* 3(1): 7–25.

Goffman, E. (1963) *Stigma: Notes on the Management of a Spoiled Identity*. EnglewoodCliffs, NJ: Prentice Hall.

Sattar, M.A. (2004) *Madrasah Education in Bangladesh and its Influence in Social Life*. Dhaka: Islamic Foundation.

14 A journey towards emerging coherence

Robyn Kemp

As an adolescent I was known as the rebel of my family, having greater concerns than complying at school and following the trajectory of my siblings into higher education – I was going to change the world. My family laughed quite a lot, and it was probably hard not to, considering my penchant for 'interesting' punk attire and music. I probably scared more people than I engaged with in those days. The punk movement in Leeds (where I lived from 1976 to 1981) was politically motivated and active, and music was a big part of this. It provided a theatre for me to explore, test and play with my contrariness and interest in the place of oppression in British society. The local branch of the Anti-Nazi League (established in 1977) together with Rock Against Racism (begun in 1976) put on regular punk, reggae and ska gigs, and was active in condemning racist attacks by the National Front (an earlier incarnation of the English Defence League and the British National Party). They gave us places and opportunities to stand up and be counted against far Right ideology. I felt that social change was truly possible from the grass roots. I also thought that the education system was elitist and I railed against it by refusing to take my O-level examinations in the way we were supposed to. Instead of answering the exam questions, I wrote long and probably rambling letters to the examiners explaining how they were part of an oppressive system that prevented us from raising the issues that were important to us and from realising our potential – what use was physics to one who had the liberation of the oppressed in her heart? It all seemed so simple then.

I came to the field of social work when I was an unemployed 17-year-old, a year after I had left home to live in what we knew then as 'the People's Republic of South Yorkshire' (aka Sheffield) with my university student boyfriend. In those days, you could claim unemployment benefit ('the dole') and housing benefit at 16, so it was possible for me to spread my wings when I needed to. A young, bright leader of the council, David Blunkett, whose political career eventually took him to the UK Cabinet, saw to it that people in South Yorkshire had such a fabulously cheap bus service that car ownership was really not necessary and we proudly declared that we had the cleanest air of any industrial city in Europe.

My mother had long held anti-nuclear views and took part in the Aldermaston Campaign for Nuclear Disarmament (CND) march in 1958; I became involved in the anti-nuclear movement at Greenham Common Women's Peace Camp nearly thirty years later. I volunteered in the Sheffield Peace Shop, which was partly funded by the council and promoted anti-nuclear and equality ideologies, and where vibrant dialogue about politics and society thrived. I volunteered through the student community action group (although I was not a student) on a play scheme for children and young people from the concrete jungle estates of Sheffield and found myself questioning whether it was OK to enjoy it so much. I particularly enjoyed playing (especially imaginative and creative play) with the children who were described as 'difficult' or 'mardy' (a Yorkshire word, meaning awkward, uncooperative, bad tempered, etc.). To me, it seemed perfectly reasonable that these kids experienced spells of being 'mardy' given the impoverished, tough realities from which they came, and they were engaging and rewarding to me. Over the next few years, I worked with people (young and not so young) who had had events, people and/or circumstances in their lives that engendered difficulty, and my passion for working with people, especially young people, grew.

In the mid-1980s, I moved to London and worked in a Hasidic Jewish school for a few months teaching girls basic, or what we then called 'remedial', maths. Before my first day, I had assumed that I would be presented with neat rows of well-behaved girls, but one of my many practical lessons in anti-discriminatory practice was about to be learned. I was ill prepared for the girls who talked loudly and endlessly, across each other and across some of their teachers, throughout their lessons. When I asked about this phenomenon, my colleagues in the staff room explained that most of the girls came from very large families (fifteen to seventeen children was not unusual) and shouting was an effective way of being heard. I quickly learned that having knowledge of different religions was not enough, and if I was to meaningfully engage with the girls I had to find out about their particular cultural contexts. My Marxist view of religion as the opium of the people began to dissipate a little as I realised that seeing all religions as a way for the powerful to keep the masses in their place failed to acknowledge the many positive aspects in religious belief (for example, having a sense of belonging, connections to spirituality), sometimes interfering with my attempts to engage, and masked my under-developed awareness of myself.

Coming into social work

At 22 years of age I decided I needed a career, and a book by Virginia Axeline (1964) given to me by my mother was pivotal in deciding on a career in social work. Axeline was a play therapist and her book described how she had developed her relationship with 'Dibs', a 5-year-old boy who didn't speak and who was thought to be mentally deficient by his mother and teachers. Through play, Dibs allowed Axeline to enter and understand his world; they discovered that he was in fact very bright, but deeply troubled emotionally. Axeline accepted Dibs exactly as he was and developed a warm relationship with him over time, and in a way that inspired me to consider connecting with children like him. A social worker friend suggested that the best way to get qualified was to work in a children's home for a year and then get a secondment. I applied for a job in Tower Hamlets and, to my surprise, got it, although it was a good five years before I was able to start my Diploma in Social Work.

Tower Hamlets is a vibrant, ethnically diverse and densely populated area of East London where migrants and immigrants have settled for centuries. In the late 1980s, there was a growing Bangladeshi community but very few Bangladeshi children came to the attention of social services, and the social work workforce was mainly white British. The home was a 'purpose-built' (although the idea of 'purpose' then was different from what it is now) 1970s building situated in the heart of the community. There were beds for ten girls upstairs and ten boys downstairs (some shared bedrooms) with three or four staff on duty, some of whom 'lived in'. Looking back, I think it was a strange place, where some excellent and some terrible work was undertaken. We took children with any problem, aged 0 to 18 years, for any length of time, most with very little referral information, and we were directed to take all, even if we had no beds. Occasionally when we were full, children slept on chairs in the office; it was really more like a holding pen than a home. We looked after those who had been abused and/or neglected, those with learning difficulties, those who had been charged with violent and other serious offences, those with undiagnosed but obvious mental health problems, sibling groups, anyone really. I don't remember ever assessing the impact of a newly admitted child on the existing group; they came, and we did our best. But I loved my work so much that I would arrive early for shifts and happily stay late, or do double or even triple or quadruple shifts. It was, for me, and still is, the best job in the world. We had a yellow minibus with 'Tower Hamlets Social Services' emblazoned on it in which we used to take groups of children to Epping Forest. I cringe now when I think of that minibus advertising the fact that children in care were within, and understand why some young people had real difficulties about being seen in it. We would aim to return with the same number of children we had left with, but sometimes finding the last stragglers required a search in the dark with a torch with very little battery left, or a strategic approach to sweeping the area to find the smokers tucked away in the hollow trunk of an ancient oak tree. I learned that getting the kids back into the van often took over an hour, especially as it was a fun game to see the staff stress out about 'losing' a child, so compensated by starting the round-up with plenty of daylight left, and kept a pair of wellington boots for use when the search took us into the mud.

In those days, we were discouraged from forming close or strong relationships with children and encouraged to establish professional boundaries that meant children and young people could not get too close; allowing children or ourselves to overstep those boundaries was seen as tantamount to abuse. Protecting oneself against allegations became first practice. At the time, this seemed reasonable – it was also about protecting children from potential abusers, like those in Staffordshire (Levy and Kahan 1991) and Leicestershire (Kirkwood 1993) (two very high-profile childcare scandals which came to the fore in the early 1990s). But the notion of professional boundaries and distance was difficult to put into practice, because most children longed for a reliable relationship with an adult and it felt as if I had to reject them. For some children, that 'rejection' itself prompted a harming reaction (whether of self or other, indirect or direct). It occurred to me that it might be helpful for children to have some written information about living in a children's home, so I made up a welcome booklet, all handwritten and drawn, and we photocopied this and gave it to each newcomer along with a toothbrush. I went on from this to become a senior residential social worker at another Tower Hamlets home, and later managed a small 'specific needs' day nursery there. The work included supervising contact between young parents with heroin addiction and their toddlers. This led me into a new and challenging aspect of social work, working with parents in a way that was respectful and non-judgemental, no matter what their past and present difficulties: a considerable challenge within a system that is designed to judge parenting ability quickly and is able to provide little in the way of specialist support.

I was granted a secondment on to the Diploma in Social Work through a government-backed residential childcare initiative (RCCI), which aimed to improve the levels of qualification for residential staff especially among managers (Utting 1991). The RCCI group at Havering College of Higher Education in Essex in 1993 was made up of twenty people from various positions in children's homes across East London, Suffolk and Essex; we were a diverse and lively bunch. The learning was fairly dialogic, which we enjoyed, and some was even quite creative, but understanding and developing relationships with clients was not an element of the programme. Undertaking the course was a personal challenge for me as my two children, Laurie and Jess, were aged 3 years and 18 months when I started, and as a lone parent I could only really get down to studying after 9 p.m. when they had gone to bed and the washing up and so on had been done. This was also when my brain capacity was not at its best. I once finished an assignment very late at night, went to save it on my computer (a very basic Amstrad) and when it prompted 'save' I accidentally pressed 'don't save'. I felt as though the sky had fallen down and had to plough on through the night until a reasonable offering could be printed. I have not repeated that fatal click since!

The main emphasis on the course was on learning about social work law and policy. It reflected what was a largely 'deficit' construction of children and childhood, informed by developmental psychology and enshrined within the recently implemented Children Act 1989 (England). We also learned about anti-discriminatory practice. The Children Act 1989 was the first piece of legislation not primarily concerned with equality which placed a duty on local authorities to give 'due consideration' to a child's racial, religious and linguistic background (section 22(5)c). I relished the discussions, though this was not an easy journey. Reading works by Lena Dominelli and Nigel Parton provided me with new understandings; *There Ain't No Black in the Union Jack* (Gilroy 1991) was a revelation despite my previous experiences and proclaimed activism. I realised that no matter how much I believed in equality, I had subconscious and unconscious discriminatory feelings and reactions and behaviours that stemmed from cultural, institutional and individual discrimination and my interpretation, or lack of interpretation, of the related realities. I came to recognise that it was crucial for me to develop an internal dialogue that included being my own most harsh critic in order to understand, take account of and counter my own leanings towards discrimination. This is an ongoing dialogue and will continue ad infinitum.

Another book I drew inspiration from was Bob Holman's (1981) *Kids at the Door*, which took a rather different view of children, families, communities and social change from that of social workers 'doing things to' families. Through this book, I learned that individual, familial, cultural and socio-economic contexts make us who we are, and as a social worker my responsibilities were to start by being alongside those I worked with, so that I understood some fundamentals about who they were before jointly creating solutions to their difficulties. The Diploma in Social Work lasted two years and during this time I learned lots about *what* social workers should do, though little about *how* we should do it; Holman's book provided insight into some of the *how*.

On qualifying, I was appointed as one of three new managers of the reconfigured children's homes in Tower Hamlets. I returned to my first children's home, now transformed into two homes, one short term/emergency, the other long term, each with six beds. Some of my friends were surprised that, having the opportunity to get out of residential childcare and do 'real social work', I chose to stay in what has always been viewed as a 'Cinderella service'. I felt strongly that by staying with residential childcare, and now with some more power, I could agree a clear direction with my team, improve the quality of care, and promote it as a positive option for children and young people, but also for other qualified social workers.

Finding social pedagogy

After fourteen years in Tower Hamlets, I spent a short while in a fostering service, while continuing my work as a trainer before returning to where my heart was: residential care. I worked for National Children's Homes (NCH) as it was then (Action for Children now) and established a new residential 'short break' service for children with disabilities, before becoming the residential service development manager. It was during this period that I started to look into social pedagogy with greater interest and felt I had found what I had been looking for all those years: *What* worked? Wrong question! I had failed to see that the *how* is crucial in residential care, together with, and perhaps starting with, the *why* – our ethical purpose. In Denmark, Germany and many other continental European countries, social work is supported by social pedagogy. There is no single agreed definition of social pedagogy, as different societal and cultural contexts determine how it is interpreted, developed and practised, but I think Hämäläinen's (2003: 71) explanation of 'educational solutions to social problems' gives a useful backdrop to a Danish social worker's explanation to me – social workers work with *what* needs to happen, social pedagogues work with the *how*. Petrie *et al.* (2006: 20) describe social pedagogies in terms of children, 'education in its broadest sense' or 'bringing up' children in a way that addresses the whole child' (ibid.), but social pedagogy is not confined to work with children, it is concerned with everyone and 'the totality of lifelong educational processes that take place in society' (Lorenz 2008: 633). In Denmark, workforce vacancies in children's homes are a rarity as they are seen as the special jobs, requiring high levels of knowledge and skill; social pedagogy provides a coherent framework for direct work that is clear about ethical purpose.

I am now a social care and social pedagogy consultant and trainer working across the UK. I work with statutory and voluntary organisations, one of which is a small community interest company, ThemPra Social Pedagogy, started by two German social pedagogues, Gabriel Eichsteller and Sylvia Holthoff, in 2007. ThemPra takes an organisational and systemic view because social pedagogy is not merely based in the practitioner; the organisational systems and policies need to be in tune with the ethos and philosophy too. Social pedagogy is not a technical or instrumental way of policy and practice; it is founded on understandings of philosophy, psychology, sociology and education, and takes an inherently positive view of the child, seeing children as competent, resourceful and active agents who are the experts in their own lives. Social pedagogy places a strong emphasis on children's and human rights and on ethics, which in turn challenges many of our UK systems and policies, especially in relation to risk (see Christensen and Mikkelsen 2008; Eichsteller and Holthoff 2009; Milligan and Stevens 2006). Social pedagogy resonates with me as it reconnected me with the ethical purpose of my work, and as it challenges the dominance of prescriptive, instrumental, technical/rational models and approaches to supporting people, and the relevance of business models in social care. I recently completed the first UK Master's degree in Social Pedagogy at the Institute of Education, University of London, and was delighted to receive a distinction.

Looking ahead

My everyday challenge is to try to find a way in for social pedagogy in the UK. The move away from direct work with clients (now referred to as 'service users' as the language of consumerism pervades the discipline) to a technical and rational approach to the work demonstrates, in my view, that social work has lost touch with its original ethical purpose. For example, the emphasis on a practitioner's responsibility to complete paperwork has reduced important relational opportunities and encourages an emphasis on a culture of 'first cover your back'. If my first responsibility as a professional is to look after myself, it makes sense that clients feel less inclined to engage, and so the cycle continues. I have already commented on the deficit construction of children and childhood in our society, which sees children as adults-in-waiting, not as important, contributing members of our society who are

MY TYPICAL WEEK

I tend not to have a typical week, but the following is one week from this year.

Monday   Start of three-day social pedagogical leadership course for a site with three secure and one open children's homes in which many staff have undertaken training in social pedagogy. Co-facilitating with a German social pedagogue, Alex, in a small and badly ventilated room within what had previously been a stately home. Wonderful grounds which the secured young people could neither see nor access. Brief but interesting discussion in a break on the classic, *Zen and the Art of Motorcycle Maintenance*. It became clear that this management team had different ideas about the vision for the service.

Tuesday   Introduced the notion of 'ethics as first practice'[1] – a clear challenge for the managers. Discussions on how the control/treat/save agenda for children in care (see Petrie 2010) often serves the financial interests of the local authority over the rights (including the best interests) of the child. Experiential learning activity with the blindfolded managers revealed excellent learning on what leadership requires from all perspectives.

Wednesday   Introduced the concepts of 'pedagogical listening' (Rinaldi 2006) and the 'pedagogy of recognition'; the Scandinavian phrase 'one cannot integrate or include a person who is negatively described' generated much useful yet not unchallenging dialogue among the management group. The course was very well evaluated by the group who had devised personal, team and organisational action plans.

Thursday   Reflections with Alex on our learning from the course, and what we would do differently next time. Conference call with two other organisations to discuss a proposal for introducing social pedagogy to fostering organisations.

Friday   Meeting with a research group from the NHS on a peer mentoring scheme for young women in care, aimed at reducing teenage pregnancies. Sadly, there is no funding to include young men, potentially giving the message that pregnancy is 'women-only' business. Tried to help the team understand the life-worlds of young women who are in and who have left care and what might be more realistic in terms of expectations. Ongoing.

Weekend   Prepare for final three-day block of social pedagogy training for a Scottish local authority which includes staff from social care, education, health and youth services. Must remember to buy eggs for the 'group juggle': an experiential learning activity that gets the group to juggle in sequence a number of objects including a raw egg. Participants rarely believe the egg is raw until one is broken!

competent and extraordinary. The UK's neoliberal culture, policies and systems, I would argue, are problematic for the marginalised in society, and for those who attempt to support them. Children in care are portrayed as needing to be rescued, treated (and if possible cured) or controlled (see Petrie 2010), and we appear to blame their troubling circumstances and behaviours on them and their families. Contributing to this and related discourses is what keeps me going; I do believe in the possibility of change! Social pedagogy may just provide an alternative paradigm within which to emphasise and reclaim the relational aspects of social work and help to reconceptualise social work more generally.

The Chinese character for crisis is made up of the characters for opportunity and danger. Looking ahead can appear rather gloomy in the current climate, especially as budget deficits and cuts hit the most vulnerable of UK society; the social inequality gap widens, but I also see opportunity in this challenge. The free market economy is now firmly embedded within English welfare services, with over 70 per cent of all children's homes and 92 per cent of elders' homes in the private sector (NCA 2009). When profit is the motivator for service provision, the danger is that the most vulnerable users of these services, funded by taxpayers' money, pay the highest price. This is where I see opportunity, for if there was ever a time when social work, locally and globally, needs a strong voice, it is now. A neoliberal focus on individualism and independence ignores that as humans we are *inter*dependent and as such, as Bauman says, we *are* our 'brother's keeper' (2007). I believe that those concerned with the individual's relationship with and within society, as individuals and collectively, have a responsibility to promote more inclusive political ideologies, policies and structures that reflect the 'collective responsibility for individual misfortune' (Bauman 2005: 2).

Social work in the UK has, in many respects, become an administrative task, focused on assessing clients' needs for services and allocating resources; the relational work, once a primary concern, is now, at most, tertiary. There is little in the way of trust, as social workers and managers seek to 'cover their backs' for fear of reprisals. Through my work and during my research with those currently practising social pedagogy in the UK, I have heard it said that 'social pedagogy is what I thought social work was about' countless times. Although inter-country comparisons are inherently problematic due to the different ways in which data are gathered and the different political and cultural systems and contexts, research examining social pedagogy in continental European countries shows that outcomes for their children in care are more positive than those for children in England (see Petrie *et al.* 2006). A family service orientation with relationships at the core appears to improve and enhance welfare and well-being for both individuals and society (Hetherington 2006). Increasing social inequalities and the free market economy have raised the profile of how we care (or not) for the most vulnerable in our society. It is my contention that the combined voices of social work and social pedagogy, informed by international perspectives that go beyond the English-speaking world, could strengthen the role of moral compass in the UK and has the potential to develop a more equal, respectful and valuing society.

Notes

1   This idea was first introduced to me by Peter Moss; see also Tronto (1993) and Steckley and Smith (2011).

References

Axeline, V. (1964/1990) *Dibs: In Search of Self*, London: Penguin.

Bauman, Z. (2005) *Work, Consumerism and the New Poor*, Buckingham: Open University Press.

Bauman, Z. (2007) 'Am I my brother's keeper?', *European Journal of Social Work* 3(1): 5–11.

Christensen, P. and Mikkelsen, M.R. (2008) 'Jumping off and being careful: children's strategies of risk management in everyday life', *Sociology of Health & Illness* 30(1): 112–130.

Eichsteller, E. and Holthoff, S. (2009) *Risk Competence: Towards a Pedagogic Conceptualisation of Risk*, retrieved from http://www.thempra.org.uk/downloads/Eichsteller%20&%20Holthoff%20-%20Risk%20Competence.pdf on 29 November 2011.

Gilroy, P. (1991) *'There Ain't no Black in the Union Jack': The Cultural Politics of Race and Nation*, Chicago, IL: University of Chicago Press.

Hetherington, R. (2006) 'Learning from difference: comparing child welfare systems', in Freymond, N. and Cameron, G. (eds) *Towards Positive Systems of Child and Family Welfare. International Comparisons of Child Protection, Family Service, and Community Caring*, Toronto: University of Toronto Press: 27–50.

Holman, R. (1981) *Kids at the Door: A Preventive Project on a Council Estate*, Oxford: Blackwell.

Hämäläinen, J. (2003) 'The concept of social pedagogy in the field of social work', *Journal of Social Work* 3 April(1): 69–80.

Kirkwood, A. (1993) *The Leicestershire Inquiry 1992*, Leicester: Leicestershire County Council.

Levy, A. and Kahan, B. (1991) *The Pindown Experience and the Protection of Children: The Report of the Staffordshire Child Care Inquiry*, Stafford: Staffordshire County Council.

Lorenz, W. (2008) 'Paradigms and politics: understanding methods paradigms in an historical context: the case of social pedagogy', *British Journal of Social Work* 38: 625–644.

Milligan, I. and Stevens, I. (2006) 'Balancing rights and risk: the impact of health and safety regulations on the lives of children in residential care', *Journal of Social Work* 6(3): 239–254.

National Care Association (NCA) (2009) *Every Budget Matters: A Survey of Current Commissioning Practices and the Health of the Residential Child Care Sector*, London: NCA.

Petrie, P., Boddy, J., Cameron, C., Simon, A. and Wigfall, V. (2006) *Working with Children in Residential Care: European Perspectives*, Buckingham: Open University Press.

Petrie, S. (2010) 'The "commodification" of "children in need" in welfare markets: Implications for managers', *Social Work and Social Sciences Review* 14(1): 9–26.

Pirsig, R.M. (1974) *Zen and the Art of Motorcycle Maintenance: An Inquiry into Values*, London: Vintage.

Rinaldi, C. (2006) *In Dialogue with Reggio Emilia: Listening, Researching and Learning*, London: Routledge.

Steckley, L. and Smith, M. (2011) 'Care ethics in residential child care: a different voice', *Ethics and Social Welfare* 5(2): 181–195.

Tronto, J. (1993) *Moral Boundaries: A Political Argument for an Ethic of Care*, London: Routledge.

Utting, W. (1991) *Children in the Public Care: A Review of Residential Child Care*, London: HMSO.

15 From the classroom to the community

Petra Matuvi

Looking back, I can vividly remember a friend encouraging me to enrol for social work training after we finished our A levels in Zimbabwe in 1991. I had already made up my mind to pursue a career in teaching and, to be honest, at that time I did not really understand what social work entailed. After training as a secondary school teacher, I taught in rural, peri-urban and urban schools. I came across children and young people from a diverse range of backgrounds, from those who were growing up in well-off families to those who were the most socially deprived. This experience made me aware of the impact that socio-economic disadvantage can have on children's well-being. Some of the children and young people were also caring for each other in sibling-led households; they were orphans who had lost both their parents to HIV/AIDS. (Child-headed families were a common feature in Zimbabwe in the early 1990s.)[1] Part of my role as a teacher was to offer pastoral support to the school students, what was then referred to as 'guidance and counselling'. I am sure that these experiences contributed to my desire to be a social worker. I also worked as a volunteer child counsellor at Childline in Harare for two years and undertook training in systemic counselling, an approach which draws on systems theory.[2] Systems theory goes hand in hand with Zimbabwean family structures because it involves examining the system and its subsystems as they are reflected in the extended family structure. Systemic counselling skills enabled me to explore contexts and networks of significant relationships within which the children and young people lived. My role centred on telephone counselling on a wide range of issues affecting the children and young people, providing them with relevant information and, in particular, lending them an ear. The regular callers were mainly children who were living and working on the streets. They had left home for several reasons, including the death of their parent/s, ill treatment or poverty. For some, working on the streets was a way of supplementing the family's meagre income. Issues about teenage pregnancies were common. To a certain extent, I also played the role of agony aunt with the teenagers as some of them raised relationship issues.

Moving from Zimbabwe to Wales in 2006 precipitated a career change for me. Having worked as a secondary school teacher for eleven years in Zimbabwe, I felt I had the transferable skills that could apply to social work, particularly the people skills. But my real motivation to be a social worker derives from my cultural background and upbringing, which have always been centred on concern for others. Altruism is a core aspect of Zimbabwean culture, and individuals are morally obliged to care for others.[3] This communal spirit is rooted in the extended family system. Both of my parents had strong ties with their extended family relatives and would always lend them a hand whenever they could. I grew up living with cousins, aunts and uncles, and even quite distant relations were still treated as part of my close family. From this perspective, my family was 'more socially than biologically constructed' (Seden 2006: 42).

Moving to Wales

My moving to Swansea in 2006 was like beginning life afresh, because I needed to learn from the start how 'the system' worked. As an immigrant who had come to the UK seeking asylum, having the right information about available services would have catalysed my integration into the community. I was on my own, since my two children had stayed behind and only joined me a year later, after I had been granted 'leave to remain'.[4] Wales was my first and final port of call. I found it easy to settle in Wales mainly because of the diverse nature of its population; there were also fellow Zimbabweans to whom I could relate.

My first few months were characterised by idleness, since I was not allowed to engage in any form of employment except voluntary work while my asylum claim was being processed. I was armed with a degree in psychology, a teaching diploma and my teaching and counselling experience, so I took the initiative to find the best pathway that would open opportunities for me. I decided to do some volunteering as a way of gaining insight into the problems experienced by young people on this side of the globe. I joined the telephone counselling service, Childline Swansea, in 2007 and underwent intensive training in basic counselling skills. I was aware from the outset that there was a major difference in terms of the approaches adopted in response to issues of abuse. The Zimbabwean approach had been quite proactive: social workers would go out with police officers to rescue a child or young person from an abusive situation. In contrast, the approach in Swansea was based on providing information, signposting and mainly listening to the child or young person from the other end of the telephone line. There were also differences between the problems experienced by children and young people in the UK and those in Zimbabwe. Bullying was the main problem which children and young people brought to the telephone counselling service in the UK.

One day, after a debriefing session with my supervisor at the end of my shift at Childline Swansea, I saw a leaflet from Swansea University on the notice-board. It contained information about a one-year postgraduate course, MA in Child Welfare and Applied Childhood Studies. I had, by then, been granted leave to remain in the UK, so I applied and was overjoyed when I was granted entry in September 2008. I remember being nervous about going to university on the first day because I did not know if I could cope. It was a totally different system and context to anything I had known before. My greatest challenge was juggling academic study with working part-time and being a mother; my two children were then aged 13 and 11, and I had to work to raise the fees for the course. I held down two part-time jobs and carried on with my volunteering as well. I offered tenancy support to individuals recovering from mental illness; my role was to support them to eventually achieve independent living. This experience allowed me to develop a better understanding of the different forms of mental illness. I also worked as a personal assistant for three women with chronic conditions: cancer, multiple sclerosis (MS) and chronic fatigue syndrome (myalgic encephalomyelitis or ME). These women had previously led independent lives, and this made me realise how such conditions can be life-changing. The women shared their life experiences with me, and through my interaction with them I learned not to take life for granted, and instead to do the best I could to give to society. It was also during this time that I thought about training as a social worker.

The Child Welfare course taught me how childhood is socially constructed across different social, cultural, historical and individual contexts. This was useful in my counselling role at Childline, since many of the children and young people I spoke to over the phone were from different cultural backgrounds. I also learned about children's legislation and policy in the UK, and about the key aspects of welfare services and social work with children and families. My cultural background inevitably influenced the choices I made on the course. For example, for my dissertation, I reviewed literature on children's participation in Family Group Conferences, a way of working with families which evolved from Māori tradition (Lupton 1998). I was especially interested in the way that the ethos of family groups resonated with my cultural background, both in terms of the value it places on kinship and extended family care and in terms of the importance it extends to children maintaining links with their families (Bell and Wilson 2006). But there was one important difference in approaches. Although families are valued highly in Zimbabwe, children are only seen and not heard. Cultural differences like this fascinated me.

Before completing my MA in Child Welfare, I applied to do the MA in Social Work at Cardiff University and was pleased when I was called for interview. Nerves got the better of me, despite being a mature student. The interview panel comprised a university lecturer, a service user and a senior social worker. I had never been interviewed by a service user before and found it daunting. It was only later that I learned that this approach was based on the concept of user involvement/participation which reflects the growing influence of the consumer on the services provided to them; active involvement of service users is part of good social work practice (Dalrymple 2002). The two years of my social work training were both enjoyable and stressful. I found the first semester of my first year particularly difficult because there were so many deadlines to meet for the coursework. I was also still finishing my dissertation for the Child Welfare MA, and when I look back I still cannot figure out how I managed to do it all! The experience has made me realise how much inner strength we have as human beings. In July 2010, I was able to attend the graduation ceremony and I felt proud when my children said, 'Well done, mum'. They have continued to be supportive throughout my social work training and have not complained about being deprived of my attention. Sometimes, however, my son has asked me when I will be finishing the course. This was his subtle way of telling me that he needed not just my attention, but also to have more quality time with me.

Social work training experience

To understand social work in Wales, it is necessary to understand the social and economic characteristics of Wales, the bilingual nature of Welsh society and institutions, national, ethnic and local identities, and Wales-specific law and policy, post-devolution (Scourfield *et al.* 2008). The bilingual nature of Welsh society demands language-sensitive practice. The Welsh Language Act 1993 sets the legislative framework with the aim of promoting the Welsh language. It is good practice that service users and carers are given choice in terms of the language they want to use in the context of social care services. However, this means not only making reference to Welsh language use, but also being aware of other ethnic minority languages and cultures, and acknowledging their significance in relation to service users' and carers' lives. Being bilingual myself (Shona is my first language), I find that there are certain nuances I can express better in my mother tongue than in English. It is also crucial to have a good understanding of legislation and policy specific to Wales, since devolution has changed the aspects of social welfare practice. This is one area I found myself struggling to get my head around – the difference between English and Welsh laws. However, working on an assignment that required demonstration of policy development in Wales helped me to gain a good understanding of this.

Postgraduate social work training in Wales (as in the rest of the UK) includes 200 days of practice learning opportunity. Experiential learning provides a link between theory and practice, and stresses the role of experience in the learning process (Kolb and Kolb 2005). For levels one and two of practice learning, I was placed with a mental health charity. I was based in one of its projects, a residential setting for people recovering from mental illness. The project was staffed by support workers and a project manager who was my on-site supervisor. When I started my first twenty days of observation, I wondered if there was anything about social work practice that I was going to learn from a team of support workers. I was very surprised when I learnt that it was not just support work, but that the work was informed by the 'recovery' model. The model challenges the presumption that service users do not understand their own mental health and involves a shift in emphasis from pathology to 'wellness', as well as building a meaningful and satisfying life by the service users themselves (O'Hagan 2007). This placement helped me to gain more insight into the issues affecting individuals with a mental illness as they related their experiences during my interaction with them. The recovery model adopts a holistic (whole person) approach that underscores addressing all areas of an individual's well-being. My role, as I see it now, was to support them on their journey (through a process of empowerment) so that they might regain control over their own lives. What I really cherished most from this practice learning opportunity was being able to spend more time with the service users, something which has become a rarity in modern social work practice, as I later found in my level three practice learning opportunity.

For practice learning level three, I was placed with a multi-disciplinary community support team which supports people with learning disabilities and other additional needs such as physical disability, health needs, communication difficulties, mental health issues and behavioural problems. I was a little anxious at the beginning about being part of such a large team of health and social work professionals, and I think that, during the first few days, if not weeks, nervousness was written all over my face. What made me more nervous was the fact that my knowledge about learning disability was quite limited, except for some university lectures and presentations from service users. However, the team was very supportive and I was able to settle in and enjoy the rest of my placement. My first few weeks involved shadowing social workers on their visits and this proved to be valuable, since I was able to learn from them the different approaches to assessments. Working in a multi-disciplinary team has also enabled me to gain a greater understanding of the roles of other professionals and their methods of intervention. This is an important aspect of social work education in the UK, and is also demonstrated in the Code of Practice for Social Workers.[5] Research demonstrates that the multi-dimensional nature of the problems experienced by socially excluded groups such as people with learning disabilities requires a multi-disciplinary approach (Lindsay and McQuaid 2008).

As well as learning about multi-disciplinary work, this placement has made me realise how much administration comes with social work. There is a lot of paperwork (and computer work) involved in my team, mainly to do with completing 'unified assessments' (UAs), care plans and case recordings. My role has involved carrying out and updating UAs, carers' assessments and drafting care plans. The exchange model of assessment (see Smale and Tuson 1993)[6] is used to generate information from the service user or carer, and this then feeds into the UA. Although in principle the unified assessment implies a coordinated approach to assessment and care management among different professionals, the administrative part of inputting information on the UA remains the sole responsibility of the social worker. I have wondered whether this, in part, reflects social work's relative lack of power in relation to the health profession (Lymbery 2006). I am aware too that the bureaucratic nature of modern social work can be at odds with the reasons why people entered social work in the first place (Williams 2007). The fact that students in Wales (and across the UK) are expected to complete the European Computer Driving Licence (ECDL) course provides just one indication of the administrative role that awaits us.

An important component of the Masters in Social Work is the research-based dissertation. Before I started writing this chapter, I had just submitted my dissertation. This was a piece of qualitative research on the experiences of asylum-seeking families in Wales. My interest in researching this topic was motivated by my personal experience as a refugee in the UK who had undergone the asylum process. My choice of subject was also related to my belief in social justice as a basis for social work values. I conducted ten interviews with women who had come to Wales seeking asylum. The interviews helped me to reflect more on my personal journey to where I am today, and I found that my experiences resonated with some of those of the women. I believe that understanding asylum seekers' experiences and how they are socially constructed is crucial, because this encourages social workers to be reflective and reflexive in their practice (Masocha and Simpson 2011). One of the major findings of my study was that structural factors in relation to the restrictive nature of asylum legislation shape and determine the lives of this social group. However, the women did not portray themselves as passive subjects but showed their active agency in their day-to-day coping strategies and in managing their situations.

MY TYPICAL WEEK

Monday	Lectures and classes in the daytime; reviewing literature for dissertation in the evening.
Tuesday	Lectures and tutorials in the daytime; helping with homework in the evening and preparation for power-point presentation on methods of intervention in working with adults.
Wednesday	Lectures in the daytime; working on an essay on carers' assessments in the evening.
Thursday	Son off school unwell, so worried throughout today's lectures; advance reading in the evening in preparation for tomorrow's tutorial.
Friday	Tutorial in the morning; pre-placement visit to a learning disability team in the afternoon – exciting.
Weekend	Catching up with reading. Time spent with my children and friends; attending church.

Hopes and fears for the future

I have a mixture of hopes and fears for the future, but the fears seem to dent my hopes. My main hope is to be a good social worker who will promote the basic values of human dignity, social justice, integrity and service to humanity. This hope can only be realised if I get a job, which brings us to my main fear: having to wait a long time before I get employment. The current economic climate of cuts confirms my fear; there are hardly any social work jobs where I live at the moment. Having to relocate is another fear I have; if I can only find work far from home, this may be necessary. I also have a more general anxiety that the heavy emphasis on administrative work in contemporary social work practice may interfere with my wider aim of bringing about positive change in service users' lives. It may also lead to de-skilling, particularly with regard to people skills; spending more and more time on the computer will distance me from the service users with whom I want to spend time. I can only remain hopeful that something will come up: that my training and experience gained over many years can be put to good use.

Notes

1   Feeney's (2001) research demonstrates that adult mortality risks in Zimbabwe more than doubled between 1982 and 1997; HIV played a critical role in this.

2   Systemic counselling is part of family therapy informed by systems theory (see Nichols and Everett 1986). Systemic counselling skills enabled me to explore contexts and networks of significant relationships within which people live.

3   See also Graham (1999, 2007) and her writing on the African-centred worldview.

4   See http://www.ukba.homeoffice.gov.uk/asylum/outcomes/successfulapplications/leavetoremain/.

5   The first-ever Codes of Practice for Social Workers and Employers in the UK were launched in September 2002. See http://www.gscc.org.uk/page/35/Codes+of+practice.html.

6   Smale and Tuson (1993) propose three models of assessment: the questioning model, where the worker is seen as expert and follows a set format of questions; the procedural model, in which the worker gathers information in order to see if agency criteria are met; and the exchange model, in which the service user is seen as expert in his or her own situation and the worker helps to provide resources and seeks to maximise potential.

References

Bell, M. and Wilson, K. (2006) 'Children's views of Family Group Conferences', *British Journal of Social Work*, 36: 671–681.

Dalrymple, J. (2002) 'Family Group Conferences and youth advocacy: the participation of children and young people in family decision making', *European Journal of Social Work*, 5: 287–299.

Feeney, G. (2001) 'The impact of HIV/AIDS on adult mortality in Zimbabwe', *Population and Development Review*, 27(4): 771–780.

Graham, M. (1999) 'The African-centred worldview: developing a paradigm for social work', *British Journal of Social Work*, 29(2): 251–267.

Graham, M. (2007) *Black Issues in Social Work and Social Care*, Bristol: Policy Press.

Kolb, A.Y. and Kolb, D. (2005) 'Learning styles and learning spaces: enhancing experiential learning in higher education', *Academy of Management Learning and Education*, 4(2): 193–212.

Lindsay, C. and McQuaid, R.W. (2008) 'Inter-agency co-operation in activation: comparing experiences in three vanguard "active" welfare states', *Social Policy & Society*, 7: 353–365.

Lupton, C. (1998) 'User empowerment or family self-reliance? The Family Group Conference Model', *British Journal of Social Work*, 28: 107–128.

Lymbery, M. (2006) 'United we stand? Partnership working in health and social care and the role of social work in services for older people', *British Journal of Social Work*, 36: 1119–1134.

Masocha, S. and Simpson, M.K. (2011) 'Xenoracism: towards a critical understanding of the construction of asylum seekers and its implications for social work practice', *Practice: Social Work in Action*, 23: 5–18.

Nichols, W.C. and Everett, C.A. (1986) *Systemic Family Therapy: An Integrative Approach*, New York: Guilford Press.

O'Hagan, K. (ed.) (2007) *Competence in Social Work Practice: A Practical Guide for Students and Professionals*, London: Jessica Kingsley.

Scourfield, J., Holland, S. and Young, C. (2008) 'Social work in Wales since democratic devolution', *Australian Social Work*, 61: 42–56.

Seden, J. (2006) 'Frameworks and theories', in Aldgate, J., Jones, D.P.H., Rose, W. and Jeffery, C. (eds) *The Developing World of the Child*, London: Jessica Kingsley.

Smale, G. and Tuson, G. (1993) *Empowerment Assessment: Care Management and the Skilled Worker*, London: NISW.

Williams, C. (2007) 'Social work in a devolved Wales', in Williams, C. (ed.) *Social Policy for Social Welfare Practice in a Devolved Wales*, Birmingham: Venture Press.

16 From Harare to Edinburgh

The professional adventures of a Shona woman

Carla Nzombe

I can safely say that I have always been interested in social work. Born and raised in Zimbabwe, I was continually aware of the social divide between the 'haves' and 'have nots'. Even though I come from a middle-class family, I was never blind to the plight of the majority of Zimbabweans living in both the rural and urban areas. As if poverty does not present enough challenges, the Zimbabwean population has been plagued by a high incidence of HIV/AIDS since the 1980s. It is currently estimated that one in ten of the population is living with HIV.[1] In the absence of an adequate social welfare and health care system, the effects have been devastating. In response, my parents always demonstrated an incredible level of social consciousness and responsibility in assisting wherever possible. This may go some way towards explaining why four of their children chose to become social workers in different countries and at different stages in our lives.

I received a good secondary education in Catholic boarding-schools. Despite the fact that I was always stronger at Arts subjects, my parents insisted that I applied for a foreign university science degree, believing that it would increase my chances of securing a well-paid job that would contribute to the technological advancement of our 'third world' nation. I secured an education grant from the Zimbabwean government and went to McGill University in Canada to study computer science. I got a real shock when I attended my first computer science class where I did not even know how to switch on a computer, while everyone else had quite advanced skills. I asked to see a student adviser and explained my situation. After finding out that I had a passion for helping disadvantaged people and an interest in sociology, economics and management, she advised me to study Industrial Relations. She explained that in Industrial Relations the issues that inevitably arise from the power imbalance inherent in the employer/worker relationship are tackled from sociological, economic and management perspectives. I was sold. I thoroughly enjoyed my education and student life in Canada and completed my first degree in Industrial Relations and a certificate in Human Resources Management three years later. After almost a year of unsuccessful attempts to secure employment in Canada largely because of immigration regulations, I reluctantly moved back to Zimbabwe in 1997 to get some relevant work experience.

Armed with a foreign degree, I secured employment quite easily, and in the four years that followed I gained extensive experience as a private sector Industrial Relations and Human Resource Management consultant. I specialised in recruitment and selection, training and development, job analysis and evaluation, performance and change management, organisational restructuring and Industrial Relations. This period coincided with the time when Zimbabwe began to experience political turmoil and a most dramatic socio-economic downturn with dire consequences for its inhabitants. Many multinational companies closed shop and relocated to other parts of the world. Workers' bargaining power was diminished and many lost their jobs, resulting in strained industrial relations and the need for objective mediation from Industrial Relations specialists. There was plenty of work for me, but while my career flourished, my conscience suffered. The firm I worked for was contracted to negotiate retrenchment packages on behalf of companies and mediate to ensure fair settlement for all parties. In reality, however, conflict of interest was inherent in our very contractual agreements. I felt we could not really be impartial when we were being paid by the company owners and prioritising their interests. It broke my heart to persuade workers to accept pay-out packages that were much lower than employers could afford. Industrial Relations work drew my attention to how critical gainful employment was to the satisfaction of people's basic needs. I realised that if I wanted to make an even greater difference to people's lives, I had to be in a position to promote the satisfaction of their basic needs and to support them in the pursuit and realisation of their rights in more areas than just the workplace. My interest in human rights was born here. In 2001, I secured a British Council scholarship to study towards a Master's Degree in International Human Rights Law in Essex, England.

After completing my studies, I moved to Geneva, Switzerland, where I worked for the International Labour Organisation (ILO), specialising in labour rights. Although I was now qualified to work in other areas, my previous consultancy experience was considered invaluable to ILO work. I prepared training materials and conducted training to help enterprises implement policies that reflected the core labour rights, with a particular focus on the elimination of forced labour and human trafficking for labour exploitation. After three years in Geneva, I again started to get the distinct feeling that the policy level work I was doing, while hugely satisfying in its own right, was pulling me further and further away from working directly with people. My yearning to focus on issues at the heart of human suffering and hardship returned, and I felt I needed to gain a qualification that would enable me to make a direct and, where possible, tangible difference to people's lives.

By this time, two of my sisters were qualified social workers in Zimbabwe, having received their training in Zimbabwe and South Africa respectively. They made social work sound very 'hands on', life-enhancing and rewarding. I used to listen in awe as they shared the challenges they faced and sometimes confronted head-on, with help from our friends and family. I remember one of my sisters organising a collection among friends and relatives for school fees for some children with whom she was working. She also routinely collected old clothes and books to distribute to her clients in direct response to their perceived and expressed needs. It is clear that social work in this context can be all-encompassing and client–worker boundaries become blurred. It is not uncommon for clients to have social workers' personal phone numbers and to call them during what we in the UK may consider unsociable hours for support. Social workers can drop in on clients outside working hours and are welcomed in people's homes. They are generally trusted and respected, and their direct contribution to the betterment of people's lives is, for the most part, recognised and appreciated. Social work is not thankless work! The fact that probably 90 per cent of social work is direct work with clients within their homes and neighbourhoods is also noteworthy. This enables workers to gain a real sense of their clients' lives and challenges and to provide tailored services in response. Of course, social work practice has evolved in response to the challenges that the context presents, characterised by limited monetary and physical resources. It is consistent with traditional cultural practices and approaches to relationships and is therefore context-sensitive. Naturally this way of doing things also has some shortcomings. It sometimes fosters what may become an unhealthy dependency on the social worker. It may also present health and safety risks to social workers' lives, and the amount of energy and sheer will-power required to sustain that level of support can potentially result in worker 'burnout'.

Against the backdrop of discussions with my sisters about their experience of social work, I decided to study towards a Master's degree in Social Work. While my Human Rights degree would have sufficed to secure work that guaranteed direct client contact, I felt I needed to understand the theoretical perspectives underpinning social work to be an effective practitioner and fully buy into social work as an instrument of social change. I applied and was accepted on to the University of Edinburgh's 'Fast Track' Master of Social Work degree programme,[2] sponsored by the City of Edinburgh Council. I moved to Edinburgh (Scotland) from Switzerland the day before my course began in August 2005.

Carla Nzombe

Social work training

Prior to starting social work training, I believed that social work practice would come naturally to anyone capable of generosity, humility, empathy, reflective listening and respect. I also believed that because I already had two degrees, the academic work would be a breeze. I couldn't have been more wrong. In sharp contrast to my other degrees, the social work degree demanded the full engagement of all my faculties: my mind, my heart, my energy and my social skills. I remember attending a Social Work Theories and Skills' group every Friday morning where we discussed theories central to social work, including attachment, resilience and loss. We had to examine our own personal experiences in relation to these theories and deal with any feelings that arose as a result of these discussions. Looking back, I understand these sessions were intended to force us to become aware of our own unresolved issues and address them before assuming the responsibility of supporting clients through their challenges. The sessions always left me emotionally shattered, as I would relive my childhood traumas and other experiences which I had thought nothing of until then. I was forced to take a cold, hard look at my own upbringing, and to reflect on the strengths and weaknesses of some social and cultural norms and practices widely accepted in Zimbabwean society. Overall, social work training challenged and necessitated the re-evaluation of my belief system and values and, in so doing, indirectly forced me to begin my personal journey of healing.

While grappling with the challenges presented by the course content, I also faced numerous social and practical problems. I had moved to a new country a day before studies commenced and had to familiarise myself with my environment. Despite having lived in the West (Canada, England and Switzerland) for a total of eight years, I had never felt a real need to engage with the communities in which I lived beyond a superficial level. I could get by with basic knowledge about the immediate area where I studied, worked and lived. The very nature of social work forced me to seek to integrate at a level that would enable me to understand the social norms, cultural practices and social class issues. At the same time as I was studying and finding my way around, I had to become attuned to the local (Scottish) accents to enable me to communicate effectively. For the first time in my life, I felt under pressure to learn as much as I could to fit into society and not to stand out as different. This pressure has persisted over the years and, at times, I feel as though my brain is going to explode with all the new information I continuously absorb and process on a daily basis. In rare moments of clarity, I accept that I will never know as much about my context as 'home-grown' social workers. When I feel particularly out of my depth, I ask myself how many local social workers would be in a position to go to my country, learn the local language, the law of the land, the cultural norms and values and to function effectively as social workers. I have convinced myself that the answer is 'not many' and this insight enables me to get on with it, and make use of my wealth of existing knowledge and experience that is transferable.

Two significant incidents occurred during my training while I was on practice placements. The first related to an experience on my fifteen-day observation placement towards the beginning of the course. I had a brief conversation with a link supervisor one morning and she asked me how I was. I have since learned that it is almost customary for people in the UK to respond, 'Fine', when asked such a question.

On this occasion, I responded honestly that I was mentally exhausted. The link supervisor did not make further enquiries about my comment, but was critical of me for 'being tired' in her placement assessment. Her interpretation of my response had been that I was not coping with the workload as well as I could have been. If she had probed, I would have told her that I had been up all night stressing about UK visa issues which would determine whether I could remain in the country to complete my studies. I had given up so much to be here and I needed to pass. I resolved that my standard response to anyone in 'authority' asking how I was from then on would be 'Fine, thanks'.

The second incident related to my first practice placement in a community care team. I was tasked with conducting a needs assessment for an elderly woman. Upon interviewing her, it became apparent that she was, in the main, self-sufficient but required someone to occasionally sweep parts of her well-kept house and also take her curtains down for washing. This situation was significant for two reasons. First, I was surprised at the type of referrals that social work received. I had only ever been exposed to social work in a developing country where poverty was rampant and social work intervention centred on issues relating to very basic needs of food, shelter, clothing, education and health. By contrast, therefore, this specific request seemed 'petty' to me at that point. This incident put Maslow's (1943) classic statement of a hierarchy of needs into context for me, highlighting the fact that developed countries are more likely to be able to afford to satisfy their citizens' basic needs and therefore the nature of social work was likely to be different. Second, owing to resource limitations, the local authority Social Work Department could not afford to pay for someone to provide this service. I was genuinely surprised when my practice teacher told me that I could not put myself forward to do this for her, even in my free time. I began to understand that social work here was different; there were boundaries and health and safety considerations to take into account that could cost me my job if I did not follow them. I had to expend more energy looking for volunteers to perform a task that I could have easily done myself.

Life as a qualified social worker

Since qualifying in 2007, I have been employed as a criminal justice social worker in Scotland. I decided to pursue this line of work for three reasons. First, I was inspired by a criminal justice social worker who had recently come to Scotland from Australia; she spoke about her work with such passion and enthusiasm that I wanted to have that experience as well. Second, relative to other areas of social work, criminal justice seemed to have the most structure, with a clear mandate to carry out work on behalf of the court and clear outcomes if the offenders with whom we are working fail to comply with the court order. Finally, and most importantly, it seemed to be the one area of social work where effectiveness did not depend on the availability of monetary resources. As a social worker, I could be the most important resource in motivating my clients to desist from offending and to lead better lives.

Criminal justice social work responsibilities primarily include: preparing criminal justice social work and related reports for court sentencing purposes; conducting assessments of the services needed to assist offenders to lead law-abiding lives; contributing to multi-agency initiatives in the assessment and management of offender risk; supervising offenders on community orders and working with their families; delivering, monitoring and evaluating planned programmes of work with offenders; participating in supervision sessions and team meetings to review practice and performance; maintaining concise, relevant and up-to-date case records; prioritising administrative work; and undertaking training programmes necessary for personal development and networking with outside agencies and the local community in respect of criminal justice services as required (see McNeill and Whyte 2007).

Many people ask me if working with 'criminals' scares me. I always respond that they are, in a way, the safest group to work with, because we are aware of what they are capable of (which is much more than we know about any people on the streets who may present even greater risks). We can therefore manage the risk they may pose as best we can. Offenders are also aware that we have some understanding of what they are capable of. I am also asked fairly regularly if I experience racism in my work. The only occasion when I experienced racism was at the hands of a client from another ethnic minority group when I was a student. She was horrified to see a black student at her door and she asked me to tell my supervisor to send someone else to help her. I was so shocked and hurt by her behaviour that I felt unable to challenge it. I also wanted to make sure that I was not being paranoid before I approached my practice teacher about the incident. The client later acknowledged how inappropriate her reaction had been, and explained that she had never spoken to a black person and had certainly not expected to see one on her doorstep. In my work now, I find that the colour difference actually serves as a good icebreaker. In some instances I almost feel as though some clients connect with me because they also consider themselves as having a 'minority status' in society. I always chuckle on the rare occasions when I have to interview clients for court reports for race convictions. I watch the blood drain from their faces when they realise that they are about to be interviewed by a black woman. Without fail, the first thing they declare is their impartiality to race and colour, and attempt to evidence this by informing me that they have black/Asian or Polish friends and neighbours!

In our line of work, it is necessary to build rapport with clients, enabling us to gain their trust. The use of clear and simple language in achieving this is key. I have learned from personal experience that clients can pick up from one's communication style and body language whether they are being heard and taken seriously; if they feel this is so, they are likely to be more receptive to any support and guidance offered. To be effective in criminal justice work one must be able to accept that despite what their criminal records may show, clients should be treated with respect and acceptance. This behaviour has to be combined with a genuine belief in the human capacity to change. As more often than not we work with people whose experience, moral and value bases may be different from our own, it is important to be role models in demonstrating that it is possible to manage difference, disagreement and life's hardships within the confines of the law. Being aware of and continually re-evaluating (1) my personal values based on my upbringing and life experiences, and (2) points of convergence and divergence from social work values and from values upheld by my clients, helps me to continue to be sensitive to these differences. (These ideas are discussed further by Trotter (2006) and Cherry (2010).)

MY TYPICAL WEEK

Monday   10 a.m.: Supervision (once every three weeks).

12 noon: Supervision appointment with a 25-year-old man on a nine-month Supervised Release Order, released from prison three months ago after serving a sentence for an 'assault to severe injury and permanent disfigurement'.

1.30 p.m.: Supervision appointment with a 59-year-old woman on a three-year probation order; first-time offender convicted of wilful fire-raising.

2.30 p.m.: Preparation of a court report. SWIFT case notes (computerised record system).

Tuesday   10.45 a.m.: Meeting with a Polish interpreter to prepare for a court report interview for a 55-year-old Polish shoplifter and persistent offender.

11 a.m.: Court Report interview with above client.

1.30 p.m.: Duty, dealing with all incoming telephone enquiries and drop-in visits from unallocated clients and members of the public. In addition, see clients on behalf of social workers on annual leave.

4.30 p.m.: Supervision appointment with 35-year-old on probation – a drug user in recovery – doing well; now heavily involved in advocacy work for drug users. SWIFT case notes.

Wednesday   10 a.m.: Team meeting.

12 noon: Court report writing.

2 p.m.: Risk management case conference – multi-agency meeting to discuss ways of managing the risk posed by a sex offender and allocate specific responsibilities.

4.30 p.m.: SWIFT case notes.

Thursday   8.45 a.m.: Visit prison with interpreter to interview Polish offender held on remand.

10.30 a.m.: Court report interview with black 23-year-old client with a prolific offending history; one of the four index offences was for domestic violence.

2 p.m.: Initial discussion with co-worker about female client on a community pay-back order (new title for probation) who has a high level of need in terms of counselling, alcohol use and social support; appointment with this client.

> 4 p.m.: Monthly home visit with a co-worker to a 44-year-old client on a supervised release order (all home visits are carried out in pairs).
>
> 5.30 p.m.: SWIFT case notes.
>
> Friday
>
> 10 a.m.: Supervision appointment with man in his sixties on life licence for a crime committed when he was 21. He is seen every six months to monitor and review, and is phoned every three months.
>
> 11 a.m.: Preparation of court report.
>
> 2 p.m.: Case management review meeting with my manager and client to review case management plan and highlight any problems.
>
> 3 p.m.: Interview with a 48-year-old man on life licence for a murder committed when he was 15.
>
> 4 p.m.: SWIFT case notes.

Looking ahead

I believe that a nation's commitment to guaranteeing equal rights and access to opportunities to all of its people must be reflected in its policies and visible in its workforce composition. I have always viewed Britain as a great multicultural nation that should be commended for its efforts to facilitate the integration of foreign nationals, while allowing them to preserve cultural values and practices within their communities as long as they are not in direct contravention of British law. The field of social work is an area where great efforts appear to have been made to recruit qualified social workers from overseas. This is in recognition of the value of incorporating knowledge and experience from other contexts that can inform, complement and improve social work theory and practice, keeping it relevant to its entire people.

Unfortunately, I do not believe that the same approach has yet been taken with regard to social work training. Anecdotal evidence suggests that a disproportionate number of international students fail social work programmes in the UK, despite the rigour of selection processes. This issue has been discussed in relation to widening participation initiatives (Dillon 2007) and international Ph.D. students in social work (Cree 2011). It may be that although the benefits of having a diverse workforce are recognised at government level, this ethos has not routinely filtered down to senior practitioners in practice teams, to practice teachers and to university lecturers who work with social work students and qualified workers from abroad. I am not suggesting that foreign social work students and workers should get preferential treatment. I am merely highlighting that it is imperative that cognisance is taken of the unique challenges faced in the adaptation and integration process, some of which I have highlighted in this chapter. Not to do so would be tantamount to missing out on opportunities to improve the responsiveness of our services to what is an increasingly culturally diverse society. I fully appreciate that the UK and other Western countries have enacted and promoted laws, policies and practices that advocate a 'colour-blind' approach to all areas of life (including the recruitment of social work students and workers). However, the challenges faced by non-UK scholars and workers may temporarily disadvantage them in political, social and economic terms. They are therefore not equal players; to treat and assess them the same as everyone else is to neglect their presence as minorities and to ignore the multi-dimensional nature of disadvantage. I therefore believe that it is imperative for developed countries to ensure that, as they open their borders to immigrants, social work values, theory and practice evolve to take account of the collective voice of the inhabitants whose needs social work is tasked with responding to. This shift must take place in education as well as in practice (see also Lyons 2006).

Looking to my own future, I would ideally love to be in a position where I could continue to contribute to social welfare in both Scotland and Zimbabwe, acting as an adviser in some capacity. This would truly demonstrate that social work was an international profession!

Notes

1 See www.avert.org/aids-zimbabwe.htm.

2 The scheme was designed to attract professionals from other fields to consider a mid-career change with an offer of a small salary to retrain on a 'fast-track' basis funded by the Scottish government. There was a contractual obligation to work for a local authority for two years post-qualification.

References

Andrade, M.S. (2006) 'International students in English-speaking universities: Adjustment factors', *Journal of Research in International Education* 5(2): 131–154.

Cherry, S. (2010) *Transforming Behaviour: Pro-social Modelling in Practice*, 2nd edn, London: Willan Publishing.

Cree, V.E. (2011) '"I'd like to call you my mother." Reflections on supervising international PhD students in social work', *Social Work Education*, first published 1 March 2011, doi:10.1080/02615479.2011.562287.

Dillon, J. (2007) 'The conundrum of balancing widening participation with the selection of suitable students for social work education', *Social Work Education* 26(8): 827–841.

Lyons, K. (2006) 'Globalization and social work: International and local implications', *British Journal of Social Work* 36(3): 365–380.

Carla Nzombe

McNeill, F. and Whyte, B. (2007) *Reducing Reoffending. Social Work and Community Justice in Scotland*, London: Willan Publishing.

Maslow, A.H. (1943) 'A theory of human motivation', *Psychological Review* 50(4): 370-96.

Trotter, C. (2006) *Working with Involuntary Clients: A Guide to Practice*, 2nd edn, London: Sage.

17 Trends and challenges of social work practice in Nigeria

Uzoma Odera Okoye

As a young girl growing up, I knew very little about social work. There was a local social welfare office, and I remember hearing people talk about married couples going there because of marital quarrels, or to make arrangements for the care of children after they had split up. I was aware that it was the place where dowries were left after a marriage had broken down[1] and I heard of men leaving money for their wives to pay for their children's maintenance after their marriages had failed. Because of this, social welfare was, for me, a place where married couples with conflict went. It was never portrayed as a place where any conflict might be settled! I always assumed that the staff of the social welfare agency must have had some form of authority from the government to be in a position to handle such family problems. However, today I know better . . .

My becoming a social worker was purely circumstantial and probably down to fate as much as anything else. I went to the University of Nigeria Nsukka, Enugu State, Nigeria in 1985 to study sociology and anthropology. Before I graduated in 1989, I married a lecturer in the Physics Department at the university and that meant I had to remain in Nsukka. My supervisor, mentor and friend, Professor D.S. Obikeze, advised me to do a Master's degree in Social Work (MSW) because, according to him, social work was 'a course for the future'. I wasn't sure what he meant by this, but I was willing to find out for myself. In order to enrol on the MSW, I had to do a ten-hour weekly field practicum for six weeks, working alongside undergraduate social work students. It was during this period that I came to understand what social work was all about and what social workers really do. The practicum was in a social welfare agency and so I learned for the first time what really happened here.

One of the first things that struck me about the undergraduate social work students was that many of them were reluctant to say that they were studying social work. On enquiry, most would say that they were studying sociology. I remember asking a student why she did this, and she explained that if she said 'social work', people would always ask her to explain what she meant by this, whereas people readily knew what sociology was all about. With this idea at the back of my mind, I decided from then on that I must be at the forefront of people making social work better known to others. When I began the course, I had to take some undergraduate courses as prerequisites in order to introduce me to social work. These courses opened my eyes to what social work was really all about, and I began to understand the difference between social work and sociology.

Social work in Nigeria: a historical perspective

Formal social work practice in Nigeria is relatively new in origin, although in pre-colonial and colonial Nigeria, extended families, social clubs, missionaries and voluntary agencies each provided social services of one kind and another. In pre-colonial Nigeria, customary arrangements and institutional provisions for organising, mobilising, administering and coordinating various forms of assistance to the poor and the needy existed among the various ethnic communities centuries before the European contact and inception of colonial administration. The traditional (pre-colonial) Igbo social structure revealed the existence of a wide variety of familial, kinship, filial organisations and networks that provided both material and non-material assistance to the needy and poor members of the society (Obikeze 2001). Furthermore, the kinship system in traditional Nigerian society provided for family welfare, child welfare, health and mental health care for older people, informal education, recreation, social planning and development (Odiah 1991). Although this traditional reliance upon the extended family has been considerably weakened by industrialisation and urbanisation, the reciprocal obligations of family members towards one another still operate quite strongly in many Nigerian communities, especially, Anucha (2008) argues, in comparison to the Western world.

During the colonial period, one of the earliest pieces of social legislation in Nigeria was the Guardianship of Infants Acts of 1886 (Ekpe and Mamah 1997). This was followed by other acts and ordinances that sought to cater for the welfare of the people. These acts by the colonial government focused on labour and child welfare, free services for the disabled and the establishment of boys' clubs to prevent delinquency among rural–urban migrants (Eze *et al.* 2000). Later, other services including social welfare agencies were instituted in order to provide such services as adoption and foster care services and marriage guidance; the establishment of remand homes followed. Anucha (2008) points out that these services set out to replicate the social work systems that existed in Britain and were underpinned by a colonial mentality which believed that anything that came from the West was superior, and therefore worthy of inclusion in Nigeria's social and economic system. However, the provision of services was limited to Lagos, Ibadan, Enugu and Kaduna, the regional capitals. It was only in 1942 that the first Department of Social Welfare was created and its scope expanded to include juvenile court services and the screening of applications of juveniles travelling to Equatorial Guinea (Mere 1988).

At the dawn of independence, social welfare services received more government attention; even the social welfare priorities that the country pursued were tilted towards programmes that benefited a newly emerging urban middle class. But the civil war brought with it many problems that the traditional welfare institutions and existing governmental social services could not handle. To tackle these problems, in 1970 the Federal government invited the United Nations Regional Adviser on Social Welfare Policy and Training to study the social welfare service situation in the country and advise on the respective roles the Federal government, state governments and voluntary organisations should play in social welfare in the country (Obikeze 2001). The Adviser's report marked an important watershed in the history of social work in Nigeria (Mere 1988). In February 1974, the Federal government passed the enabling decree, Decree No. 12, also known as the Social Development Decree, and, through this, launched the country into a new orbit of social work philosophy and practice. This is because it led to the creation, in 1975, of a separate and totally independent Ministry of Social Development, Youth, Sports and Culture, responsible for the coordination of social development activities and the training of social workers in Nigeria (Mere 1988).

Initially, staff members at the ministry were sent overseas to acquire professional social work training and learn how to manage and organise social welfare agencies. The social workers who were sent to the West studied Western social work theories and methods and the administration of Western social welfare systems, although critics felt that Western-based education and training was irrelevant to what Nigerian social work students needed to know in order to practise at home (Odiah 1991). As time went on, various levels of training institutions came into being, with the aim of producing a core of indigenous professional staff. One such institution is the Federal School of Social Work, Emene Enugu, in Enugu State, where it is possible to take a certificate course in social work. Nigerian universities were also not left out in the training of social workers. For instance, the University of Nigeria, Nsukka, with the help of a grant from the Federal government, established a two-year diploma programme in Social Work in their Department of Sociology/Anthropology from the 1976/77 session. The programme has since grown to include a three-year B.Sc. degree programme for those with a two-year diploma;

a four-year B.Sc. degree programme; a postgraduate Diploma in Social Work; an M.Sc. in Social Work; and a Ph.D. in Social Work. Other Nigerian universities also have one form of a social work programme or another. Graduates from all these programmes form the core of social work practitioners, social work administrators and educators as well as policy analysts in the country. There are three main social work associations in Nigeria: the Nigerian Association of Social Workers (NASOWS), the Nigerian Association of Medical Social Workers and the Nigerian Association of Social Work Educators.

Graduating with an M.Sc. in Social Work

Before I graduated from social work, we (the graduate students who were working on our theses) were put in charge of the undergraduate field practicum. Part of our duties involved going to their various agencies to supervise them and interact with the agency supervisors, reading, correcting and grading the students' fieldwork reports and organising field practicum seminars for the undergraduates. In doing this, I came to realise that the agency supervisors did not really know what was expected of them where the students were concerned. This was probably because none of them at that time had a Certificate in Social Work, with the exception of the supervisor in Nsukka Prison (one of the field practicum agencies). This affected the quality of guidance they were giving undergraduate students in the field; in some cases, they were not providing any guidance at all.

On graduation, the department offered me a full-time job as a lecturer, and I readily accepted because I felt (and still feel) that producing quality social workers is what is needed in order to make our social agencies and services professional in nature. I have been doing that now for fifteen years.

Social work practice in Nigeria: an educator's perspective

As a social work educator, one of my duties is to assign students to agencies for their field practicum. There are not many agencies where students can go for field practicum, and we usually assign them to schools, hospitals, markets, communities, prisons, homes for motherless babies and, most importantly, social welfare agencies. In Nigeria, every local government council area has a social welfare agency. This agency is usually in charge of issues relating to children and families; workers deal with cases which include child abuse and neglect, child adoption and fostering, marital problems and teenage pregnancy. However, many of the duties of social welfare agencies today are being undertaken by new government agencies and NGOs. This is because many of the social welfare agencies are not staffed by trained social workers and they are also underfunded. Because of this, cases are not always handled the way they should be. In fact, students on field practicum in social welfare agencies report some highly unethical practices at times. For instance, in one welfare agency, couples were being granted divorces by the Chief Welfare Officer, when such cases should have been referred to the courts! This is not surprising, because many of those who work in these agencies have academic backgrounds in sociology, psychology, counselling and the law, but lack social work skills and knowledge. There are also other challenges facing the social work profession in Nigeria, which I will now discuss.

In most Western countries where social work has been recognised as a profession, there are certain requirements both on the part of the institution and on the part of the individual that must be fulfilled before degrees in social work can be awarded. For instance, in the USA, the Council on Social Work Education (CSWE) sets standards for social work education, and promotes and improves the quality of education in social work programmes. Students who attend schools with accredited programmes are assured that the quality of education meets national standards and generally have an advantage in securing employment following graduation, because social welfare agencies prefer hiring graduates from accredited programmes (Zastrow 2004). However, this is not so in Nigeria, where individual universities set standards as they deem fit. The result is that there is no harmony in the courses taught and credits required in order to qualify on any of the programmes. Many students upon graduation from Bachelor's programmes find it difficult to pursue postgraduate programmes abroad because they are unable to provide evidence of an accredited programme. Many get frustrated and some start fresh social work programmes abroad. This has not helped the growth of the social work profession in Nigeria.

Just as there is no accrediting body, so Nigeria lacks a board to license social work practitioners. Licensing is a process by which a government agency or other jurisdiction acting on a legislative mandate grants permission to individuals to engage in the practice of a particular profession. By ensuring a level of safe practice (through professional education and experience), the licensure process protects the public (Morales and Sheafor 2004). There is no such board in Nigeria; anybody can lay claim to being a social worker and this has hampered, in no small way, the development of the profession in Nigeria. Various attempts have been made to remedy this situation, but because most current social work practitioners in Nigeria have no qualifications, there is a reluctance to act because of fear that people may lose their jobs.

As already stated, there are three professional associations in Nigeria. Membership of the Nigerian Association of Social Workers (NAOSWS) includes 'all those who hold relevant degrees, diploma certificates from recognised universities or other institutions and have successfully completed a training in social work approved by the institution' and 'all those who have had full-time paid employment of not less than five years in any area of social work'. From this, it is clear that membership is very open and, because of this, it has been difficult for the Association to make any impact or even influence policy, since members may have such diverse, and at times competing, interests.

A profession should protect the public from those who abuse their position. In order to carry out such self-policing, every profession must establish standards and develop procedures for evaluating complaints and imposing sanctions if a member engages in incompetent or unethical practice. Licensing boards perform this protective function by withdrawing the legal rights to practise as a social worker if such violations occur. In the USA and the UK, Codes of Ethics spell out in detail the social worker's ethical responsibilities to clients, colleagues, practice settings, other professionals, the profession of social work and the broader society. In Nigeria, such checks for misconduct do not exist. Although there is a paper called the Code of Ethics, it is unfortunately not implemented in any way (Idyorough 2001). Cases abound of social workers who engage in one form of misconduct or another. For instance, we hear of social workers who engage in illegal adoptions or grant divorces (as already referred to). In all these situations, no form of sanction is meted out against the perpetrators and so the profession is greatly undermined.

I have noted that there are very few institutions where social work is taught in Nigeria. These institutions rarely have qualified personnel to teach the courses. For example, in the University of Nigeria, Nsukka (the first university to start a fully fledged social work programme), there is no professor of social work on the staff. In addition, there are not enough teaching staff. This has led to many core courses not being taught, because there is no one to teach them. Similarly, there is a lack of teaching materials, especially textbooks and journals. Many libraries stock sociology textbooks, thinking that this is the same as social work. Not only this, but most of our textbooks come from the USA and UK. Nearly all the case examples in some of these books are not what Nigerians can readily appreciate or understand. One of the challenges facing us as teachers is how to use local examples to portray some of the social work issues. This means that staff and students have to operate under very difficult conditions.

There is, however, another key problem here. The field practicum is the core of social work training, but due to the fact that many of the staff members in agencies are not trained, there is minimal supervision in the agencies where students go for their practice. We have had situations where students have had to teach the staff their job, and this has sometimes led to students being rejected by fieldwork agencies. Some examples may illuminate this further:

- On one occasion, students in a hospital setting were expected to contact friends and relatives of patients who were defaulting in payment of hospital dues. They were merely used as debt collectors.

- On another occasion, students posted to a home for motherless babies were made to wash nappies and mop dirty floors. When they protested, the management told them that it was the only job they could allow the students to do.

- In social welfare agencies, students were expected to collect child support from defaulting fathers and sometimes to participate in cases that involved dissolving marriages.

- There was one school where social work students were put in charge of 'catching' latecomers and flogging them. Some teachers also insisted that the students teach their classes and mark students' exams and tests.

There are many more examples. However, these problems arise because we do not have trained social workers in these agencies, and so the students are not well supervised. One of the ways we have tried to solve this problem is to organise workshops for our 'agency supervisors'. This has had some success, in that some of them now know what is expected of them. There are also other reasons for optimism.

As I have said, new Federal government agencies and NGOs are emerging and are gradually taking over the duties of the social welfare agencies. Many of these agencies are currently run by trained social workers, and it is hoped that the trend will continue (Okoye 2008).

MY TYPICAL WEEK

My typical week goes like this:

Monday	Lectures start at 8 a.m. and end at 2 p.m.
Tuesday	The day starts at 7 a.m. with the inspection of students as they board vehicles to travel to their various agencies for field practice. (The inspection is necessary so as to make sure that they are well dressed.)
	4 p.m.: Fieldwork practicum seminar. Students share experiences about the field practice for the day.
Wednesday	Lectures start at 8 a.m. and end at 2 p.m.
Thursday	As Tuesday, I start at 7 a.m. again.
	4 p.m.: Fieldwork practicum seminar. Students share experiences about the field practice for the day.
Friday	10 a.m. to 12 noon: Meeting with students to discuss their final year projects, theses and dissertations.

Looking ahead

I believe that the future for social work is bright in Nigeria. Currently, many students are applying to study social work in university as their first choice of course. This is indeed remarkable, because in the 1980s and 1990s those who applied tended to be rejects from other social science courses. In addition, many more universities now have a social work programme and attempts are being made to professionalise social work, aided by a Canadian government-sponsored project, 'Social Work in Nigeria Project' (SWIN-P).[2] The aim of the project is to create awareness about the social work profession in Nigeria. Already there has been some collaboration with the University of Benin and this has resulted in the setting up of a new Department of Social Work there, admitting its first set of full-time students in the 2011/12 academic year. In addition, the American International Health Alliance (AIHA) has established a new partnership through its HIV/AIDS Twinning Center Program that will support the US President's Emergency Plan for AIDS Relief (PEPFAR) by training social workers and para-professionals to provide much-needed care and support to Nigerian children orphaned or made vulnerable by HIV/AIDS in the West African nation's Enugu State. Hunter College School of Social Work in New York City is partnering with the Federal School of Social Work, Enugu and the Department of Social Work at the University of Nigeria Nsukka, both in Southeast Nigeria. Together, partners will work to strengthen the capacity of both Nigerian institutions to provide in-service and pre-service training in social work, case management, leadership, and other skills necessary to ensure that comprehensive services are available to children and families affected by HIV/AIDS in Enugu State.[3] The Federal government of Nigeria has also made it compulsory for every Federal government-owned health institution to have a social welfare department that will employ only trained social workers. This has created many job prospects for graduates of social work and is also helping patients in these hospitals to benefit from social work services. But there is a lot still to be done if social work is to occupy its rightful place in a country like Nigeria which is riddled with problems that are begging for professional solutions.

Notes

1   In Southeastern Nigeria, when a man marries, he pays a dowry (in cash) to the bride's family. If the marriage breaks down and the woman wants to remarry, family members are expected to return the dowry to the man's family. Sometimes the man's family refuses to take the money to prevent her from remarrying, and in these situations the money is handed into the social welfare agency. The woman is then free to remarry and the man's family loses all rights to get its money back.

2   This is led by Dr Uzo Anucha from York University, Canada, with a grant from the Canadian International Development Agency (CIDA). See http://www.acdi-cida.gc.ca/home.

3   This partnership is the Twinning Center's first in Nigeria, and was established with support from PEPFAR and CDC/Nigeria in close cooperation with Nigeria's Federal Ministry of Women's Affairs and Social Development.

References

Anucha, U. (2008) 'Exploring a New Direction for Social Work Education and Training in Nigeria', *Social Work Education,* 27(3): 229–242.

Ekpe, C.P. and Mamah, S.C. (1997) *Social Work in Nigeria: A Colonial Heritage.* Enugu: Unit Oriental Press.

Eze, C.A., Ezea, P.C. and Aniche, A. (2000) *Fundamentals of Social Work.* Nsukka: Liberty Printing Press.

Idyorough, A.E. (2001) *Techniques and Principles of Social Casework Practice.* Abuja: IBV and Associates.

Mere, A.A. (1988) *Social Work Education and Professionalism in Nigeria.* FMSDYS, Report of the National Seminar on Social Development Policy in Nigeria, Vol. II.

Morales, A.T. and Sheafor, B.W. (2004) *Social Work: A Profession of Many Places*. Boston, MA: Pearson Education.

Obikeze, D.S. (2001) 'Social Work Services in Nigeria in the Emerging Years'. Lead paper presented at the Workshop on Social Services in Nigeria. Nsukka: University of Nigeria.

Odiah, C.A. (1991) 'Identification of Gaps in Social Work Education on Nigeria'. Unpublished Ph.D. dissertation, Toronto, Canada: University of Toronto.

Okoye, U.O. (2008) 'Awareness of Social Work Profession in Nigeria: A Challenge to Social Workers'. Paper presented at the Second International Social Work Day Celebration on the theme Social Work: Making a World of Difference, Abuja, Nigeria.

Zastrow, C. (2004) *Introduction to Social Work and Social Welfare*. Belmont, CA: Brooks/Cole–Thomson Learning.

18 Can we do it better?

Sally Paul

Emily was extremely angry. She had been told that she had to leave the residential summer camp programme she was attending for girls with insulin-dependent diabetes and return home. This decision had been made as a last resort, owing to fears for her safety. In the past forty-eight hours she had attempted to run away fourteen times, and most recently had been found by the camp lake, looking like she was about to jump in. Emily could not swim. She was 12. I was 24. It was my fifth summer working at the camp. Due to the resignation of the Resident Director, I had suddenly become accountable for over a hundred girls and sixty-five staff, and was thus responsible for ensuring Emily's safety. Other staff members and I had spoken with her numerous times over the past two days. She had repeatedly said she enjoyed camp and had made lots of friends. She could not explain why she was running away and she had no idea where she was running to. She explained that she was currently staying with foster carers because of her diabetes and had been told that if she completed camp successfully, she would be allowed to go to live with her mum. She said that this was what she wanted. She had completed nine days at camp and had only three left when her behaviour changed. We had tried various techniques to help Emily to stay, but to no avail. Her behaviour began to escalate and she was increasingly placing herself at risk. Thus it appeared that the only decision was for her to return to her carers, a decision which they supported. Emily was not happy with this and grew increasingly angry while waiting for them to arrive. Screaming that she wanted to be left alone, she attempted to run out of the campsite into the dark country lanes yet again. Hitting, kicking and spitting at staff members who attempted to bring her back, she was eventually restrained until she calmed down. The foster carers arrived and took a calm and apologetic Emily home. A call to them the following day revealed that Emily had already been transferred to an inpatient psychiatric hospital at her social worker's behest. A brief conversation with the social worker revealed that the decision for her to attend hospital had been part of Emily's care plan should she be unable to sustain the two-week programme; we had not been informed of this 'owing to confidentiality'. All she would tell me was that Emily would be safe and well cared for.

This situation really affected me and I was left with lots of questions: Why had the camp not been informed about Emily's home situation? Was it right that home should be a reward for attending a diabetes camp? What did Emily actually want? Did she understand what was happening? Did her behaviour warrant admission into a psychiatric ward or was she a young girl confused about what was happening in her life? Was restraint the best option? Why did 'confidentiality' prevent joined-up working? Why was camp not valued as a service that could support Emily through some of her difficulties and provide insight into her care plan? Could we/I have supported Emily better? I also remember feeling utterly helpless. I had used all the skills and experience I had gained over my previous years working with children to build a relationship with Emily. Nevertheless, her time at camp had resulted in her liberties being taken away from her, something which, despite not knowing all of the background, I thought was unnecessary. It was after this incident that I made the decision to apply to do social work. I believed that social work training would equip me with the answers that I needed to enable a better outcome for Emily and for all of the other children I would work with in the future.

The yellow brick road to social work

Although this was a turning point that resulted in my applying to university to study social work, there had been different, earlier influences which had also led me to this choice of career. My original degree was in Drama, Film and Television Studies and I had undertaken this degree with ambitions of becoming a director or performer. This was quite an unusual step within my social circle. I grew up in a relatively deprived area of Manchester, England, with little concept of university education. My dad was a bus driver and worked lots of overtime to keep the family afloat. My mum worked as a school dinner lady during the day but primarily looked after my brother and me. My dad was from a family of eleven children and had been encouraged to leave school as soon as possible to start work and contribute to the household. I think, because of this, he felt he had missed out on opportunities, and so was supportive and encouraging of any education I wished to pursue. Although I failed the exam to get into grammar school, my parents enrolled me at a high school outside my neighbourhood. It had a good reputation and they thought it would give me a better education. I later moved to the grammar school to complete my A levels, an experience I did not particularly enjoy. Here, social class became an issue, significantly perpetuated by staff, and people from my part of town were definitely stigmatised; this was perhaps surprising in the late 1990s. It felt wrong and uncomfortable, and this encouraged in me a fighting spirit against what was expected of me. Thus, when all of my fellow students applied to 'red-brick' universities to study subjects such as dentistry, law, English and pharmacology, I decided to head to London and study drama. My mum and dad were incredibly proud that I was going to university and I remember them dropping me off at the halls of residence, making a tearful goodbye, and handing me ten pounds to 'keep me going'. Luckily at this time, students who were from a limited income background were given grants to study, which paid for fees and accommodation costs. I also worked, probably too much, in a variety of jobs to fund my additional living costs. This included working as a sales assistant in a clothes shop, a fairground attendant, an office assistant and as part of a film crew for a local theatre company.

Four months after starting university, I was diagnosed with insulin-dependent diabetes. I remember health care professionals telling me, 'You can't do a lot during this time'; 'You can't eat this, you can't do that and you really can't go back to university until next year'. It was the latter that ignited a new ability to self-advocate. I was 18. I had made new friends. I was having fun. I did not want to miss a year of university. It was difficult at first to sway the doctor's decision but with some pleading, lots of self-study about diabetes, and then phone calls between professionals, it was agreed that I could return on the condition that I saw a specialist once a week at a hospital near the university. I decided at that moment that diabetes would never stop me being me. Against the advice of the doctor (I had only had diabetes for three months at this point) I applied to work in the USA at any summer camp that would have me. By coincidence, or pure luck, I was given a job as a lifeguard at the Barton Centre for Diabetes Education in Massachusetts,[1] much to the relief of my parents. It was through this experience (where some years later I met Emily) that I became increasingly aware of the effects of discrimination, disadvantage and the notion of empowerment. I also realised that I enjoyed working with children very much. This encouraged me to take a Community Drama course in my final year at university, which involved facilitating drama workshops with young carers. During this process, the children decided that they wanted to develop a play they could perform to their families and the community to highlight their experiences of being a young carer. This opportunity brought a whole new dimension to my love of the performing arts and working in groups. Instead of being something of personal enjoyment/ expression that entertained, it became something which enabled children to build self-esteem and confidence, make friends, celebrate their lives, find a voice to share issues that affect them, and challenge preconceived ideas. I strongly began to believe that, for me, this was a much better use of drama and decided to continue developing and using these skills so that other people could benefit from them. So I began to consider what a career in social work might hold. I kept these thoughts with me while I took time out doing a whole range of jobs, from English-language teacher to working at a ski centre, until I met Emily.

Training and working

I completed my Masters of Social Work (MSW) in 2004 at the University of Glasgow. Most of my fellow students had qualifications in sociology, psychology and theology which, given my background in drama, I found somewhat daunting. The course was hard work not only academically but also on a personal level as our values, morals and life experiences were constantly being challenged. It did not necessarily give me all the answers I was looking for on how best to work with children, but it encouraged critical thinking and research-mindedness. I found the placements particularly useful in exploring the links between theory and practice as well as enabling a realistic insight into the social work task.

I graduated at a time when there was a huge recruitment drive for social workers. Newly qualified workers were being offered 'golden hullo's' of significant sums of money if they committed to working in a local authority area team for two years. Most of my fellow students took up this option and, although I had also provisionally accepted such an offer in a Glasgow children and families area team, I decided to take a more unconventional route. Staff at the Barton Center had heard I was graduating and contacted me, informing me that they were recruiting for the Resident Director post and asking me to apply. This post involved managing and developing the year-round residential programme for children with diabetes and their families. Having a Masters qualification meant that I was able to apply for the post and obtain a working visa for the USA. Which post to take was a very difficult decision at the time but I felt that living and working in the USA was a rare opportunity and one that should not be missed. I greatly enjoyed my time at the Barton Center and gathered a great deal of experience working with children and parents/carers, managing staff and budgets, developing residential programmes that sought to enable children with diabetes to live long and healthy lives, and working within US law and social work procedures.

On returning to the UK a year and a half later, the job market had changed considerably and there were very few social work positions available. Many of my friends had completed their obligatory time in statutory services and were desperate to leave. They complained of feeling burnt out and fed up with carrying increasing caseloads with very little support, but were caught in a trap of earning a wage that other positions and/or councils could not offer. While looking for a permanent social work position, I was accepted as a contract researcher at the Scottish Institute for Residential Child Care (now called 'The New Centre').[2] My work involved evaluating a number of residential and secure projects across Scotland, taking into account staff and user perspectives. Several months later, I became a residential social worker at a residential unit that was about to open. The newly hired team was responsible for developing the unit, from furnishings to policies, and I felt that the position linked well with my previous development work at the Barton Center as well as the research work, which I was able to continue with due to the nature of working shifts. Working and researching in the same environment proved to be beneficial and frustrating in equal measure. It enabled me to gather different perspectives and experiences of residential social work and to bring this learning back to my workplace. It was difficult, however, to give this research a voice among the busy-ness of the practice world, focused as it was on specific (and speedy) task management and decision making. This issue continues to be a challenge for social work and one that has shaped my continuing career.

Practice and research: my current job

I moved from residential childcare to take a position as a social worker at Strathcarron Hospice[3] where I am currently employed. This was a newly created position that involved coordinating the hospice's plans for setting up a children's bereavement service, as well as completing other social work tasks within the setting. This was an exciting opportunity, and my senior and I spent a great deal of time liaising with the local community and service providers to design and facilitate the service. Referrals were much greater than anticipated, confirming the level of unmet need, and six months after I started we were already holding bereavement groups for children and their parent/carers two (sometimes three) nights per week. In 2009, the service was awarded the National Health Service 'Celebrating Success Award' for the most innovative service in the Forth Valley. This was a great achievement and one that confirmed the necessity for such support. The children's service runs alongside other social work duties which include: providing one-to-one support for children and adults (pre- and post-bereavement); family work; training and supervising volunteer staff; contributing to the hospice multi-disciplinary team; liaising with/advising external professionals; promotional work; benefit checks; community care assessment and planning; nursing home referrals; providing clinical supervision to other hospice staff; contributing to the development and facilitation of training courses; and participating in hospice research and audit. It was a very busy time.

Three years after I started work at the hospice, the management invited staff to put forward potential research ideas. My experience of working with children who were bereaved meant that I was increasingly aware that the social taboo surrounding death and dying often resulted in children being excluded from important conversations about significant aspects of their lives. I thus put forward an idea that involved researching possible interventions for working proactively with children in the school setting, to demystify and normalise death and dying so that children are better prepared for, and more able to talk about, loss. This idea was accepted, and in October 2010 I was funded to study for a Ph.D. in Social Work at the University of Edinburgh for three years, continuing to work one day a week as a social worker in the hospice (see 'My typical week').

My Ph.D. studies have so far been interesting, enjoyable and challenging. They necessitate a different pace to practice, although equally demanding, and initially it took me some time to adjust to the change in focus. I am currently coming towards the end of my first year which means spending time refining my research design so that I can proceed to fieldwork in year two. The research involves exploring how hospices and schools can work together from a health-promoting palliative care perspective that seeks to address the social taboo of death and dying with children (see Kellehear 1999). The research aims to directly influence practice within my organisation, which has provided a number of challenges in terms of the Ph.D. research process. Significantly, I am also aware that the focus on practice, coupled with my social work values, influences my research design, which will involve participatory methods (see De Koning and Martin 1996; Holland and Blackburn 1998). I do miss the face-to-face work of social work practice, but I am enthused and motivated by having an opportunity to develop research capacity and shape practice within the fields of palliative care social work and health-promoting palliative care. This area, like most social work, is not easy either to work or to research in and can be emotionally challenging. I think what keeps me going is my commitment to the philosophy of palliative care which 'affirms life and regards dying as a normal process' [4] and my belief in promoting children's ability to thrive. This has also been aided by developing a broader understanding of theories connected to adapting to loss and change, such as the dual process model (Stroebe and Schut 1999) and the four tasks of grieving (Worden 2009), and how they normalise what are extremely difficult experiences.

MY TYPICAL WEEK

Please note that all names have been changed to ensure anonymity.

Monday	Hospice day. Catch up with colleagues, check emails and then visit John (aged 10) at school. His father died of cancer last year. This is our fourth session together. Later met Claire (aged 18) who had self-referred for one-to-one support. Both of Claire's parents have died and as a result she has been living in homeless accommodation for over a year with her younger brother, until a property was recently found. Meeting with an occupational therapist in the afternoon re introducing different activities for patients. Followed this with a quick discussion with the volunteer coordinator, before having supervision with my line manager. Ended the day with emails again.
Tuesday	Check emails and then complete reading on Standpoint theory (Collins 1991) for Social Theory class. Attend class. Spend afternoon in library composing argument for the social theory assignment which involves relating Lukes' theory of power (Lukes 2005) to talking (or not) to children about death. Email this to lecturer. Prepare for presentation for tomorrow.
Wednesday	Complete reading for today's class and then review presentation for this afternoon. Also start reading for my literature review around involving children in research. In the afternoon I attend 'Listening to Children' class followed by 'Advanced Issues in Social Work' class, where I present my research design to other social work Ph.D. students for feedback. Check emails and respond where necessary. Prepare presentation for tomorrow.
Thursday	Meet with my research supervisors first thing to discuss progress of Ph.D. Complete reading for afternoon class and review presentation. Attend Research Design class followed by a group tutorial where I present on ethical issues relevant to my research design. Meet briefly with other social work Ph.D. students to share ideas and catch up on progress.

Friday	Check and respond to emails, followed by writing up minutes of yesterday's meeting with my supervisors. Spend the rest of the morning trying to find articles on health-promoting palliative care activities and follow-up links from emailed newsletters. The afternoon is spent reading some of the identified articles and writing up notes. Also begin drafting essay plan for social theory assignment.
Weekend	Try to do some reading or writing on at least one weekend day and spend time with my family and friends.

Looking ahead

I am aware that I am in a fortunate position as a social worker who has been funded by their own organisation to complete a Ph.D. project. I hope that as we look towards the future this is something that will change. Social work research is needed to both inform professional practice and influence policy development (Orme and Powell 2007). I fear, however, that this will be a continuing challenge for the profession. Heavy and demanding workloads mean that research is often not prioritised within practice settings; yet it is essential in ensuring social work's identity as a professional and competent workforce. I am strongly committed to social work research. I hope that by building my own expertise through completing a Ph.D., I can continue to sustain both research and practice in my future career, thus contributing to enhancing and informing practice that will ultimately change lives.

My time as a qualified social worker has been mainly spent working for voluntary agencies. Here I have found that new ideas have been embraced and creative responses to meeting need have been encouraged. My friends and colleagues within the statutory services constantly complain that they are merely 'case managing', with little time for therapeutic intervention. Although there sometimes seems to be a hierarchy in social work where only statutory child protection is considered to be 'real social work', I am aware that voluntary services fulfil an essential role in service professions (Kendall 2003). I hope that this will continue, that funding will be made available for this, and that voluntary services continue to get the recognition they deserve. At the same time, I also hope that statutory services are prioritised in local government budgets so that social workers no longer have to shoulder unrealistically heavy caseloads. Only then will they be able to provide the service which they are trained to do.

Notes

1   For more information, see http://bartoncenter.org/bcsite/front_page.

2   To find out more about the centre's activities, see http://www.thenewcentre.org.uk/.

3   For more information, see http://www.strathcarronhospice.org.

4   See http://www.who.int/cancer/palliative/definition/en/ (last accessed 25 March 2011).

References

Collins, P.H. (1991) *Black Feminist Thought: Knowledge, Consciousness, and the Politics of Empowerment*, New York; London: Routledge.

De Koning, K. and Martin, M. (1996) *Participatory Research in Health: Issues and Experiences*, New York: Zed Books.

Holland, J. and Blackburn, J. (eds) (1998) *Whose Voice? Participatory Research and Policy Change*, Rugby: ITDG Publishing.

Kellehear, A. (1999) 'Health-promoting palliative care: developing a social model for practice', *Mortality* 4(1): 75–82.

Kendall, J. (2003) *The Voluntary Sector: Comparative Perspectives in the UK*, London: Routledge.

Lukes, S. (2005) *Power: A Radical View*, 2nd edn, Basingstoke: Palgrave Macmillan.

Orme, J. and Powell, J. (2007) 'Building research capacity in social work: process and issues', *British Journal of Social Work* 38: 988–1008.

Stroebe, M. and Schut, H. (1999) 'The dual process model of coping with bereavement: rationale and description', *Death Studies* 23(3):197–224.

Worden, J.W. (2009) *Grief Counselling and Grief Therapy: A Handbook*, 4th edn, New York: Springer.

19 Social work with adults

Risks and relationships

Richard Pearl

I was born and brought up in Surrey in Southeast England and was sent to a private school. It was single sex until the sixth form and I was a day pupil in a boarding house, at school from 8.30 a.m. to 8.30 p.m. My parents did this with the best of intentions; they and my grandparents had all been privately educated so it was the normal thing to do in my family, but for some reason I never felt comfortable with this. As a youngster, I felt embarrassed and guilty about my private school status and denied it wherever possible. Overall, it was an existence far removed from the realities of the economic recession and high unemployment which characterised 'Thatcher's Britain' in the 1980s.[1] It also, perhaps surprisingly, gave me my first experience of social care. At 15 years of age, I was asked to leave the school's Combined Cadet Force because I was told I had nothing to offer. I had to choose instead between woodwork, metal work and what was then called 'community work'. Lacking any practical skills, I chose community work, and found myself engaged in hospital visiting every Wednesday afternoon for the next year. My home town, Epsom, was the site of a cluster of psychiatric hospitals built between 1896 and 1924, all of which have since closed (see Thornicroft and Bebbington 1989). I visited different wards in the hospitals and spent time talking with the patients or joining in with planned activities such as tea dances. Over time, I built relationships with some of the patients and it seemed that in a small way we visitors made a difference to their lives.

Looking back, I think it was also important to me that I was accepted and valued, in spite of the private school blazer that I wore and tried to hide!

Going to university

I applied to study psychology at university because I was interested in how people's minds worked and why we behave in certain ways. Swansea University offered me a place and I arrived in September 1990, still quite naive about people and society. I remember being surprised that one of my new friends at university did not come from a two-parent or even a two-car family! I struggled to adjust to my independent life away from home, and in my first year I experienced several periods of very low mood. I went to one counselling session but didn't go back, because I didn't feel immediately better. I tried to speak to other people about what I was going through, but it was only when I spent the summer working that I began to feel more in control of my life again and my mood lifted. A couple of friends had started a project with Student Community Action and I joined them, going out on social activities with young people in hostel accommodation. We had little training or supervision and the outings were sometimes chaotic, but as with my volunteering experience at school, the focus was on relationships and I loved it. I also became interested at this time in the work of Horace Dobbs, a former research scientist who took depressed people to swim with dolphins.[2] I contacted him and arranged to undertake a piece of analysis for him, evaluating feedback questionnaires which explored the therapeutic effects of listening to a recording of dolphins and music on people with depression. I was later able to use this work for my Honours dissertation.

Life at university was still difficult at times. In my third year I began to experience panic attacks after a series of difficult personal situations including a relationship breakdown and being assaulted in a 'road-rage' incident. Occasional cannabis use did not help either, encouraging paranoid thoughts and, I now believe, starting the panic attacks in the first place. These attacks were distressing and debilitating, but they have proved useful in subsequent years when working with people who have also experienced such attacks. Much to the surprise of everyone who knew me, I became a Christian at this time after a friend prayed for me in the midst of a panic attack. My faith has become increasingly important to me, giving me security in the face of an uncertain future and a hope and purpose in everyday life.

When I graduated from university, I got a job working for a housing association in a unit for people with mental health difficulties and, at the same time, undertook Christian counselling training, spending time working with an experienced counsellor. He advised me to apply for the Diploma of Social Work as a good qualification for supporting people. Looking back, I see that it was the career that I had been heading towards since my first experience of social care at school. If I am honest, I also wanted to give something back in return for my privileged upbringing and education.

Social work training

The best part of my social work training (apart from meeting my future wife in the first tutorial!) was the placements. Prior to these, I really knew little about social work and I am aware that my written assignments were wonderfully idealistic and completely unrealistic. Practice placements helped to ground me in the 'real world'; I think it's great to get experience in as many different settings as possible while studying social work.

My first placement was in a community development project in a large village in South Wales. I quickly discovered that this was not for me; I much preferred one-to-one work, whereas my practice teacher thrived on organising a roomful of teenagers. My second placement was in a hospital team. My practice teacher worked me very hard; I was grateful for this when I started my first job. I believe that the practice teacher role is vital to the future development of social work and I am pleased that Welsh Assembly guidance for the continuing professional development (CPD) of social workers includes practice education as both a key area of competence and an expected responsibility for a social work practitioner (Care Council for Wales 2010). Tutors/lecturers are important too. It is interesting to note that my favourite lecturer on the social work course only taught part-time because he was still a practising social worker. Although other lecturers were good, he could bring more practical examples to illustrate theory. He was also still doing the job we were training for, so we tapped him for information on 'what it was really like'.

I have recently undertaken an Introduction to Practice Teaching award which I found extremely interesting. I enjoyed the chance to read up on academic journals and the latest research, although this highlighted the gap between research and practice, at least in my experience. Wherever I have worked, practitioners haven't had the time to read research, except for a quick scan of a magazine with sandwiches at lunchtime. Marsh *et al*.'s (2005) study found that the nearer a person is to practising social work, the less likely they are to be involved in the research production process. Marsh and his colleagues advocate a bridging of the gap between social work practice and academia, suggesting this might be achieved through the role of lecturer-practitioner, as is already present in professions such as nursing, engineering and theology.

My current job

I currently work in a community team for adults over the age of 65. We deal with everything from assessing a person for support to wash and dress or make a meal, to full Protection of Vulnerable Adult (POVA) investigations.[3] As a man, I am often allocated cases of men with 'challenging behaviour', which has been defined as 'culturally abnormal behaviour(s) of such intensity, frequency or duration that the physical safety of the person or others is placed in serious jeopardy, or behaviour which is likely to seriously limit or deny access to the use of ordinary community facilities' (Emerson 1995). Our team is seeing more and more cases of older men who are physically well, but who are unable to manage living independently, often due to long-standing drug and alcohol issues, accompanied by lifestyles that do not fit with current services for older people. This remains a large gap in terms of social care provision. One of the issues I have to face when working with this service user group is the discrimination that older people face, not least from the welfare benefits system; many benefits in the UK stop at 65, or mutate into lesser versions of themselves. But does the government think, for example, that when a person reaches 65 they have less need to access transport?

I am always fascinated by the fact that you never know the situation you're going to meet once you step through a person's front door. Sometimes it can take a couple of visits even to get through the door, if a person has a particular distrust of Social Services; occasionally you never get in at all. I believe that the relationship between service users and social workers is crucial (see Gilburt *et al.* 2008; Huxley *et al.* 2009), and the best results are achieved after time has been spent building such relationships. In our world of local government performance targets, it seems that two of the least measured skills have been those of relationship-building and the manner in which we work with people.

Protection of Vulnerable Adults (now known in Wales as 'Safeguarding Adults') is becoming an ever-greater part of my role. We have strong links with the POVA team in the local police force and are currently part of a pilot project for risk assessments in domestic violence, 'honour-based' crime[4] and stalking cases. In my experience, money is often a factor in the abuse of older people in particular by family members, although prosecutions are rare: it is a big decision for a parent to take their child to court. If an adult has the mental ability to make decisions and chooses to remain in an abusive situation, there is usually nothing we can do to intervene. This can be extremely frustrating as a practitioner. It is also misunderstood, at times, by the public and even occasionally other professionals who cannot understand why we cannot just 'put someone in a home'. Good working relationships with colleagues from other disciplines and organisations are vital. When these work well, there is a sharing of knowledge and values that can benefit the service user. It's always good to do favours for other professionals so that you can 'call in' these favours during a service user's time of crisis. It doesn't always work, though. I shall never forget the doctor who, when I asked him to attend a Mental Health Act assessment for a man who was in grave danger of blowing up himself and his tower block by leaving the gas on and smoking, told me that it was Friday night, it was none of his business and he was going home!

Social work in our sector, as in other service areas, remains balanced between two seemingly opposing sets of priorities. On the one hand, we are rightly encouraged to work according to the principles of personalisation, defined as both 'the way in which services are tailored to the needs and preferences of citizens' and the means by which the state empowers citizens 'to shape their own lives and the services they receive' (Department of Health 2008: 4). At the same time, government budget cuts are not just potentially affecting the delivery of care to many vulnerable people but are impacting upon their lives in other ways, for example with cuts to welfare benefits or loss of funding to voluntary agencies. The effect on staff of being pulled in two directions can be profound. Attempts to work in a more radical, person-centred way can also be stifled by the amount of time it takes to complete the current level of bureaucracy, although thankfully this is being addressed.

I think the social work role has changed considerably over my thirteen years of front-line practice. My first job was at a field office on the edge of a county, some distance from the main council offices. Perhaps because of our location, and perhaps because of the staff who were there at the time, we were able to practise community-based social work. We cleaned houses, tramped across fields to remote dwellings, made arrangements with local pubs to deliver meals, and engaged with a generation for whom the idea of community was rapidly being replaced by neighbours who kept themselves to themselves. I moved five years later to a larger city and to a team based in the main council building. The volume of work was considerable and I remember being clearly told by a manager that I could not do 'social work'; we were only to undertake 'care management', that is, the setting up and monitoring of care packages. Along with similar-minded colleagues, I baulked at the idea of being called a care manager – I am a social worker! There have been some improvements in recent years, however. We have become more flexible in our approach to meeting people's needs, so that 'day care' does not automatically mean a local day centre; similarly, 'respite care' (giving carers a break) does not have to be 'one week, no more, no less'. It is clear that as the population continues to age, and there is an increase in demand for both assessment and provision of services, we cannot go on as we have done in the past. It seems possible that social work may have survived the onslaught of care management and is returning to its more radical roots. I believe that there are many resources in the community that we are not making use of and that we need to reconnect with the neighbourhoods in which we work. Our team is currently piloting a community development project where staff members have been compiling a directory of resources in our area. Informal meeting groups have been set up in local pubs and many links made with community groups. The project has been a great success, both in terms of benefits to individuals and through improved community cohesion.

Keeping going!

I would be lying if I said I had not considered changing career over the years, and at times I have had to look for ways to keep myself motivated. I enjoy reading research, and have spoken with friends and colleagues in the local university and my own authority to explore the possibility of undertaking research of my own. I also recently became practice teacher for a second-year social work student. She was keen and enthusiastic, and wanted to know the reason for each action I undertook with a service user or carer. It was extremely challenging to have someone watching your every move and it made me review my practice and my attitudes. In particular, it made me think more deeply about each case and how I was practising; for example, how much was I really working with the service user to enable them to achieve an outcome *they* wanted and how much of my own feelings were coming into my work? Mentoring a student also made me realise how far I had come in my career in terms of knowledge and experience.

In the past few years, senior management and development officers have been working to transform our Adult Social Services towards a more outcome-focused and less bureaucratic style of working. A project based in the west of Swansea aimed to improve social work practice and outcomes for service users by more actively involving all stakeholders in the process (see Andrews *et al.* 2009). This approach is part of a growing movement back towards inclusive relationship-based social work which has encouraged me to remain a social worker. In addition, our Director of Social Services funded a private company with a proven track record of working with businesses to undertake transformation work within Adult Services. They turned some control of planning and development over to us and talk in the office has turned to about how we can make changes. This has been extremely unsettling as, deep down, none of us really likes change, but it has also been exciting to think we have been given greater control. We have been looking at alternative ways of working, and have actively been listened to by senior management. As a result of this project and the other transformation work being done by the authority, barriers have begun to break down within different parts of social services. This is already making a difference and improving practice and service delivery.

MY TYPICAL WEEK

Monday   a.m.: Deal with emails and phone messages. Go through my caseload and update 'to-do' list.

p.m.: Multi-disciplinary meeting involving the Police, Ambulance, A&E, Mental Health Services and Emergency Social Services Team regarding the behaviour of one gentleman.

Tuesday   a.m.: Training – not a weekly occurrence, but interesting as we are introduced to a pilot project, developed by the Police, which attempts to predict risk in complex situations.

p.m.: Visit a service user who was being victimised by neighbours and whom I have supported to move to a new location. He informs me that a 24-year-old female has been asking him for money and he has given her £400.

Wednesday a.m.: Find out that a service user has not been allocated a care package due to a temporary lack of staff at weekends. Look for alternatives while requesting that a care package be started anyway.

p.m.: Supervision with team leader – helpful. Called to an emergency visit – a gentleman I work with has been drinking a litre of vodka daily and refusing all offers of help. He is now extremely ill. Attend the situation and call 999 for Emergency Services – man is admitted to hospital.

Thursday   a.m.: Urgent referral received to assess an ex-street homeless gentleman living in a temporary hostel. Visit and speak with him for ten minutes before he storms out to return to the streets.

p.m.: Panel meeting confirms service user can have care Monday to Friday; community psychiatric nurse will monitor how she manages over the weekend. Visit a service user who now lives with her daughter and son-in-law. Everything is going well – a positive way to finish the day.

Friday   On emergency duty. Called to assess a service user who has lost the ability to stand during the past twenty-four hours. Doctor says hospital is not appropriate and our rehabilitation beds in a local authority home are full. Prompted by her family, the woman decides on a care home. Explain the complex funding procedure while we look for a suitable vacancy, though I hope she gets better and can return home. Return to the office to complete the case notes and make a note in my diary to follow this up next week.

The future of social work

I am grateful that my local authority is attempting transformation and looking at different ways of working rather than merely raising the eligibility criteria and withdrawing services. I firmly believe that social workers should be involved in both research and development work, as indeed should service users and carers, in fact everyone involved in the grass-roots delivery of care. Expanding the social worker role to include research and development might provide an alternative for experienced social workers who are looking for a change but who don't want to move up into management. I would also love to see greater links between social work practitioners and social work academics in universities, as is starting to happen in our area.

Longer term, I feel that practitioners and academics have lots to share with each other, including research and development and encouraging interest in working with students. There is a growing movement of academics, practitioners and voluntary groups as well as some local authorities who are seeking to return to outcome-focused, relationship-based work where the social worker is valued as a service in themselves. I feel this is not just a good way of working for service users and carers but it also allows for greater expansion of the social work role and hopefully more job satisfaction and retention of staff.

Social work worldwide has to address the needs of a changing and growing population. Fertility rates are dropping and the proportion of people aged 60 or older on the planet is estimated to increase from 11 per cent in 2009 to 22 per cent in 2050.[5] People are also expected to live longer, with a greater number of people with chronic health problems and also people living longer before these problems develop. This produces two groups with different needs: a larger percentage of the population who will need services from health and social care but also a larger percentage of the population who are able to participate actively in society. While this is not just the concern of social work, we are perhaps uniquely placed to champion the values of older individuals and their potential contribution to society. If we can focus on the skills, knowledge and talents of people then we can encourage and enable them to use these assets for the greater good of society and for themselves as senses of value and self-worth increase. A project running in my local authority encourages care homes to speak with residents about how they could contribute to the home. In one home, a resident wanted to make staff members cups of tea. The staff struggled with this as they felt that it was their job to make the tea; however, they were won round when they saw the difference it made to the person concerned. In most countries, older people are becoming more involved in volunteering and childcare for their grandchildren. In both areas, social workers can support and develop older people's ability to manage the situations and reach their potential. For the group of people – mostly older but not always – who have extreme health or personal care needs, even here social work can promote independence and self-worth to some degree.

Social work can also challenge some of the deep-rooted prejudices that still exist in our world. Valuing disabled children, refugees, older people, people of different castes and creeds helps to dispel discrimination. Enabling and encouraging people to live independently, challenging oppression and protecting the vulnerable are fundamental to social work and I believe that these values can be actioned on a much greater scale. In recent times, we have seen popular uprisings against repressive governments in many parts of the world. Global social work has much to offer the current world, but I believe we need a louder voice and presence than we have at the moment. I am not suggesting that social workers should become the new revolutionaries, overthrowing governments. But we can and should be agents of social change, challenging discriminatory attitudes and empowering and protecting the vulnerable in our societies, wherever we are living.

Notes

1   Margaret Thatcher led the neoliberal Conservative Party in government for eleven years, from 1979 to 1990. See Vinen 2009.

2   See http://www.horacedobbs.com/.

3   The Protection of Vulnerable Adults (POVA) scheme was introduced in July 2004 under the Care Standards Act 2000 to protect vulnerable people aged 18 years and over in care settings in England and Wales. See http://www.scie.org.uk/publications/newsletters/scielineMar09.pdf.

4   There is no specific offence of 'honour-based crime'; however, the Crown Prosecution Service and Association of Chief Police Officers in England and Wales use the definition: 'Honour based violence is a crime or incident, which has or may have been committed to protect or defend the honour of the family and/or community.' See http://www.cps.gov.uk/legal/h_to_k/honour_based_violence_and_forced_marriage/#a02.

5   United Nations Yearbook 2009-2010 http://unstats.un.org/unsd/demographic/products/dyb/dyb2009-2010.htm.

Richard Pearl

References

Andrews, N., Driffield, D. and Poole, V. (2009) 'All together now: A collaborative and relationship-centred approach to improving assessment and care management with older people in Swansea'. *Quality in Ageing* 10(2): 12–23.

Care Council for Wales (CCW) (2010) *Continuing Professional Education and Learning: A Framework for Social Workers in Wales.* Cardiff: CCW. http://www.ccwales.org.uk/development-and-innovation/social-work-education/c-p-e-l.

Department of Health (2008) *Transforming Social Care*, Local Authority Circular DH (2008)1. London: Department of Health.

Emerson, E. (1995) *Challenging Behaviour: Analysis and Intervention with People with Learning Difficulties.* Cambridge: Cambridge University Press.

Gilburt, H., Rose, D. and Slade, M. (2008) 'The importance of relationships in mental health care: A qualitative study of service users' experiences of psychiatric hospital admission in the UK'. *BMC Health Services Research*, biomedcentral.com, available at: http://www.biomedcentral.com/1472-6963/8/92/prepubyours.

Huxley, P., Evans, S., Beresford, P., Davidson, B. and King, S. (2009) 'The principles and provisions of relationships: Findings from an evaluation of support, time and recovery workers in mental health services in England'. *Journal of Social Work* 9: 99–117.

Marsh, P., Fisher, M., Mathers, N. and Fish, S. (2005) *Developing the Evidence Base for Social Work and Social Care Practice.* London: Social Care Institute for Excellence. Available at http://home.kanto-gakuin.ac.jp/~akiyak2/deveEBSW.pdf.

Thornicroft, G. and Bebbington, P. (1989) 'Deinstitutionalisation – from hospital closure to service development'. *British Journal of Psychiatry* 155: 739–753.

Vinen, R. (2009) *Thatcher's Britain: The Politics and Social Upheaval of the Thatcher Era*, London: Simon & Schuster.

20 Steel tempered by fire

June Sadd

Social work with a difference! I am not a qualified, registered social worker, so should I be writing a chapter in this book? Oh, the identity question again. Identity is hugely important to me, as it must be to all of us. I believe that what I do is social work. It is rooted in community development and relationship-based practice and is underpinned by personal and social work values. How much more 'social work' can you get than that? Sadly, I believe that there isn't always the opportunity for 'social work' in mainstream social work services today.

My journey into social work and my identity journey are completely connected. I am going to tell the story of my journey in reverse, because this is the way that makes sense to me and I hope to you too. I don't want to start from a victim position. No, better for me to start from one of empowerment. It has been hard fought for.

Regaining my identity: 'for now'

Much of my current work is focused on social work education in England, nationally, regionally and locally. I advise on strategy and policy at pre-qualifying, qualifying and post-qualifying levels and I am involved in the design, delivery and evaluation of several social work programmes. I also work as a 'Visitor', the formal term given to service users and carers who inspect, approve and re-approve social work programmes. So how did I get to do all this? Through the service user movement, that's how. I self-define as a survivor of the psychiatric system, an extremely crucial identity to me. I have established my credentials as a survivor consultant and I bring added value to the role, using wider experience and expertise. What I do now has its foundations in the collective nature of the service user movement, as I will go on to describe.

National activities

I have worked using a community development approach to support collective advocacy over the past seventeen years, and I now bring this experience to the strategic role I play in social work education at the national level.

I was a member of the Education Working Group of the Social Work Reform Board,[1] a grouping set up to implement recommendations made by the Social Work Task Force to improve the quality of social work in England. I have been part of three subgroups, developing the Professional Capabilities Framework, the Social Work Degree Curriculum and Practice Learning. I am currently a member of the College of Social Work's Education Advisory Implementation Group which is working towards the same aims. I have also been involved in work on the future direction of service user and carer involvement in social work education, supported by the Social Care Institute for Excellence (SCIE)[2] and the Social Work Reform Board's Education Working Group. Following consultation with service users and carers, I have produced a report entitled *We Are More than Our Story* (Sadd 2011) which will contribute to the guidance on best practice to be held by the College of Social Work.[3] This is especially important because there is widespread concern that service user and carer involvement in education may be lost if it ceases to be a mandatory requirement in the regulation process. The possible loss of the Department of Health funding which has supported service user and carer involvement in social work education in recent years will also have a detrimental impact on participation in the future.

I have already said that I also work as a Visitor. In 2008 the General Social Care Council (GSCC) invited service users and carers to train as Visitors to accompany their Inspectors in their work. This was in recognition of the value of the user and carer perspectives, experience and expertise in inspections. I am presently involved in the inspection of the post-qualifying training for Approved Mental Health Professionals (AMHPs) in England.

I am also involved in research. I am working with a research team of service users and academics to review the impact of the Independent Mental Health Advocacy Service[4] in England. This is a nationally commissioned project combining quantitative and qualitative research methods; what I bring, as always, is my long-standing commitment to an emancipatory and participatory approach. Shaping Our Lives (SOL)[5] figures heavily in my work schedule; at the time of writing, I was a non-executive director of this national organisation which is user-controlled, as distinct from user-led. Much of SOL's work gives government agencies the opportunities to listen to the voice of service users. For example, in working with the Office for Disability Issues, I supported service users to review two strategic documents: the United Nations Convention on the Rights of People with Disabilities, and the Independent Living Strategy. I lead on SOL's work with the Department of Health's Strategic Partners Programme, a conduit for the voice of third sector and user-led organisations directly into government.

However, SOL does not compromise its independence in its work with the Department of Health. There is much to campaign about in the present climate of cuts, oppressive practice and discrimination experienced by disabled people and service users. There is an increasing need to ally ourselves with campaigning organisations which promote social justice and rights. This structural oppression can only be effectively challenged through the power of the collective, bringing together allies with different backgrounds and perspectives but with a common agenda to fight social injustice. I am a member of the Social Work Action Network,[6] an international collective of service users, practitioners, academics and students which seeks to do just that. We must never lose sight of the fact that social work is a political activity.

Regional and local activities

Moving to regional and local activities, the main focus of my work is developing service user and carer involvement in social work programmes in Southwest England. I have introduced the 'Hub and Spoke Model' to many universities, thus providing a strategic framework for involvement.

I continue to use my community development skills to promote to service users and carers opportunities for involvement in the design, delivery and evaluation of social work programmes. I designed the Hub and Spoke Model to provide a structured approach to involvement in the recruitment and selection of applicants, in teaching and assessment, and in designing and quality-assuring social work programmes in the academic environment. I am now using the Hub and Spoke Model to introduce opportunities for more meaningful involvement in placements. During these pilot projects in placements a student comments: 'the service users are in charge of my learning'; and a service user describes their supervision sessions with the student as 'keyworking in reverse'. This innovative work goes some way to redressing the power imbalance between students and service users as the dynamics of the relationship change.

I am also a qualified Practice Educator/Practice Assessor. I gained the Practice Teaching Award in 2004, but was involved in practice teaching and assessing social work students for ten years prior to this.

MY TYPICAL WEEK

Monday   Meeting with the University Coordinator and the Chair of the service user and carer forum to renegotiate my contract as the development worker.

Teleconference with academic researchers to discuss the next stage of the research project. Phone conversation with university tutor re presentation I am doing at a practice assessor's briefing session the following day. Final edit of the report on the benefits of service user and carer involvement in social work education written for SCIE and the Education Working Group of the Social Work Reform Board. Evening rehearsal for a musical concert in two weeks' time. Continuing with the summative assessment of the Final Portfolio for a final year social work student. Catch up with emails.

Tuesday   Two-hundred-mile return journey to a southwest university for a Practice briefing day to deliver a presentation on the meaningful involvement of service users and carers in practice learning. Return home and continue the assessment of the Final Portfolio.

Wednesday   Meet with the student to agree the summative assessment and sign off the Final Portfolio. Deal with emails. Travel five hours to Northwest England in preparation for the Approved Mental Health Professional (AMHP) inspection.

Thursday   AMHP inspection.

Friday   AMHP inspection and travel six hours home. Work on the train dealing with emails.

Reclaiming my identity: I survived

After a period of my most intense exposure to the psychiatric system, I joined my local user network, one of the biggest in the country, and, surrounded by peer support, I healed. I became a worker in the organisation, first in a community development role and then in management, ultimately becoming Chief Executive of the organisation. Over these fourteen years, I learned my craft.

As a development worker, I supported the growth of peer and collective advocacy. I developed the first mental health user forums countywide where service users challenged commissioners and providers to improve services. There were many gains for service users as a result of the forums' campaigning work. Services were commissioned differently to meet the needs which service users identified; they were invited to contribute to the monitoring and reviewing of services and the setting up of new services through interviewing tendering organisations. Service users were also involved in interviewing applicants for key posts in the local Mental Health Trust and Social Services.

I then changed my focus to the development of groups for people with learning difficulties to have their voices heard; for example, in genuine person-centred planning. People with learning difficulties were supported to take part in local planning groups and partnership commissioning boards, and in interviewing applicants for posts. Using the same community development approaches, further work in collective advocacy was done with older people and with people with physical and sensory impairments so that they too were involved in planning, commissioning, interviewing and selection, and monitoring and review processes.

In the area of individual advocacy, I set up and managed a number of advocacy projects for mental health service users, for people with learning difficulties and for older people. We recruited and trained volunteer advocates who became skilled in developing rapport and empathy to support service users to obtain their rights and entitlements. Advocates always worked to the service users' direction, even if they were doubtful that the outcomes required by the service users could be achieved.

I helped set up other projects to support independent living; for example, a transport project which supported people to gain confidence in travelling independently, and a project to support service users to influence housing plans with regard to accessibility. And, of course, one of the key areas in which I participated has been the development of service user involvement in social work education provided by local higher education institutions.

Losing my identity: no way home

I had a happy childhood in India where, as an only child, I was cosseted and pampered. My parents and I identify as Anglo-Indians and I grew up in a close-knit community in Calcutta. Anglo-Indians held elite positions in India before and after independence from Britain in 1947. I accepted the status quo (as children do) but with this acceptance of privilege, manifested in an excellent education and comfortable living conditions, came unease on my part about the very real deprivation experienced by whole families who were street-dwelling. Witnessing and being part of perpetrating social injustices undoubtedly influenced the later direction I took in my kind of social work.

My life changed completely when I was 9 years old and we emigrated to England, the 'mother country'. England was not a nurturing mother. It was a time before race relations legislation had been passed; 'no dogs, no blacks, no Irish' signs were displayed on doors of boarding houses, and Enoch Powell's 'rivers of blood' speech[7] soured the atmosphere. A timid child, I stood no chance against the open racism shown towards me and my family. My own experiences at school were difficult at times, but they were nothing compared to the oppression shown to my parents by systems and structures. Life got marginally better for me after I passed my 11-plus examination (thanks to my education in India) but not for my parents. We all hurt.

Much as it hurt to be treated as inferior, it also hurt to lose my identity. I had to deal with an identity crisis, actually more of an identity implosion! We Anglo-Indians were left by the British to continue to run the bureaucratic institutions like the Civil Service, the railways and the police; the old traditions remained, and I mean old. In the 1950s, we still lived in the manner of the colonial masters of previous generations. Meals were prepared by servants; afternoon tea was taken at 4 o'clock and dinner at 8 o'clock. It was obligatory to dress for dinner which was provided by a cook and servant waiting at table. Servants did our laundry and cleaned our house, and my ayiah (nursemaid) cared for me. Our privileged position did elicit much covert resentment from the Indian people but that did not impact upon my idyllic existence as a child growing up in India.

Coming to live in a back-street, terraced house in the North of England was very different. From being a lady of leisure, shopping and directing her household, my mother now held two jobs; her work in the day was followed by an evening shift in the local sugar beet factory. I had to cope with seeing her less at the very time when I needed her more. My father wasn't able to pursue his previous white-collar profession and became a manual worker, often working long days and at weekends on overtime to make up the family income.

No one could understand who we were, and consequently we were reshaped into the identity which was most comfortable for others. I didn't argue, and became more and more introspective. Our family became isolated and turned inwards, drawing on the little emotional strength we could offer each other. There were about five other Anglo-Indian families in our town and we shared a fundamentalist Christian faith. Increasingly, my life revolved around school routines and educational achievements, and the requirement to adhere to the strict rules of the Church. We were told by our elders and Church leaders to be 'in the world but not of it'.[8] Added to this, old-style colonial norms adopted by my parents included chaperoning, so I was kept on a tight rein. There were high expectations of me both educationally and morally.

The following poem, which I wrote in June 2009, describes this cataclysmic loss of identity at the age of 9 which was the start of my journey down the ever-constricting path of mental illness.

The breaking of June

Sun, hot, rain, warm, not cold, ever, colour, flowers, clothes,
everywhere colour, always warm, people warm, warm family,
happy, happy, happy

      I am lovely   I am important   I am loved

Fog, smog, cold, grey everywhere, grey skies, grey people, grey clothes, grey food, grey looks, no one smiling, and always cold, can't get warm, so cold, and the cold people always looking

I'm scared, help me mum, dad – but you can't because you are scared too. Isolated, lonely, so alone

People say –   You don't belong here;   go back

But I do belong here. I am part of you, your forefathers created me, love me.

I'll be good. What do I have to do to please you? I'll change, tell me what I have to do, I'll change, I am trying to please you, all of you, please love me

You don't want to, You can't . . .

It's me, I am not good enough, I am worthless, you can't love me, I can't love me.

I want to go home, where is home, I am lost, I HAVE LOST ME.

For so many, many, many years – growing up, growing down

Fear, Confusion, Madness

For so many, many, many years – growing up, but all the time growing down

I was very unhappy between the ages of 9 and 18. I increasingly questioned the norms which set me apart even further from my contemporaries at my girls' grammar school. Still scared but trying to keep some control, I became quietly rebellious, sneaking out to innocent venues for teenagers that were frowned on by the Church and forbidden by my parents, until finally, at the age of 18, I escaped to university. I took with me the seeds which had been planted during these formative years regarding a career in social work. A hospital almoner had visited our school to talk to us at a careers session and so I opted for a combined degree in sociology and psychology with a career in a 'caring' profession in mind.

I thoroughly enjoyed the freedoms of university life when I went there in the early 1960s, but after underachieving in my first year (too much play and not enough study), I made a vow that if I passed my resits I would return to the strict religious path. I did pass and then had to deal with a massive crisis of identity again. I couldn't cope, developing obsessive compulsive disorder (OCD) in my second year. I did achieve my degree and then, for the next thirty years, went between periods of wellness and illness. I was able to conceal my OCD at work as I progressed up the ladder in personnel management. But as periods of hospitalisation increased, I could no longer hide from my employers the fact that I was using psychiatric services.

Most employers were sympathetic, but one woman was not, and she unknowingly contributed to my change process, for which I have to thank her. During that period of employment (my last in personnel management), I was subject to a Section 3 detention under the Mental Health Act 1983 (Amended 2007),[9] and experienced being broken by the system and putting myself back together the best way I could manage; feeble beginnings but nevertheless the catalyst for change. My employer was intent on getting me out of the job against the advice of the organisation's medical officer and I felt forced to quit an unbearable situation which was stacked heavily against me.

This was the beginning of my journey of self-empowerment. My community psychiatric nurse gave me a flyer for the local user network saying that I believed I had things to say and no one was listening. Another person I have to thank. This was in 1994; the rest, as they say, is history.

June Sadd

The future

So what of the future? Playing with my new grand-daughter features heavily. Connecting with my spiritual side, this time in a positive way, is important to me too. I am also kept busy with amateur dramatics, acting, singing and dancing to my heart's content. Never forget that the heart needs fulfilment, absolutely essential to well-being. In between times, I will continue to strive to make a difference. Challenging social injustices is a fight worth continuing. Independence, autonomy and empowerment, all the things that service users want, figure heavily on my agenda.

I believe that the future of social work lies in community approaches, and for me that means initiatives started by 'small people' rather than by the 'great and the good'. Protecting people's rights, choice and control is fundamental to the aims of our communities and this is what keeps me going in my work. I have been privileged to work with some amazing people, such as one woman who could only communicate with the movement of her eyes and who still influenced provider and commissioner decisions, not only for herself but also for others.

It is all getting so much harder. Because of the economic recession in the UK, more and more people are becoming victims of class and poverty struggles. Social work is under pressure politically and financially, at a time when it is most needed; social workers are becoming burnt out and stressed with heavy workloads and low morale.

The way forward, I am sure, must be through community and people empowerment; that we can learn lessons from the ventures in some of the most deprived areas of the world where women have taken charge of literacy and farming projects, with just a little 'seed' money to start them off. Here in the UK we, too, have seen community initiatives started by mothers, for example mothers of people who misuse substances. This approach makes a lot more sense than adopting tired and morally bankrupt business models in social and health care systems which don't and won't work.

My vision for the future of social work is therefore akin to my own personal journey. I believe that solutions lie within the strength and strengths of people coming together in collective action with peer support. In my own private troubles, this is what turned me around, and having experienced it I am committed to spreading the sight, sound, feel, taste and sweet smell of self-empowerment and, yes, the sense of self-worth: our true identity. As the inspirational American community worker Saul Alinsky wrote: 'Denial of opportunity for participation is the denial of human dignity and democracy. It will not work' (1971: 123).

Notes

1 See http://www.education.gov.uk/swrb/.

2 See http://www.scie.org.uk/.

3   See http://www.collegeofsocialwork.org/.

4   Statutory access to an Independent Mental Health Advocate (IMHA) has been available since 2009 in England to patients subject to certain aspects of the Mental Health Act 1983. See http://www.dh.gov.uk/en/Healthcare/Mentalhealth/InformationontheMentalHealthAct/DH_091895.

5   SOL began as a research and development project but became an independent organisation in 2002. It is a federation of local user-controlled organisations; the organisation for which I was working is a member of SOL and was instrumental in setting SOL up. See http://www.shapingourlives.org.uk/.

6   SWAN first came together as a grouping in 2004 when a manifesto was published: *Social Work Manifesto for a New Engaged Practice*. Conferences bring supporters together each year. See http://www.socialwork future.org/.

7   This infamous speech was delivered to a Conservative Association meeting in Birmingham on 20 April 1968. Enoch Powell argued that that immigration should be contained or else there would be fighting on the streets. See http://www.telegraph.co.uk/comment/3643823/Enoch-Powells-Rivers-of-Blood-speech.html.

8   This is a quotation attributed to Jesus in John 17, verses 14–17.

9   This allows for detention for treatment and may be for up to six months.

References

Alinsky, S. (1971) *Rules for Radicals: A Pragmatic Primer for Realistic Radicals*, London: Random House.

Sadd, J. (2011) *We Are More than Our Story: Service User and Carer Participation in Social Work Education*, SCIE Report 42, London: Social Care Institute for Excellence.

21 My life's journey

A journey into social work

Gaylene Stevens

Mau ki to mana ahua ake
[Cherish your absolute uniqueness]

(Ruth Tai)

I was born in 1962, and raised as the second eldest of seven children in a small saw-milling and farming community in the most southern part of Te Waipounamu (the South Island) in Aotearoa (New Zealand). We carry in our hands a 'kete' (flax basket) handed down to us from our mother at birth; a 'kete' for gathering information on our journey. The weave has come from a community richly entwined in 'tikanga' (customary rule), 'kawa' (ceremonial protections) and 'whakapapa' (genealogy) inherently Māori from the East Coast of Te Ika O Maui (North Island of New Zealand). Its 'whakapapa' has within it a tradition of healing, orators, great leaders and advocates both male and female. On our backs we carry a duffel bag handed to us from our father, a sturdy, versatile bag for working-class people. It had journeyed from England through Scotland then down through New Brunswick in Canada before arriving in Aotearoa with my great-great-grandfather, the Reverend Andrew Stevens, a Presbyterian minister who disembarked the 'Cariboo' at Port Chalmers in 1865 and, soon after, looked after a parish at Wallacetown in Southland.

There were only two Māori (indigenous) families living in Tuatapere when I started school. Within the first decade, I learned very quickly to hide my kete inside my duffel bag, already having experienced the pernicious effects of racism and sexism. Confusion quickly clouded my world as I cast everything into the duffel bag. Occasionally feeling a sense of shame, I pondered why I kept my kete hidden in there. I remember one teacher ripping my book in half and yelling at me, 'Your work is not worth putting in a book'. Before the age of 10, I had been exposed to varying forms of abuse and witnessed domestic violence brought about by excessive use of alcohol. Maturation was fraught with dysfunction and the incongruous cornerstone of mistrust became firmly embedded. As a 10-year-old part-Māori girl living in a totally 'Pakeha' (white) world, I had embarked on a journey that appeared to be full of paradoxes, contradictions and conflicts.

I always had a feeling of disjuncture; a feeling of not quite fitting in. It followed me into my second decade as I continued schooling in a Eurocentric system. I struggled with learning, even though I seemed to manage it. I represented the school in hockey and athletics but never felt as if I was very good at anything. I walked through my schooling with a sense of shame and a lack of self-confidence. During this decade, my 'whanau' (family) started going to church, and family life as I knew it changed for the better. Whanau outings became more frequent and we spent many a happy day down at Blue Cliffs beach and Monkey Island gathering kaimoana (seafood). I remember one holiday when mum, dad and at that stage five of us kids piled into the Zephyr, the back seat taken out and replaced with mattresses so that we could all fit comfortably, and dad drove us around the South Island. At night we parked up on the side of the road and slept; it was safe to do so then.

I developed a more optimistic outlook on life while attending church and discovered that there is a force far greater than you and me; thus I learned to have faith and hope in things I could not see. None the less, in contrast I added to my duffel bag the ability to externalise behaviours and events so that I was no longer responsible for them, to accredit God with the good deeds and blame Satan for the bad.

I moved away from home before the start of my third decade, still involved in the Church, and entered the workforce as a clerical cadet for Māori Affairs in 1980. A window of opportunity presented itself as my work took me to Rehua Marae, a traditional Māori meeting place in Christchurch. It was here that I experienced a harmonious awakening of my 'Wairua' (spirit). My kete seemed nothing more than a distant memory but, when coupled with this environment, it seemed so familiar and comforting. However, the disparity between Church and Māori seemed contrary; this, coupled with the destructive forces of unresolved grief connected to the sudden death of my father, made it easy for me to slam shut this window and take denial as a good friend for a while.

However, this did not stop Ruamoko, the earth mother's unborn child, the god of earthquakes, from becoming unsettled in the depths of my 'puku' (stomach). I ignored the movement and for the next seven years or so worked harder in order to ignore the calls. I mastered the art of managing chaos and thrived on its urgency. However, the 'karanga' (calling) of my inner child became too loud to ignore; she wanted attention and attention is what she got. I was arrested and appeared before a court. This crisis shattered my world and provided me with a second opportunity to take out the kete from the duffel bag, an opportunity for me to find my identity and be grounded in it. It led me into the social work arena and, ironically, returned me to Rehua Marae, a place I had run away from some ten years earlier. Karen Brown, a Māori woman, came beside me and offered me an opportunity to work in a small social work team alongside urban Māori disadvantaged by colonisation. Until this time, I had mistakenly confused the culture of poverty and the ethnicity of Māori as synonymous. It was here that I started to unpack a social norm that I had carried with me on my journey, a thought that cluttered up my thinking – one that said Māori are 'dumb and useless'; how liberating to discover we are not!

I completed a Certificate in Social Work, inadvertently still driven by the need to 'fix' my own problems. The learning continued to stir up my inner child and so I finally decided to stop running from myself and relinquished denial as my friend. Two years of counselling helped me empty out a lot of clutter and it was here that I rediscovered the kete my mum had given me at birth. I found that I no longer needed two bags, so I blended the weave of my kete with the practical nature of my duffel bag and now I wear a 'piko', a woven backpack that encompasses both Māori and Pakeha values and beliefs.

Another person who had a major influence on me at this time was the late Heemi Rihari and together we have a beautiful daughter, Jazz Kahurangi. I met him going into my fourth decade. He was a Māori man of Ngapuhi (a northern tribe) descent. He acquainted me with his Māori worldview, its customary rules and ceremonial protections handed down to him through generations. He told Jazz stories that connected her to him, him to his parents, his parents to his grandparents and back through the generations to Io, the Supreme Being. I felt a pinch of envy, as my grandparents on both my mum's and my dad's sides died before my parents became adults themselves. The storytelling in my world stopped at my mum and dad: my grandparents were the missing links in our storytelling chain. I am often left wondering what my grandparents were like, what attributes they passed down to us, how our lives would have changed had we lived in their world for just a little while. For that reason there are lots of unanswered questions, and I am ever determined to strengthen and maintain the connectedness to my whanau (family), 'hapu' (extended family) and 'iwi' (tribe).

So, still within the fourth decade, I moved to Gisborne with my daughter to learn Te Reo Māori (Māori language) and live among my mother's tribal people, Ngati Porou. It is here that I discovered my Turangawaewae, my footing in a Māori world, a little place called Uawa, Tolaga Bay, a place where my grandparents lived, a rural community steeped in tradition and exuding 'whanaungatanga'. Whanaungatanga to me is best described as a way of life rather than a concept that can be easily translated; it includes people-making, maintaining and strengthening relationships. It is about making connections and includes exchanging stories rather than just exchanging genealogical ties. It is here that I found some of the missing pieces, some stories reconnecting me with my grandparents, and stories that helped me understand my mum's journey.

My fifth decade, and my daughter Jazz was due to start intermediate school, the transition into high school, and so the time had come to take my daughter to her father's people in the north, to Ngapuhi. Heemi's extended whanau wrapped their 'korowai' (cloak) of 'manaaki' (support) around us on arrival and looked after us really well. I continued my social work journey with Ngapuhi Iwi Social Services in Taitokerau (Northland). This time I worked with rural Māori who lived in close proximity to their extended whanau and in most instances their whanau marae (meeting place). I was employed as a social worker in schools and then as supervisor for this team. The focus of my role was managing the 'Social Workers in Schools' contract for the organisation. We were fortunate to live in a wonderful settlement called Waitangi in the picturesque Bay of Islands, a place of historical significance for Aotearoa. Waitangi is the birthplace of the treaty which was signed between Māori as tangata whenua, people of the land, and Pakeha as manuhiri, the visitors who came and settled here after Māori. This document is formally known as Te Tiriti o Waitangi and promotes four principles that ought to influence policy-making in Aotearoa New Zealand. The principles are partnership, protection, participation and pastoral. The education sector works hard to incorporate this document as foundational to most study undertaken at tertiary institutions. This leads us into another facet of my social working journey: study.

Tertiary study had begun three years after I started social work with Rehua Marae. My daughter was three months old then, and I completed a 'Care and Protection' Certificate in Social Work at the University of Canterbury with her by my side. Returning to study was a struggle for me as memories of a shame I carried through primary and secondary schooling came flooding back when I entered the classroom; I experienced a strong emotional block that cluttered my thinking and consequently my learning. I often felt confused and could not access the teaching easily. It was as if the teaching was being handed out in the form of cuttings taken from the English rose and, somehow, I was meant to graft this cutting into my 'harakeke' bush (a native flax bush). The grafting did not take and, needless to say, the shame continued to grow and the confidence continued to diminish. Somehow I had got my wires crossed; I was trying to link Pakeha knowledge to a Māori worldview, rose cuttings to flax. This mismatch linked learning with shame and the two became inseparable. It took me a long while to work out this grafting process (academic learning) and to disentangle the emotional baggage attached to it. However, I was not easily deterred and continued on to complete a Certificate in Te Reo Māori at Tai Rawhiti Polytechnic, a Bachelor of Arts double-majoring in Māori and Education at the University of Canterbury and a Certificate in Adult Teaching at Christchurch College of Education.

While I was working with Ngapuhi Iwi Social Services, I started supervising social workers and felt confident to complete the 'mahi' (tasks) associated with this role. I had been under the illusion that supervision of social workers was simply a matter of line management. That illusion was soon dispelled as I began to read literature on supervision and how to supervise practitioners. In my search for simplicity, I discovered complexity, but I had to make the journey into the complexities of supervision in order to come back out understanding it more simply. Māori have a symbol that best depicts this action; it is called 'Awhiowhio' (Webber-Drendon 1999), spiralling down into the whirlpool to discover what is there and then spiralling back up with the answers. There was, of course, very little literature written by Māori about 'kaupapa Māori' supervision at that time (Bradley *et al.* 1999); as a new Māori supervisor, the little information I found was invaluable.

In September 2006, I attended supervision training at Massey University off-campus at Ngatokowaru Marae, Ngati Pareraukawa. This was training for staff in NGOs that were Māori providers of social work services. In preparation, participants were asked to bring with them a symbol that best represented their model of supervision. I jumped off the plane into the hired car and made a quick stop at the 'Two Dollar

Shop' on my way to the marae. Time was against me as I tried 'thoughtfully' to look for something awe-inspiring that would reflect my model of supervision. I grabbed a ball of string. From that moment, consciously or subconsciously, I started forming ideas that connected my ball of string with a potential model of supervision. Ironically, much later on into the evening I realised that *this* was my model of supervision: not the string, but stopping at the 'Two Dollar Shop' amidst the haste of business to grab something that would make me look prepared!

That evening, I stood in the 'whare tupuna' (meeting house) with the ball of string. I was nervous because I felt that my unpreparedness would be exposed. Many participants had come and had obviously put a lot of time into their presentation, and here I was standing there with a piece of string. My 'tinana' (body) standing still, my 'wairua' (spirit) and 'ngakau' (heart) took a moment to settle, my 'hinengaro' (mind) was quiet and then something magical happened. I opened my mouth, hinengaro took the floor, and tinana, wairua and ngakau, now aligned, all joined me in a captivating presentation. My piece of string became 'Te Aho'; an invisible umbilical cord that connected me firmly to Papatuanuku, my earth mother. I gently took 'Te Aho' in my hands and it became the live link connecting me to the rich symbolism of the whare tupuna. It connected me to tupuna korero; stories of my ancestors, to atua; the gods, to whakapapa; genealogy, to whanau, to the past, the present and future. The magic became intrinsic as I used 'Te Aho' to make connections to Māori theorists like Maui, Hineahuone, Rahiri and Porourangi; tupuna (ancestors) who orally passed information down through their whakapapa, and then, 'ka taka te kapa', the penny dropped! Even though I did not know these people as theorists, for the first time in my academic journey I understood the concept behind theorists, people who lend their thinking to academic learning as a way for others to make sense of something. That was a magical moment for me, a 'wana' (full of awe) moment, a moment of realisation; Māori were so 'on to it', they were so clever, they just recorded their knowledge in a different way and now I knew how to read from this great library of Māori knowledge. 'Te Aho' became the key to unlock the encoded knowledge for me. It didn't stop there. An illusion was dispelled and a huge block in my learning moved as I realised that I too am a theorist in the making and the scholarly did not seem so untouchable any more. I instantly felt an increase in cerebral confidence to manage this academic journey and continued on to complete a Master's in Social Work (Applied) in 2009. Shame does not reside here anymore and I know that I have a contribution to make in growing new knowledge.

I completed a research project as part of the requirements of the MSW (Applied). This project involved interviewing five Māori women who are supervisors/trainers of kaupapa Māori supervision. I held two focus groups that explored core components, investigated cultural constructs and considered what synergises the supervisory relationship in magical moments for kaupapa Māori supervision. The findings of this project inform us that whakawhanaungatanga is the ngako that creates magical moments in kaupapa Māori supervision for Māori supervisors and Māori supervisees. There are four core components that support the ngako to synergise the supervisory relationship into magical moments. They are: the willingness of the supervisee to discover something about themselves; the 'mauri' (life force) of the supervision space; the fact that cultural constructs are essential for kaupapa Māori supervision; and the ability of the supervisor to become selfless.

When these components are synchronised, magical moments can happen at four different levels: 'mana motuhake' (with self), 'mana tangata' (with people), 'mana tupuna' (with ancestors) and 'mana atua' (with God) (see also Eruera and Stevens 2010).

So here I am at yet another crossroads. I stand with my piko (woven backpack) on my back, the values, beliefs, ethics and morals handed down to me from my parents. On one side I have a kete (woven flax basket) that draws from both Pakeha and Māori knowledge bases. On the other side I have a kete that is filled with skills I have gathered from a multitude of people and experiences along my life's journey. I felt that I became a better social worker once I had worked as a supervisor. I became a better supervisor once I had managed a contract. My work has matured and I have a good working understanding of the operational tensions that exist between the management and delivery of services. I made lots of mistakes along the way but, after twenty years, I finally feel as if I am so much better equipped and ready to do social work.

Social work: the journey continues

In my social work journey, I have a clear understanding of the social work process and utilise a strengths-based approach (e.g. Saleeby 2006) from two worldviews. My goal is always to be open to magical moments for whanau. I am able to complete a comprehensive social work assessment and know that good information gathered informs good intervention plans and, in turn, achieves good outcomes. I advocate clear goals completed *with* whanau and not *for* whanau. My supervision looks at four main areas: the workplace (the operational systems that support the worker in the field, such as policy and procedure, contractual obligations, codes of ethics, standards of practice, etc.); the work (the outputs and outcomes, contracted volumes, proposed, actual and variances); the worker (what tools – skills, knowledge and experience – workers have to complete the mahi and what areas need to be strengthened); and finally, the working (how practice is being performed, what models are used, how networks are utilised, how whanau strengths provide whanau solutions). Social work seems straightforward now, and yet I procrastinated for some time about writing this part of the chapter. Lots of things have changed over the past year.

Christchurch suffered major devastation with three big earthquakes, loss of life, continuous after-shocks, the central city 'red zoned', two unexpected snowstorms, iconic buildings demolished, people displaced and lives absolutely shattered to a desensitising numbness. While this has all been traumatic, I sit here today in a sun-filled room, peacefully surrounded by birds chirping, a neighbour mowing his lawn, a lovely phone call from my mum, the All Blacks have won the Rugby World Cup, my daughter and her partner are at work . . . yet another epiphany . . . after the birth of my daughter, my life was spent looking after her and now she is at work! My motivation for getting into social work has changed, my environment has changed and so too has the nature of the social work I want to be part of. I am now 49 years old and nearing the end of my fifth decade. We have left the warm embrace of Ngapuhi and returned to Te Waipounamu (South Island). My mum is 71 years old and I need to dedicate the next part of my journey to being with her. I have been running around in the name of helping for a long time and now I want to refocus my participation in social work to include my whanau.

I am employed today by the Anglican Māori Diocese of Te Waipounamu as the Kaihautu for Te Whare Wananga, the education arm of the Diocese. My role is to coordinate a training programme for clergy and laity in order to strengthen clerical and pastoral care skills. I took on this job in August and our first quake was in September. Setting up social work training for 'minita-a-iwi' (ordained clergy) and laity has been one of Bishop John Gray's long-term goals. He would also like to establish social work services for the Māori Diocesan. This is where I come in. I was originally employed to further develop a basic social work course called 'Awhi Whanau' and we have just completed the pilot programme. The programme starts by examining social work from three worldviews: mainstream social work, Māori Awhi Whanau and Christian Pastoral Care. The programme teaches that the most important thing in the world is people, 'ko te mea nui o tenei ao, he tangata', and woven through this fabric are threads of scripture; for example, 1 Corinthians 13 talks about how the attributes of love can be evidenced in a worker. The framework for Awhi Whanau utilises Māori cultural constructs and provides guidelines for the programme and in turn the worker:

- 'Ko Au' (me) – 'Ko Koe' (you): the importance of knowing yourself and how your environment has influenced your journey before you engage with someone else. Once you understand your world you will then have an idea of how to explore someone else's world with respect.

- 'Ko Koutou' (you and yours) – 'Ko Tatou' (both of us and ours): whanaungatanga happens by exchanging stories and making connections with whanau until 'kua ea' you are satisfied koutou has become tatou. Now the work begins.

- 'Ko Ratou' (others, not you or me) – 'Ko Tatou' (both of us and ours); sometimes we will need to engage someone else to help us whether that be whanau whanui (extended family) or networks; again whanaungatanga happens with others until 'kua ea ratou' becomes tatou and the work continues.

MY TYPICAL WEEK

There is no such thing as a 'typical week'; my work varies from day to day. Two weeks ago we were hosting a National Ministry Training. Last week we were in Wellington presenting a proposal seeking approval for a similar training and accreditation programme. This week I am helping the Bishop to look for a food caravan that can be used to Awhi (support) Whanau here in Christchurch post-quake. Next week I will begin to make up a teaching manual for our two pilot programmes, Manaaki Hauora and Awhi Whanau, the training and accreditation of Hospital Chaplains and Social Workers respectively who work alongside whanau Māori. While both programmes come from quite different disciplines, the framework, epistemology and pedagogy are very similar. Amidst this, there are the usual administrative tasks of reviewing, maintaining and strengthening operational systems and setting up ongoing residential ministry training programmes. The training includes five residential block courses a year and four two-day regional training events to follow up modules completed at the kura (residential training). Clergy and laity can complete a Certificate in Ministry and then move on to a Licentiate in Ministry; added to this are the two new programmes: the Advanced Certificate in Manaaki Hauora and the Advanced Certificate in Awhi Whanau.

The future for social work

In Te Ao Māori there is a saying, 'You go into the future looking back'. I would like to take a minute to pull some threads through from my life's journey, in order to highlight how my journey may influence the setting up of the Awhi Whanau Ministry for the Anglican Māori Diocese of Te Waipounamu. I would also like to share how our current situation has helped shape the pathway forward for Awhi Whanau and its development.

- I bring through some threads that validate the importance of celebrating difference. I bring my piko acknowledging two worldviews: my dad as Pakeha and a spiritual belief in Christianity, and my mum as Māori and spirituality in Te Ao Māori that says all things are connected. I live in both worlds, and my values and beliefs are valid and attributed to them both. Awhi Whanau training will allow students the opportunity to examine social work from three worldviews: mainstream social work, Māori Awhi Whanau and Christian pastoral care.

- A thread from working with urban Māori, Māori who moved away from tribal living in search of employment. When the work stopped, poverty and benefit dependency crept in and continue to jealously hold onto families; in turn their children are not always able to return home to their Turangawaewae, their footing in a Māori world, and become displaced from their home. This is coupled with a thread from the rural communities of Ngati Porou and Ngapuhi, reinforcing the importance of whakapapa, genealogy and belonging, the importance of tikanga and kawa, my learning about whanaungatanga as a way of life, about the connectedness of all things. About the need for tapu and noa, safe boundaries.

- A thread from tertiary education within a Pakeha institution; the realisation that rose clippings should be grafted on to rose bushes; if you are creative you can introduce a hybrid rose, new information to be added to the valuable knowledge stored in libraries. There are also other commonalities with gardening – tending to the soil, the need for light and moisture to create the best environment to grow plants. This parallels humanitarian thinking; people are people no matter what culture, ethnicity, religious belief or political view they hold. However, it is a reminder that the rose bush has different needs to the flax bush and so it is with people, whether in study or working alongside them in social work.

- A thread from 'Wananga Māori', that there is an amazing wealth of knowledge encrypted and stored in the Arts, storytelling, song and symbolism. Māori have a term, 'ako': a process that encourages reciprocity of teaching and learning, encouraging Hui, people gathering together to talk collectively about their knowing. The ministry of Awhi Whanau will encourage people to work with a collective consciousness as opposed to an individualistic approach.

- A rather special thread is that of storytelling . . . let's not complicate it. Storytelling is a dying art and yet crucial when working with whanau. The ability to allow people the time to tell their stories. The ability of the worker to make connections with whanau until koutou (them) becomes tatou (us). Quite simply, it is the whanaungatanga that exists between me and you. If our focus is about whanaungatanga, then the issues we have become so accustomed to in social working will fall away as people are validated in their knowing.

- Another thread comes from the experience of Cantabrian people in the first two to three days after the quake. Just as the quake shook buildings to the ground, it also shook away the barriers that keep people apart. Magic happened; attitudes, social norms, social status and prejudices were, for that moment in time, no longer important. People mattered, neighbours helped neighbours, the young helped the old, the poor helped the rich, volunteers swamped the central city, prepared to risk their lives to help clear away the rubble in search of those still trapped in buildings. Magic happened because there was no bureaucratic clutter (said respectfully). Rescue slowed right down as local and central government intervened to manage the 'state of emergency'. Volunteers were kept at bay, and professionals were sent in to manage compliance.

- A thread of well-being and reclamation. Counselling helped clear away the clutter from my hinengaro and ngakau; God helps clear the clutter from my wairua; Zumba, with John Gray and Innate Rhythm, has helped clear away the excess kilos I have been carrying around for years and has given me back my life. Awhi Whanau has taken on a more practical approach to social work and promotes the total well-being of whanau.

- A thread woven through it all is the importance of knowing God, the Supreme Being; a thread that comes through from the beginning of time. It is this spiritual thread that has bought me through to where I am today. It guides my journey in this world. Awhi Whanau as a ministry and as a training opportunity will, first, consider God, 'Ko a ia te timatanga me te mutunga o nga mea katoa' ['He is the beginning and the end of all things']. Second, it will consider people, 'Ko te mea nui o tenei ao, ko te tangata' ['The most important thing in this world is people'].

'Ma te Atua koutou e manaaki i roto i to koutou haerenga.'
[May God look after you all in your journey.]

References

Bradley, J., Jacob, E. and Bradley, R. (1999) 'Reflections on Culturally Safe Supervision, or why Bill Gates Makes More Money Than We Do', *Social Work Review*, December: 3–6.

Eruera, M. and Stevens, G. (2010) *Te Whiriwhiringa o te Kete. Weaving the Past into the Present for the Future*, Presentation for Supervision Conference held at the University of Auckland, May.

Saleeby, D. (ed.) (2006) *The Strengths Perspective in Social Work Practice*, 4th edn, New York: Pearson Education.

Webber-Drendon, E. (1999) 'He Taonga Mo o Matou Tipuna (A Gift Handed down by our Ancestors): An Indigenous Approach to Social Work Supervision', *Te Komako III Social Work Review*, 11(4): 7–11.

22 Becoming a reflective social work practitioner

A story of a Hong Kong-born Chinese woman

Pauline Sung-Chan

I have been practising social work for almost three decades in different parts of the world, but mostly in Hong Kong and the Chinese Mainland. Social work is a field of practice which is diverse with many different kinds and types. I believe that to be a social worker is an existential choice each practitioner has to make from time to time; another important decision is what kind of social work to do and what not to do. In this chapter, I will highlight the key figures and theoretical frameworks that have shaped my choice of certain social work models to guide my practice. I will begin by telling you a brief story about myself. Setting a stage around this biographic information, I hope that readers will appreciate how social work as a profession has given great meaning to the life of a young Chinese woman who was born in Hong Kong.

Growing up in a British colony in the 1950s

My father was born and raised in Shanghai, in China. He left his homeland to emigrate to Hong Kong (then a British colony) with my grandfather in 1948, leaving his elder brother and mother behind; he did not see his family again until twenty years later. My father, like many migrants at this time, lost everything he had in China and had to start all over again to build a new life in a strange city. Despite being a university graduate, he was unable to make a successful career in Hong Kong. My mother was born and raised in Hong Kong. Because she was a girl, she had very little schooling. She became a housewife after marrying my father in her early twenties. I was born in Hong Kong, the second of three daughters. In my growing-up years, I was exposed to both Western and Eastern cultures which significantly cultivated my orientation towards multiculturalism. Consequently, I have always sought to live and work in different cultures. My childhood experiences taught me something else as well, however. Seeing my parents' struggles to survive inspired me to decide to make a different life for myself. But the pathway to a successful life for a girl was to marry someone rich. How could I do things differently in a social environment saturated with strong traditional Chinese beliefs about what women should do? The Hong Kong government had established an educational system enabling all children to receive basic education, regardless of their sex; investing in education for girls is the best way to support them to lead a different life, including a life without poverty. The opportunity to receive formal education gave me a head start in life. I did not need to follow in the footprints of my mother, who was very bright but had been deprived of the opportunity to go to school.

College and work in Canada in the 1970s

With a strong desire to pursue a college education and escape from family pressures, I decided to leave Hong Kong in the early 1970s. I was thrilled to leave home because I was longing to go to a place where I would be nurtured to be a thinking person. I was like a bird who struggled hard to fly away from an iron cage! In my first year at college, I majored in Human Geography with a goal to become a map maker. I changed my major after I became a Christian in the same year. I saw human services as more attractive, since my religion called us to serve the poor and marginalised. I had the most wonderful time in college as I came to acquire knowledge in different disciplines: studies in urban planning, geography, psychology and counselling laid a good foundation for my future career in human services. I was transformed from a shy Chinese girl into a confident young woman. My university education gave me a different outlook on life. It had also planted a new belief that I could be economically independent, with no need to rely entirely on a husband to support me and to give meaning to my life.

After my graduation from the University of Waterloo, Ontario, Canada, I was fortunate to find a job as a community worker in an old neighbourhood in Toronto. I was responsible for coordinating services to the adults in the community. There were many service gaps, but the settlement house where I worked did not have the required resources. Taking up a proactive stance, I had pressed the Ministry of Culture and Recreation hard and demanded grant money to support new projects for adult residents in this low-income neighbourhood. Working in the settlement house allowed me to see the advocacy role of social work in protecting the marginalised groups in the local community. My success in my first job in community work assured me that I could make a difference in the lives of others.

A gap year in Hong Kong and taking up social work training in the late 1970s

After two years working in Toronto, I travelled back to Hong Kong to work in a secondary school as a youth counsellor. Taking up this offer required me to give up a good job and a promising career in Canada, but I wanted to make a contribution to my home city. So I embarked on a new journey, despite the fact that I was travelling against the mainstream: the trend at this time was for young people to move overseas. Leaving my comfort zone was not easy, especially because by this time, my family had themselves migrated to Toronto. My parents no longer wished to be in Hong Kong because my father's relatives had suffered greatly during the communist rule in the Chinese Mainland. In retrospect, the decision to leave Canada was significant, marking not only a new page but a new book in my life. This was the beginning of my decision to practise social work in different Chinese societies.

Building up a social work career in Hong Kong in the 1980s

After an exciting year working with young people in a school setting, I had to decide what to do next. If I wanted to continue practising as a social worker, I would have to have formal social work training. A good friend, Angie Tsang, whom I had come to know in Toronto, was a graduate of the University of Hong Kong and she encouraged me to apply. I joined the Master of Social Work class at the Hong Kong University with a group of eighteen students from diverse backgrounds. It was a very intensive training programme based primarily on British social work models, under the leadership of Professor Peter Hodge, who showed us the importance of social policy and of bringing together a macro and micro focus in social work.

I graduated in 1981 and experimented with various forms of social work practice for a few years. My first assignment was to help build a new multi-service centre in an old neighbourhood in Hong Kong, under the leadership of Mary Lam, an expert in mental health. In 1983, I decided to take on social work teaching as a career and became a practice teacher at the Chinese University of Hong Kong. I enjoyed this very much, because I could work with students in different settings, including governmental and non-governmental organisations. I liked practice teaching because I did not have to divorce teaching from practice. I taught and worked for six years in different social work settings. Through this, I gradually moved from being a novice to becoming an experienced practitioner-teacher. I saw myself becoming more and more professional and mainstream and took on a more 'expert' role through a specialisation in case work. I was systematically applying social work theories to guide my practice and the practice of my students. But underneath this, I was extremely doubtful about the usefulness of theories which had been developed in the West and I found it strange to apply them in a Chinese context. When I could not get insight from theory, my other option was to seek practice wisdom from local experienced practitioners. However, this was equally disappointing, because the practitioners made their practice wisdom mysterious; their expert knowledge was elusive. I struggled with what I saw as a chasm between theory and practice. How did I cope with this career/life crisis? Leaving Hong Kong was an option. My husband was taking sabbatical leave at Harvard University in the USA in 1989 and I joined him as a visiting scholar at the Simmons School of Social Work, Simmons College in Boston, Massachusetts.

There was another reason for taking sabbatical leave, however, as external events coincided with my career crisis. For years, I took for granted my identity as a Chinese person in Hong Kong. As a second-generation migrant, I had moved steadily upwards and enjoyed a life with good career prospects and income. I was not at all paternalistic towards China and did not see myself as having any relationship with her. However, events in China on 4 June 1989 radically changed my perception.[1] I felt the need to revisit my identity as a Chinese woman and my responsibility with the Chinese people there. The sabbatical year allowed me to ask what a middle-class social worker might do in a country which valued only economic development, and which held ideas about democracy and human rights that were vastly different from the West.

Experiencing a reflective turn/a paradigm shift in social work practice in the USA

I settled down in Cambridge, MA, in 1989. This new social, cultural and intellectual context provided a special space to address my career crisis, similar to what Erikson (1956) has called a moratorium: a special context in which teenagers can experiment with different ways to address their identity crisis. Living abroad exposed me to a new horizon of knowledge which, in turn, gave new direction to my social work development. I realised what I (as a Chinese social worker from Hong Kong) could do to make a difference to social work development in China.

Systems theory tells us that systems are likely to remain in the same equilibrium which has evolved over time (Bertalanffy 1968). From this perspective I had maintained a sense of sameness/constancy gained over my ten working years in Hong Kong. If I wanted to make changes to my familiar ways of practising social work, I had to have new stimulation from the outside. Exposing myself to new knowledge and a new community of academic scholars in social work and family therapy in the USA opened up some new ways of understanding the nature of social work and what social work could do, and I experienced the meaning of the dictum, 'knowledge is power'.[2] I realised painfully that my professional practice was based on a technical-rational approach derived from positivism. One of the pitfalls of this epistemological stance was that I regarded myself as the expert who had privileged knowledge to unilaterally change and manipulate my clients from the outside. I was a fallen angel! What dismayed me most is that no one had ever challenged this framework over my ten years in practice.

At Simmons School of Social Work, I was introduced to postmodernism, social constructionism, second-order cybernetics and feminism which all challenged the positivistic framework I had sub-scribed to previously. Some of the major figures I learned about were Sophie Freud, Carlos Sluzki, Marcelo Pakman, Lynn Hoffman and Carol Gilligan. I began to question the notion that there is an objective reality which can be deciphered by professionals who have privileged knowledge, and which is not accessible to our clients/service users; also that as 'experts' we could maintain a value-neutral stance in relation to our clients. It became clear to me that I had helped to create a world of practice in which I had ignored the importance of participation and collaboration with our clients. I was astonished to understand for the first time that we use our professional knowledge to oppress our clients, and we do so by saying that we involve clients in the helping process. I began to ask whether I liked what I had been doing. What were some of the unintended consequences?

Pursuing a reflective approach to practice in Hong Kong in the 1990s

Approaching the end of my sabbatical, I received an offer to help develop a new postgraduate programme in family-centred social work at the Department of Applied Social Sciences of the Hong Kong Polytechnic University. Many people were surprised by this career move. I chose this department because the Head, Professor Diana Mak, was an advocate of a post-positivistic epistemological stance to social work practice and was conversant with current developments in social work throughout the world. She was a strong supporter of educating social work practitioners to be critical and reflective. She introduced me to the work of Donald Schön (see 1983, 1987, 1991). He argued that one reason for the crisis of confidence among professionals was that professional schools had built their curriculum on a technical-rational approach which had played down the need to develop practice knowledge to deal with the uncertain and complex practice world. Schön (1983) asserted that professional artistry is embedded in direct action and is tacit in nature, and practitioners know more than they can tell, but they normally find it hard to make explicit this kind of tacit knowledge. He called this 'reflection-in-action' or, as it is commonly called, a reflective approach to practice.

I first met Don in 1991 in his Newton home. He had hurt his back while playing volleyball with his students. He understood I had come a long way to see him, so instead of cancelling the meeting he arranged for us to meet in his home. Lying on his couch, he devoted almost two hours to a stranger from Hong Kong, showing great interest in discussing two important issues in social work: reasons for the gap between theory and practice, and appropriate methodologies to generate theories from practice. At the end, I asked whether I might do my doctoral studies with him; I subsequently worked with him until his death in 1997. I formally enrolled in a Ph.D. programme at the University of Nottingham in 1993, where I also had the privilege to study with Professor Olive Stevenson from the UK. I benefited tremendously from this cross-cultural study experience. I was Don's first and possibly only social work student. His influence on me was not only through his theories related to professional artistry and education. He also showed me how to conduct research that could develop knowledge from, in and for practice. Following the intellectual traditions of Kurt Lewin and John Dewey, he and his long-term collaborator, Professor Argyris from the Harvard Business School (see Argyris and Schön 1974), advocated a research method called 'collaborative-action research' to generate knowledge from practice. Both men were strong proponents of training practitioners to be researchers who could make use of their daily practice to experiment with existing theories, with a mission to develop new knowledge for improving practice.

These theories came to me like a light from the end of a tunnel. Over the next twenty years I learned to employ collaborative-action research to make use of my daily practice to creatively synthesise Western knowledge and local practice to address many practice challenges in both Hong Kong and China. I will share two of these experiences to illustrate how I facilitated communities of social work practitioners to become reflective practitioners/researchers, in order to develop useful practice knowledge for improving the existing social services.

Building a reflective community in Hong Kong in the 1990s

My Ph.D. fieldwork began in a collaborative-action research project set in the context of the youth services. A government report had expressed concerns that existing service delivery models were no longer adequate to assist young people in becoming responsible, contributing members of society (Working Party on Review of Children and Youth Center Services 1994). Service models adhered rigidly to service boundaries, resulting in fragmentation and duplication of service, and failure to address service gaps and respond to community needs. This provided a golden opportunity for cooperation between practitioners and academics. Since youth agencies lacked the resources to train front-line workers, they welcomed academics' assistance, not only in supporting them to learn new approaches for delivering a new integrated service model, but also in conducting research to test the usefulness of the new approaches.

I approached Yolanda Chiu, manager at a well-established, non-governmental youth organisation. She was keen to join the action research because their current approaches were not working well with complex problems such as drug abuse, adolescent suicide and adolescent psychosomatic illness. For the past twenty years, the prevailing approach to school social work had been individual. To improve their effectiveness, they needed a wide range of theories and intervention methods for a better understanding of the problems young people encountered. They knew that the family played a significant role in young people's development. Thus, they considered it worthwhile to try a family-systems perspective to determine whether it was more applicable to the situations they faced on a daily basis. Participation in my action research would give them the necessary support to experiment with this approach with their clients.

Twelve social workers joined the action research. Over a period of two and a half years, we formed six family teams, consisting of social workers and family therapy interns from the HKPU, and a reflective approach was employed to examine the usefulness of the intervention. All the interviews were video-taped, and observers (including me) watched from behind a one-way mirror. We conducted reflection sessions after the interviews, allowing us to examine how well Western family therapy worked in facilitating the family to address life issues of importance to their teenage children. These sessions served as a context for research and professional training. Critically examining one's own practice with other colleagues was a scary process as we had to make explicit our private practice to a community of practitioners/researchers. We also created a parallel process by involving the family in researching their ways of framing and solving their problems. Inviting families to be our co-researchers made it easier for us to find out whether or not Western family therapy approaches worked well for them. Building in an evaluative element was crucial to our goal of generating local knowledge for improving practice. We had to substantiate our claims if we asserted that certain interventions were useful.

Our findings were similar to the outcomes of other studies (Pinsof and Wynne 1995; Pinsof *et al.* 1996), which point to the efficacy of family treatment. One outcome measure is to assess the extent to which the clients' symptoms were reduced. Of the eleven families we studied, only one failed to change. The remaining clients were able to remain at home rather than being placed in institutions; we were able to support them by strengthening the capacity of their families through acquiring new knowledge to relate differently to their children.

After numerous action-research cycles, the practitioners/researchers were thrilled to produce practice-based evidence to explore how well Western family therapy could offer help to the local families. The practice-based evidence was later systematically theorised into a framework which explained the processes that facilitated and prohibited the local families from adopting a family-systems perspective to address family conflicts. The process of constructing local knowledge was powerful, as it allowed us to experience an unprecedented sense of agency and a contribution to social work practice (see Sung-Chan 2000).

Building a reflective community in the Chinese Mainland in the 2000s

In 2000, I decided to experiment further with this methodology in the Chinese Mainland, a very different social-economic and cultural context (Sung-Chan and Yuen-Tsang 2007). The first experiment was carried out through the community-based Women Networking Project in Beijing, and commissioned by the All Federation of Women in China. The aim of the project was to facilitate unemployed women to find new ways to tackle the social and economic problems that had arisen during the transition from a planned to a market economy. Our biggest challenge was deciding how to foster a community of social work practitioners/researchers to practise a new method to promote change in China; the task of the practitioners/researchers would be to guide the unemployed women to master a new strategy for coping with unemployment, unlike their customary dependence on government.

Collaborative-action research provided the way forward. The reflective community included not only trained social workers but also participants from the local community. The Beijing project comprised eight local, untrained social service workers (commonly referred as cadres), four social work student practitioners, thirteen unemployed women and two social work teachers. Over the next two years, four iterative stages of the action-research cycle were worked through (Lewin 1948). In the first stage, the practitioners helped the women to find their personal voices and map their existing approaches to problem-solving through a process of oral history interviews. In the second stage, the women reflected critically on their existing approaches to problem-solving and sought new frameworks. In the third stage, they experimented with their new, proposed practice framework. In the final stage, they reflected on their experimentation and refined their newly acquired practice frameworks, thus gaining agency over their own destinies.

How did we do this? Contrary to endorsing the familiar approach of depending on 'experts' to deal with their problems, our project invited women to learn new approaches to dealing with change. This required a change as radical as a paradigm shift (Kuhn 1962). Our efforts to support this group in their search for new ways to understand and construct their realities were fraught with tension, uncertainty, disillusion, excitement and contentment. We encountered numerous social and cultural challenges. Socio-cultural discourses play an important role in shaping cultural understandings, as well as the market, the state and social control (Schön and Rein 1994). When the women sought new solutions to their unemployment problems, they experienced the domination of the two prevailing social-cultural discourses, namely the 'grand narrative of progress' and the 'return home' paternalistic discourse. Since they lacked alternative discourses to fight against this, they took on the voice of government, a strong advocate of these dominant discourses. Hence, their own authentic voices were marginalised. At first, we were frustrated that they gave up their endeavour to develop a different voice so easily. We then critically analysed the ways in which the social and cultural discourses determined the women's voices and narratives. We moved from despair to excitement as we witnessed these women recognise, first, their subjugation to these unhelpful social-cultural discourses, and second, that using these discourses kept them powerless and without distinct, authentic voices. Their willingness to challenge the premises underlying their entrenched ways of understanding their unemployment gave us the incentive to move on with the collaborative-action research with them. In order to support the women's efforts to resist these discourses, we also engaged the officials of the local government (especially during stages three and four of the project) to reflect on their role in reproducing these discourses.

> **MY TYPICAL WEEK**
>
> One-third of my time is currently engaged in educational administration; one-third is devoted to providing postgraduate teaching; while the last third is spent in conducting action experiments to generate new knowledge for tackling concrete social problems. I am at present leading a multi-disciplinary team which is employing collaborative-action research to generate practice knowledge for childhood obesity prevention.

Looking ahead

As a reflective social work practitioner, I have sought to keep to the fore the ideas of Kurt Lewin, who wrote, 'Action, research and training are a triangle that should be kept together for the sake of any of its corners' (Lewin 1948: 211). I am committed to employing collaborative-action research to conduct research in action as well as educating practitioners using it to promote social practice. Having accumulated two decades of experiences of training reflective practitioners/researchers, I am determined to continue working with my long-term collaborators to further this work in different parts of the world, especially in Mainland China.

Notes

1   On 4 June 1989, hundreds of people were killed in the Chinese capital of Beijing as soldiers and tanks moved to clear Tiananmen Square of pro-democracy demonstrators.

2   This quotation is said to be from Sir Francis Bacon's tract *Religious Meditations, Of Heresies*, published in 1597, although this has been disputed.

References

Argyris, C. and Schön, D. (1974) *Theory in Practice: Increasing Professional Effectiveness*, San Francisco, CA: Jossey-Bass.

Bertalanffy, L.V. (1968) *General System Theory: Foundations, Development, Applications*, New York: George Braziller.

Erikson, E. (1956) 'The problem of ego identity', *Journal of the American Psychoanalytic Association*, 4 (56): 56–121.

Kuhn, T. (1962) *The Structures of Scientific Revolutions*, Chicago, IL: University of Chicago Press.

Lewin, K. (1948) *Resolving Social Conflicts*, New York: Harper and Row.

Pinsof, W.M. and Wynne, L.C. (1995) 'The efficacy of marital and family therapy: An empirical overview, conclusions, and recommendations', *Journal of Marital and Family Therapy*, 21: 585–613.

Pinsof, W.M., Wynne, L.C. and Hambright, A. (1996) 'The outcomes of couple and family therapy: Findings, conclusions and recommendations', *Psychotherapy: Theory, Practice and Research*, 33: 321–331.

Schön, D. (1983) *The Reflective Practitioner. How Professionals Think in Action*, London: Temple Smith.

Schön, D. (1987) *Educating the Reflective Practitioner*, San Francisco, CA: Jossey-Bass.

Schön, D.A. (1991) *The Reflective Turn: Case Studies In and On Educational Practice*, New York: Teachers Press, Columbia University.

Schön D.A. and Rein, M. (1994) *Frame Reflection: Toward the Resolution of Intractable Policy Controversies*, New York: Basic Books.

Sung-Chan, P.L. (2000) *A Collaborative-action Research into the Teaching and Learning of Systemic Family Practice to School Social Work in Hong Kong*. Unpublished doctoral dissertation, Nottingham: University of Nottingham.

Sung-Chan, P. and Yuen-Tsang, W.K. (2007) 'Reflections on building a reflective practice community in China', in S. White, J. Fook and F. Gardner (eds) *Critical Reflection and Professional Development: The State of the Art*, London: Open University Press: 57–72.

Working Party on Review of Children and Youth Center Services (1994) *Report on Review of Children and Youth Center Services*, Hong Kong: Hong Kong Government.

23 Social work across four continents

Neil Whettam

Social work was not my first choice of career. I grew up in Kent, the 'Garden of England', and worked on a farm every Saturday for a friend's father. It was not surprising that when I left school at 16, I enrolled at an agricultural college, determined to become a farmer myself. It was not to be. I soon learned that because I didn't come from a farming family, the best I could hope to achieve would be to be a farm manager of a large commercial farm – the very last thing I wanted. My dream in tatters, I got a job as a stockbroker's clerk in London, commuting each day and hating every second of every day. Life at home was difficult too. I was an only child and my father was bipolar. He had spent periods of my childhood in and out of psychiatric hospitals while my mother struggled to keep the family together, working in commercial banking and looking after my father. During one particularly unhappy episode my mother became ill herself, and I was cared for by the parents of schoolfriends and my mother's relatives. By the time I left school, I lived for my free time, which was spent completing the community element of a Gold Duke of Edinburgh Award.[1] Looking back, I see this and my father's illness as the triggers that led me into a career in social work. I began an introductory course in social care at a local college, and on completion of my studies, applied for jobs all over the UK. My first job was in a residential childcare unit for emotionally disturbed 10- to 16-year-olds in Aberdeen in the North East of Scotland at the age of 19, not understanding a word anyone said to me![2]

I had a great time in Aberdeen; I made lifelong friends and still see the 'Granite City' (Aberdeen) as my 'home'. But it was far from easy at the beginning. Scottish Nationalism was very strong at this time and I was often called a 'white settler' or even a 'Sooth moother' (literally, a person with a southern way of speaking) by the families with whom I was working. The aim of the residential unit was to help children and young people to return home to their families, schools and communities, but it soon became apparent to me that my job was much more than the job description led me to believe. This has been a theme throughout my working career. I also became involved in the Boys' Brigade, a Christian youth organisation which was first set up with deprived youngsters in Glasgow in 1883.[3] A year into the job, I went on to take a two-year social work qualification at a local college of education, through an employment-based learning route. I then applied and was accepted for Voluntary Service Overseas (VSO),[4] taking two years' unpaid leave from my job. This was the beginning of over fifteen years of social work overseas.

A baptism of fire: working in Belize, Central America

My first assignment was in Belize, in Central America, as a Social Work Adviser. (Belize was formerly a British colony known as British Honduras. It became independent of Britain in 1981.) My work here was superficially similar to that in Aberdeen: I was based at a juvenile detention centre, where I lived and worked on site. But here the similarities ended. The centre was far from the nearest town, with intermittent water and electricity and a two-mile walk to the nearest highway. Many of the young people detained there had committed crimes such as armed robbery, burglary, theft and assault; others were locked up because their behaviour was deemed uncontrollable. In my first six months there, my house was burgled on many occasions. It transpired that my burglar was a young man who was the scapegoat of other youths. He stole money, clothes and personal possessions in order to distribute them to his peers. In exasperation, I had a brainwave and made the young man my watchman. Whenever I was away, he would sit on the porch and make sure that no one entered the house. I was never burgled again. This account demonstrates that social work is about building trust and building relationships. It is also about empowerment, about giving others a purpose and sense of responsibility (see Adams 2003).

Conditions in the centre were basic, and in many ways it was out of sight of the community and society as whole. Perhaps because of this, it was run on lines which would have been familiar in British Victorian times. Lashing with a rope was a common method of chastisement. I remember vividly the first time I saw a young lad of 13 years old being lashed for disrespecting an officer; yet from what I had seen the officer had been extremely disrespectful to the young man. On another occasion, I decided to intervene in an altercation between a 16-year-old and an officer. The youth was being punched and kicked by the officer, and I stood in between the two and shouted for the attack to stop. I too received a few blows until my voice could be heard around the campus shouting for the officer to leave. This young man was known as 'top dog' to his peers. He was a notorious gang member who had often threatened me in the past, verbally and physically, and on one occasion had taken a machete to my head for challenging his bullying of others. After I stepped in to protect him, he sank into my arms, crying like a baby, and asked if I would help him. This was the start of our work together. He said he wanted to change his life, so we began to look at each aspect of his life, beginning with education. He enrolled again in school and got involved in sport, something for which he had a natural ability. I didn't expect him to withdraw from the gang – after all, it had provided him with the attachment he had craved in his childhood after he had been abandoned by his parents (see Howe 1995). But I hoped that by becoming part of another network, he would come to feel included in his wider community. Sadly, on a visit to Belize this year, I was told that he had been killed in a gang-related attack.

Life at the detention centre was made all the more bearable for me by the strong friendship I built with the centre's Director, who went on later to become a lecturer in social work at the University of Belize. He also lived on site with his young family, and I spent many happy weekends at his family home discussing social work, as this was something new for him, and we began to discuss how we could make changes in the centre and introduce new opportunities for training and development for the detainees. After a year, thanks to our efforts, lashing was discontinued and every young person was delighted. But the changes were not welcomed by all staff members, who felt that their control and power had been taken away. Six months later, a new, forward-thinking government permanent secretary[5] responsible for children and young people asked what should be done about the centre. The centre's Director and I recommended that it should be closed; we felt that staff members were simply too entrenched in their attitudes and we saw no way of changing this situation. The permanent secretary respected our views, and the centre was subsequently closed. The young people were relocated to a new centre fifty miles away in Belize City, where most of them had come from before their detention. The centre Director was appointed Director of the new institution, and I, again, became its Social Work Adviser. We began to put in place the systems which we knew would make a difference in the young people's lives, and before I knew it, my two years were up and I was back in Aberdeen. (I am pleased to report that over the past ten years, the whole legislation pertaining to children and young people has been overhauled in Belize.)

I was glad to see my friends in Aberdeen again; I had not been able to afford to return at all during my placement owing to the prohibitive cost of travel. But it was not easy going back to being a residential social worker again after my time spent on high-level government committees and influencing policy. I returned to Belize for two short trips in 1997 and 1999, when I delivered training on a variety of social work topics to the departments of Women's Affairs, Youth Affairs and Refugees. It was an exciting time in Belize. Social work was a new area of practice and some US-trained social workers were returning home to work. A Faculty of Social Work was being established for the first time at the university.

A new assignment: Kosovo

Before long I was on the move again, this time to Kosovo in South-Eastern Europe, as Country Director for Social Work for an international NGO, EveryChild.[6] I arrived just after the NATO bombing of Yugoslavia at the end of 1999, with Kosovo on the brink of collapse, utilities and banks closed down, and an interim government created by the international community.

Much of my work in the early months was to allow people to verbalise what they had endured and gradually to support the rebuilding of their lives. I was responsible for the delivery of a range of programmes and also had to satisfy donors that their funds were being used appropriately to help those in most need. I had to juggle the needs of my own staff members too; they had all suffered greatly and were supporting their own extended families. Kosovo remains one of the least developed areas of Europe today. Although undergoing major social, economic and political transformation, the disintegration of old systems has not yet been replaced by viable new ones. For example, around 50 per cent of adults are currently unemployed, with all the damaging consequences this brings for individuals, families and communities (International Federation of Red Cross and Red Crescent Societies 2010).

I was responsible for the work of eight national staff in Kosovo. Together we introduced the Newpin model[7] into family support programmes. Much of my supervision with staff was spent in allowing them time to cry and reflect, but also to share as a group. I like to see this as the building of a community where no money exchanges hands or deals are done, but instead there is open communication and honesty is applauded and appreciated and not condemned, with permission given to move on when appropriate. I stayed for a year only, finding myself emotionally drained by the situation and not wanting to become like so many of those in the emergency international field who survived on little more than strong coffee and chocolate. I was frustrated that I was expected to chase funding, write proposals and do *to* rather than work *with* people – a recurring theme of my experiences to date. I felt that my social work values were being fundamentally compromised and I had to do something to recover my sense of what a social worker could and should be.

And then: Kyrgyzstan

Another continent and another risk took me to Kyrgyzstan in Central Asia, at the time leading up to the events of 11 September (2001). In many ways, I felt like one of the children I was going to help; I was a child on the move! But, unlike them, I had been able to make choices.

Kyrgyzstan had become an independent state with the collapse of the Soviet Union in 1991. In the ten years which followed, political and ethnic conflict had been fuelled by poverty and corruption, and hundreds of children and young people had taken to the streets as never before. The state's solution had been to institutionalise these children; my task (still working for EveryChild) was to act as Social

Work Adviser, developing social work practice at the state's Street Children's Centre. This was hugely challenging for me. I believed that what the children and young people needed was not an institution but a temporary shelter and services on the street, such as health, food and education. They needed to learn to trust adults again, and I felt that whisking them away to somewhere unfamiliar was not helpful to them. I, like them, had been thrust into a culture I did not know, living under rules that seemed complex and that were made to control me and not protect me. For the first time I was missing home, and this reminds me of one young person who came to the centre. He was an 8-year-old who arrived late one cold night escorted by the police, wearing just a pair of ragged old knee-length shorts and a grubby yellow T-shirt. He was slight in stature, had a mass of black curly hair, and cuts to his face and arms on his black skin. (This was an ex-Soviet state where 85 per cent of the population has blond hair, blue eyes and white skin.) The boy looked as out of place as I felt. How had he come here and how was he going to be understood? For weeks, we were not able to say anything to each other because neither could understand what the other said. We were both living in a world we could not understand. I was taken back to my early years as a very 'green' social worker when I was thrust into a world where chaos in the families I was working alongside was the norm. How was I going to begin to understand these families? I believe that the word 'understanding' is overused in social work and has lost its true meaning. No two situations are ever exactly the same; we can never fully understand what another person is going through. I rarely use the term now and prefer to say, 'I hear what you are saying and acknowledge you want this to change, let's talk how we are going to do that.' My work with the boy began by observing and giving my feedback to see if my analysis was right. We did this with pictures at first. I would hold up or draw a picture and point at it and at him and he would either nod or shake his head; then, as time went on, he gained confidence and either drew or scrambled to find another picture to evidence what he wanted to say. Only then could I begin to fit all the pieces of the jigsaw together. As social workers, we are good at fitting all the pieces of the jigsaw together and offer this skill to the world when looking at developing and supporting change.

Returning home

I stayed in Kyrgyzstan for fifteen months before returning to the UK in 2002 to cover a maternity leave post in Norfolk at a children's hospice. My parents were living nearby, and although this was emotionally demanding work (I was a family support practitioner, supporting families pre- and post-bereavement), I knew that I needed time to recover and rebuild my strength. Kosovo had been an extremely stressful place to live and work in and then I had gone straight to Kyrgyzstan. I had seen many of my colleagues in the international social work scene living on a knife edge between sanity and insanity, and I didn't want to end up like that.

I had always wanted to go back to Aberdeen, so when a job as a social worker with a fostering and adoption team came up I applied and got it. I was responsible for two years for the recruitment and training of foster carers in North Aberdeenshire, and then went on to become the Employee

Development Officer for Social Work/Social Care in Aberdeenshire. My work covered a large geographical area and 5,500 staff. I stayed for four years, returning to Kyrgyzstan once each year under the auspices of UNICEF to deliver training for residential childcare staff, evaluate and provide training for street children's projects and advise the government on foster care standards (this was at a time when foster care was being introduced for the first time).

In 2008, I moved to East Lothian to become a social work training officer for Children's Services and, significantly, a volunteer with Waverley Care[8] in Edinburgh, sitting on its Advisory Board and acting as a 'buddy'/befriender. Because of my previous work, the agency's Director invited me to contribute to a Scottish government-funded project for HIV education providers in Malawi, targeted at those working with disaffected youth in rural communities, commercial sex workers, men who have sex with men, and prisoners. I went out to Malawi in May 2010 with another worker from Waverley Care and, since then, have gone on to give advice on the implementation of the education and training programme. I also joined the British Association of Social Worker's International Committee at the same time, and have since attended meetings regularly across the UK as well as the 2010 World Conference in Hong Kong.

And finally: the Balkans

I have now taken another two-year career break to become the Regional Child Protection Adviser for another children's charity, this time Terre des Hommes (TDH)[9] in the Balkans.

MY TYPICAL WEEK

My typical week is spent in each of the delegation countries where TDH has a presence. I leave home in Bucharest on a flight every Sunday afternoon ready to begin work first thing on Monday morning and return back home on a Friday evening. A typical week would be spent working with TDH staff responsible for the capacity-building of the child protection networks. This might include following up from training I have delivered to them and they have delivered across the centres of social work they are supporting and advising. We will discuss developments since my last visit. There are also complex case discussions to be held, and I must attend UN meetings on social welfare development where there is a heavy UN presence. In one month, I am likely to be in four different countries, hearing several different languages and supporting and advising complex cases where there are few resources, but the need is the same. This takes me back to the early days in social work in the UK when we had little to offer but ourselves.

How do I survive such a strenuous schedule? Well, apart from my addiction to chocolate, thank goodness for the invention of modern technology, which means that no matter where I am,

---

I can chat to family and friends with the push of a button and now see them as we gossip about what is happening back home and in the lives of our friends. To help clear my mind and allow me some 'head space', I try to swim every day if possible – those Soviets certainly knew the importance of building open-air pools in the heart of cities for citizens to enjoy and help keep them healthy. Otherwise, I wander through the Bucharest parks at the weekend and sit with a pot of tea, reading every word in my *Guardian Weekly*. I am still very new here, but I very much look forward to making friends with some local people so that I can enjoy lively discussions around the dinner-table and go and see a trashy Hollywood movie to escape into. I guess I am quite a resilient person and always have been, until someone sweeps me off my feet and I settle for a life in the Highlands of Scotland with a log fire, my CD collection of music from around the world, and a wonderful man to cook for me.

Looking ahead

So what can we hope for our profession? 'Social work' and 'social worker': does our title match what we do? If so, how, and if not, why not? Sadly, I believe that for many of us in the UK, being a social worker has become being an administrator. Yet our contribution can be enormous. When I embarked on a career in social work, I knew that I was entering a world that was going to view what I do as interfering; that I was likely to be seen as a 'do-gooder' and a waste of taxpayers' money. But I also knew that I would be entering a profession which had the needs and rights of the world's citizens as its foundation and could help people realise their full potential. I have not been proved wrong on either point, and I can say without a shadow of doubt that even at the most stressful and difficult times in my life, I would not wish to have done anything different. I believe that as a profession, social work can achieve more than any other without spending a penny, because we offer support and guidance and create a space for people to achieve their own goals in their own way. For me, it is very simple, whether working overseas or at home in the UK: 'If you have come here to help me, you are wasting your time. But if you have come because your liberation is bound up with mine, then let us work together.'[10]

Notes

1 The Duke of Edinburgh Award scheme is a UK charity which aims to give 14- to 24-year-olds the chance to develop skills for work and life, fulfil their potential and have a brighter future. See http://www.dofe.org/.

2 The regional variation of 'the Doric' which is spoken in the North East of Scotland, especially around Aberdeen City and the County of Aberdeenshire, is quite different to English not just in the words that it uses, but also in the way that English words are spoken. See http:// www.scotslanguage.com/.

3 There are companies of the Boys' Brigade throughout the world. See http://www.boys-brigade.org.uk/.

4 VSO is the world's largest independent international development organisation that works through volunteers to fight poverty in developing countries. See http://www.vso.org.uk/.

5 The government minister has since gone on to become UNICEF's Deputy Representative in Eritrea.

6 EveryChild is an international development charity which aims to stop children growing up vulnerable and alone. See http://www.everychild.org.uk/.

7 Newpin is a service which began in England, targeting families with identified needs who were seen as ready to be actively involved in making changes for themselves and their children. See, for example, Family Action Southwark Newpin, http://www.family-action.org.uk/uploads/documents/Southwark%20Newpin%20%28 referrers%29.pdf.

8 Waverley Care is Scotland's leading charity providing care and support to people living with HIV and Hepatitis C, and to their partners, families and carers. Education and training form an important aspect of its work. See http://www.waverleycare.org/.

9 The Terre des Hommes International Federation is a network of eleven international organisations working for the rights of children and to promote equitable development without racial, religious, political, cultural or gender-based discrimination. See http://www.terredeshommes.org/.

10 This is a motto for many activist groups in Australia and elsewhere, originally credited to the Aboriginal Activists' Group, Queensland, in the 1970s.

References

Adams, R. (2003) *Social Work and Empowerment*, 3rd edn, Basingstoke: Palgrave Macmillan.

Howe, D. (1995) *Attachment Theory for Social Work Practice*, Basingstoke: Palgrave Macmillan.

International Federation of Red Cross and Red Crescent Societies (2010) *Plan 2009–2010*. Accessed 5 July 2011 at http://reliefweb.int/sites/reliefweb.int/files/resources/02799191387E54DAC12575050055DFF8-Full_Report.pdf.

24 Social work

A global profession

Viviene E. Cree

In reviewing the book as a whole, three issues emerge as central in the accounts of the contributors. The first may be described as the process of *becoming* a social worker; that is, the ways in which the authors explain their decision to enter a career in social work. The second focuses on what it is like to *be* a social worker: the paths people have taken in social work and their feelings about the job of social work, today and in the future. The third issue reflects the different *contexts* in which social work is located in different parts of the world. The accounts demonstrate that there is no single way of becoming a social worker and no unitary social work task. In spite of the multiplicity of social work settings, however, shared ideas and practices shine through the contributors' stories of their lives and work. The narratives also afford insight into the ambivalences and complexities that surround becoming and being a social worker in a global (or perhaps more accurately, 'glocal') world (see Robertson 1992). From this, it is evident that becoming and being a social worker is accompanied by ongoing tension between the self and others, the individual and society, the local and the global, as social workers negotiate and renegotiate their lives and work on a daily basis.

Becoming a social worker

Although there is no single explanation for becoming a social worker in this book, there are (as in the first edition) a number of recurring themes that contributors draw on to explain their choice of social work as a career. These include:

- childhood and family background;

- experiences of education and work;

- the influence of significant individuals;

- the value-base of social work.

Childhood and family background

Some authors describe their childhoods as happy and secure. They grew up in caring, supportive families, brought up by parents who loved them and who passed on their values to them. They describe an awareness of their own good fortune, as well as inequalities in society. This is sometimes expressed as a need to make society a fairer place for those less privileged than themselves. Other contributors outline a childhood marred in some way by loss or adversity. They grew up knowing what it was like to feel 'different' or an 'outsider'; they experienced disadvantage and injustice (and sometimes racial oppression) first hand. This, in turn, led them to have a deep-seated desire to do something about it; again, to challenge injustice and change society.

Experiences of education and work

Some authors point to their undergraduate university studies as being instrumental in giving them an intellectual and political language and, alongside this, a *raison d'être* for coming into social work. For example, subjects such as sociology helped contributors to make sense of the relationship between themselves and the society in which they were growing up.

Employment experiences are also critical in the development of an understanding of social work as a career. Authors came to social work from a very diverse range of backgrounds, including forestry, legal and insurance services. But many more were involved in 'caring' professions of one kind or another, working as teachers, personnel officers, care assistants and unqualified social workers, either during vacation from university or after graduating, before they chose professional social work as a career. While gender may have played a part in this for some people (girls today are still likely to be channelled towards 'caring' occupations), this was clearly not the case for the men who have written for the book and who have had to overcome traditional gender stereotypes to become social workers. This is significant because occupational gender segregation is found to persist across most countries, 'irrespective of the level of economic development, political system and religious, social and cultural environment. It is an enduring characteristic of labour markets around the world' (Watts 2003: 631). See also Miller and Hayward's (2006) UK study, which identified that school pupils aged 14 to 18 (especially boys) still see jobs in segregated terms.

The influence of significant individuals

Significant others have been hugely important in influencing some authors' decisions to become social workers. Sometimes this person was a parent or family friend; at other times it was a lecturer, colleague or another social worker who encouraged them to apply for social work. For some people, it was simply an awareness of the pain experienced by another human being – a child or a person with mental health problems. Witnessing this caused a jolt and led to the realisation that they should try to help in some way.

The value-base of social work

All the contributors, whatever their context, describe how the value-base of social work 'fitted' their own personal belief system. This was not only about having concern for others; it was about being prepared to do something about it. Underpinning all the accounts in this and the first edition of the book is a sense that the authors felt they had to take action. It was not enough to have sympathy with oppressed people or even to understand theoretically the origins of inequality and injustice; something had to be done to bring about change in individuals and society, and the contributors felt that they had a personal contribution to make to that process. This comes close to the rather old-fashioned idea of social work as a vocation or 'calling'. While some authors in the book express this in religious terms others do not; either way, the effect is the same. The impulse is to do something for humanity, however this is put into words (see also Le Croy 2002).

Reviewing the narratives overall, the explanations given by most contributors for becoming social workers include a number of different reasons. These reasons are not separate from one another; they do not exist as 'either- or'. Instead, they are likely to be 'both- and' (Derrida 1978); together they demonstrate the complex and, at times, contradictory ways in which we, as human beings, tell and retell our life stories, always seeking to find meaning in the journey of our lives (see Connelly and Clandinin 1990).

This is worth reflecting on further. If becoming a social worker is a journey, where does that journey begin and where does it end? To be accepted on to most social work training courses, applicants must demonstrate a minimum of one (and sometimes two) year's experience in some aspect of social work or social care. This suggests that becoming a social worker begins long before the point of entry to a social work course. It begins in childhood, in voluntary work undertaken with older people or younger children, in youth clubs and uniformed organisations. It may then continue into young adulthood, through volunteering or through paid work, as students work in care homes to pay for their fees and accommodation. Or it may continue as adults go through the process of building relationships, having children, and then looking after their own parents in older age. But where does it end? Does it end when a training course begins, or perhaps when a student goes on their first practice placement? Or does a student 'become' a social worker when their course ends and they start their first job as a qualified social worker? Research conducted in the UK in the 1990s and early 2000s suggested that students often do not feel ready to practise at the point of qualification; there is still a great deal of 'becoming' to do once qualifying training is over (Marsh and Triseliotis 1996; Pithouse and Scourfield 2002). The relatively recent emphasis in social work on post-qualifying training, and on continuing professional development, must be seen in part as recognition that there is no fixed end-point at which the process of 'becoming a social worker' ends, also highlighted in the 2012 Munro Review (discussed in the Introduction and in Chapter 6 above).

Being a social worker

The contributors to this book have much to tell us about the 'real world' of social work today: about its successes and failings, its joys and frustrations, its hopes and fears. The chapters do not cover all possible social work settings; given the diversity of social work, that would be an impossible goal to achieve. Nevertheless, what the individual accounts show is that in spite of the differences across countries, work settings and even job titles, there is a level at which shared knowledge and values underpin professional practice in social work. This is not always straightforward. The contributors demonstrate that the contexts in which social work operates across the world have changed dramatically over the past forty years, and are changing still, as I have discussed in relation to social work in the UK (see Cree 2009). Moreover, knowledge and values are themselves always contested. For those who are currently working in the 'Southern' countries of the world, there is a realisation that theories and models built in the Global 'North' cannot and should not be transported 'lock, stock and barrel' to countries in the Global 'South', as has undoubtedly happened in the past. Social workers today are fighting to retain their own local knowledge and practices, valuing traditional, 'indigenous' (sometimes called 'regional') ways of thinking and doing, just as Māori people have done very successfully with Family Group Conferencing, and as Graham (2002 and 2007) has argued that we must do now in terms of valuing African-centred practice.

The context in which social workers are working

Perhaps the strongest impression I am left with in reading the chapters again is the degree to which people writing in this book demonstrate the impact of globalisation. Travel, journeys, cross-cultural understandings feature in a significant number of the chapters. This highlights the reality that many of those who are living and working in the UK today were born in another country; many UK authors have worked (or are working) overseas; many authors from the Global 'South' travelled to the Global 'North' for their education; some have returned to their country of origin while others have not. A small number of people have made multiple journeys over the years. Of course, this, in part, reflects some of the choices I made in inviting people to tell their stories; I wanted to interrogate the global nature of social work today. However, I believe it also demonstrates a wider truth: that we are living in a global world, and social work is affected by globalisation (for good and bad) as we all are, in all areas of our lives.

There is, nevertheless, one final point for consideration here. Globalisation for some is accompanied by localisation for others (see Bauman 1998). It is the poor, unemployed and oppressed who are unable to move, and who experience restrictions on their movements through repressive immigration policies. As social workers, it is our responsibility to work with the casualties of globalisation; with those whose movement in time and space is limited in some way, by age or gender, class or caste, imprisonment or infirmity. Bauman (2000) argues that social work must be conceived essentially as a *moral* activity, not a technical-rational one (see also Smith 2011). Our response must therefore be one of humility and respect, just as has been demonstrated throughout the chapters in this book. I finish with Bauman's words on this:

> Being one's brother's keeper is a life sentence of hard labour and moral anxiety, which no amount of trying would ever put to rest. But this is good news for the moral person: it is precisely in the situations social workers are daily in, in the situations of difficult choices, of choices without guarantee and without the authoritative reassurance of propriety, that the responsibility for the Other, that foundation of all morality, comes into its own.
>
> (Bauman 2000: 7)

References

Bauman, Z. (1998) *Globalization. The Human Consequences*, Oxford: Polity Press.

—— (2000) 'Am I my brother's keeper?', *European Journal of Social Work*, 3(1): 5–12.

Connelly, F.M. and Clandinin, D.J. (1990) 'Stories of experience and narrative enquiry', *Educational Researcher*, 19(5): 2–14.

Cree, V.E. (2009) 'The changing nature of social work', in R. Adams, L. Dominelli and M. Payne (eds) *Social Work. Themes, Issues and Critical Debates*, 3rd edn, Basingstoke: Palgrave.

Derrida, D. (1978) *Writing and Difference*, Chicago, IL: University of Chicago Press.

Graham, M. (2002) *Social Work and African-centred Worldviews – A Theoretical Perspective*, Birmingham: BASW/Venture Press.

—— (2007) *Black Issues in Social Work and Social Care*, Bristol: Policy Press.

Le Croy, C.W. (2002) *The Call to Social Work. Life Stories*, Thousand Oaks, CA: Sage.

Marsh, P. and Triseliotis, J. (1996) *Ready to Practise? Social Workers and Probation Officers: Their Training and First Year in Work*, Aldershot: Avebury.

Miller, L. and Hayward, R. (2006) 'New jobs, old occupational stereotypes: gender and jobs in the new economy', *Journal of Education and Work*, 19(1): 67–93.

Munro, E. (2012) *Munro Review of Child Protection: Final Report – A Child-centred System*, London: DoE.

Pithouse, A. and Scourfield, J. (2002) 'Ready for practice? The DipSW in Wales: views from the workplace on social work training', *Journal of Social Work*, 2: 17–27.

Robertson, R. (1992) *Globalization: Social Theory and Global Culture*, London: Sage.

Smith, M. (2011) 'Reading Bauman for social work', *Ethics and Social Welfare*, 5(1): 2–17.

Watts, M. (2003) 'The evolution of occupational gender segregation in Australia: measurement and interpretation', *Australian Journal of Labour Economics*, 6(4): 631–655.

Index